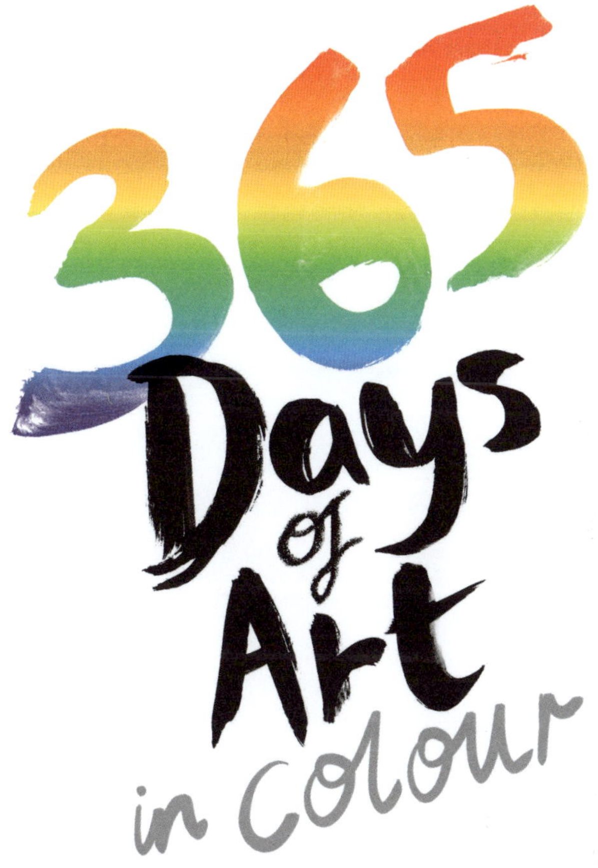

This book belongs to:

365 Days of Art in Colour

CREATIVE ART PROMPTS
FOR EVERY DAY OF THE YEAR

LORNA SCOBIE

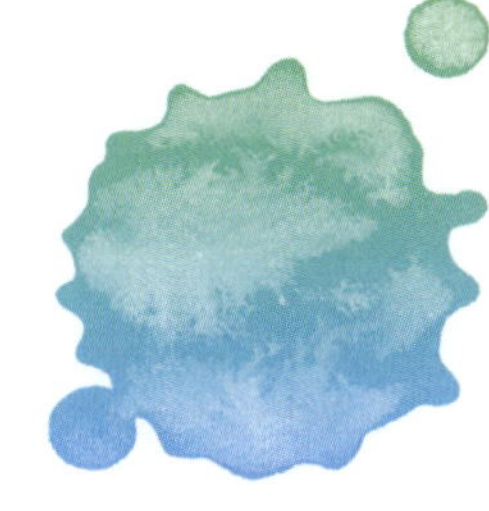

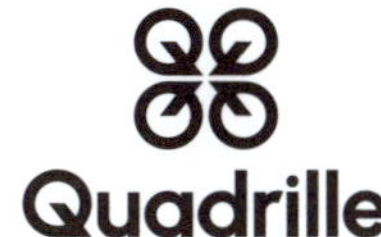

Quadrille

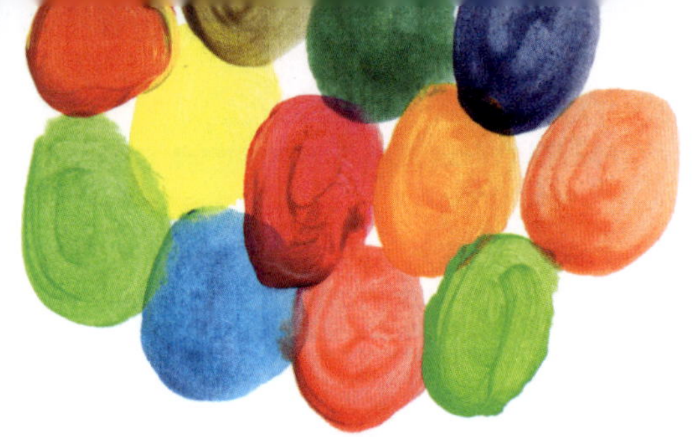

Welcome to 365 Days of Art in Colour!

I absolutely love using colour in my art – filling a page with vivid greens, blues, reds and oranges brings me joy! In the past, however, I found using colour a bit intimidating and I'd stick to colours that felt familiar and 'safe' rather than using the colours I loved. Through playful exploration and plenty of happy 'mistakes', I learnt to let go and fully embrace using a vast spectrum of colour. I hope that this book encourages you to also feel excited and energised by colour.

Or perhaps you already do! This is a book for people who love colour and would like to use it more in their art, as well as a book for those who feel nervous about using colour and unsure about where to start. Adding colour can be daunting for any artist at first, as it can seem like there are so many decisions to make: which colours should I use, and where, and how? This book challenges the idea that there is a 'right' answer to these questions, and instead encourages you to make instinctive choices about colour. As your confidence builds, you'll begin to trust your instincts and just go for it.

In these activities, I will introduce some elements of colour theory, but mainly I'll create a safe space where you can relax, unwind and have fun. As with all my *365 Days* art books, these tasks have been designed to be suitable for everyone – regardless of skill level, age or prior experience.

Art has the power to make us *all* feel good. Although we often have the desire to be creative, it can sometimes be tricky knowing where to start. So I've provided a colour-themed prompt for every day of the year, sometimes with an example or a starting point. This book will encourage you to leave your comfort zone and try new colours, combinations and themes, and through your exploration perhaps you'll discover fresh techniques to use in your art. I'd recommend trying activities even if it feels out of your comfort zone, as you may discover something new! You can also adapt the tasks in any way, so that they work best for you.

Approach these activities with confidence. Don't worry about making mistakes on the page – in my opinion there is no such a thing as 'bad' art, and if you've enjoyed the time spent creating, and perhaps even learnt something new, it was worth it! So just pick up a pencil, pen or paintbrush, make a mark and enjoy the moment.

You can work through the book in order, or choose prompts based on how you feel in the moment. Be guided by your own intuition, and don't feel like you have to complete one every day – life is busy and there's no need to put extra pressure on yourself. Some activities can be accomplished relatively quickly, so you may like to squeeze one or two into a break during the day. Or perhaps you dedicate time once a week to spend on your art, really getting stuck in and letting your mind focus solely on creating. As you finish an activity, cross it off on the 'activities completed' grid to record your progress.

The activities are categorised to give you an idea about the nature of each task, and provide the opportunity to explore colour in four key areas:

The **learn** tasks introduce colour theory. You'll gain a greater understanding of how colour behaves and how to mix colours, and the chance to explore what you've learnt. Definitions of colour are sometimes used in a variety of ways and some words are interchangeable. I've used them in the way that works for me, but you might come across alternative definitions. Don't let the words and meanings hinder your creativity, use whichever terms work for you. And remember, in this book there's no right or wrong way to use colour. It can be useful to learn the artistic conventions, but then it's up to you how you apply them in your art.

Some activities encourage you to **play**, forget the rules of colour and be experimental! Challenge yourself to think differently and have fun without any fear of making a mess. Create art in an environment where you feel relaxed and free to be yourself, perhaps with friends, or while listening to music. This is a chance to let your imagination run wild, be mindful and enjoy the process.

There are activities that offer a chance to **observe** the colourful world around you. Rather than just seeing, practise actively *looking* at your surroundings. The observational tasks may require a little more time and concentration than others. Embrace taking these moments to focus entirely on your art without distraction, and at the same time you'll be building your artistic skills.

Different colours can evoke different feelings and moods, and we can harness this within our art. Explore this in the **feel** tasks. The emotions you experience will be personal to you – be guided by your own responses in these activities and enjoy thinking a little deeper when you create.

I believe *everyone* is creative, and thanks to the *365 Days of Art* community I have been lucky enough to see how art can bring happiness into people's lives, every day. Your art can be just for you and there's no need to share it, but if you do feel like it, do so with confidence! Use the hashtag **#365DaysOfArt** to share your art with the online community and see what else has been created.

Activities Completed

KEY: Learn Play Observe Feel

1	2	3	4	5	6	7	8	9	10
11	12	13	14	15	16	17	18	19	20
21	22	23	24	25	26	27	28	29	30
31	32	33	34	35	36	37	38	39	40
41	42	43	44	45	46	47	48	49	50
51	52	53	54	55	56	57	58	59	60
61	62	63	64	65	66	67	68	69	70
71	72	73	74	75	76	77	78	79	80
81	82	83	84	85	86	87	88	89	90
91	92	93	94	95	96	97	98	99	100
101	102	103	104	105	106	107	108	109	110
111	112	113	114	115	116	117	118	119	120
121	122	123	124	125	126	127	128	129	130
131	132	133	134	135	136	137	138	139	140
141	142	143	144	145	146	147	148	149	150
151	152	153	154	155	156	157	158	159	160
161	162	163	164	165	166	167	168	169	170
171	172	173	174	175	176	177	178	179	180

181	182	183	184	185	186	187	188	189	190
191	192	193	194	195	196	197	198	199	200
201	202	203	204	205	206	207	208	209	210
211	212	213	214	215	216	217	218	219	220
221	222	223	224	225	226	227	228	229	230
231	232	233	234	235	236	237	238	239	240
241	242	243	244	245	246	247	248	249	250
251	252	253	254	255	256	257	258	259	260
261	262	263	264	265	266	267	268	269	270
271	272	273	274	275	276	277	278	279	280
281	282	283	284	285	286	287	288	289	290
291	292	293	294	295	296	297	298	299	300
301	302	303	304	305	306	307	308	309	310
311	312	313	314	315	316	317	318	319	320
321	322	323	324	325	326	327	328	329	330
331	332	333	334	335	336	337	338	339	340
341	342	343	344	345	346	347	348	349	350
351	352	353	354	355	356	357	358	359	360
361	362	363	364	365					

Materials

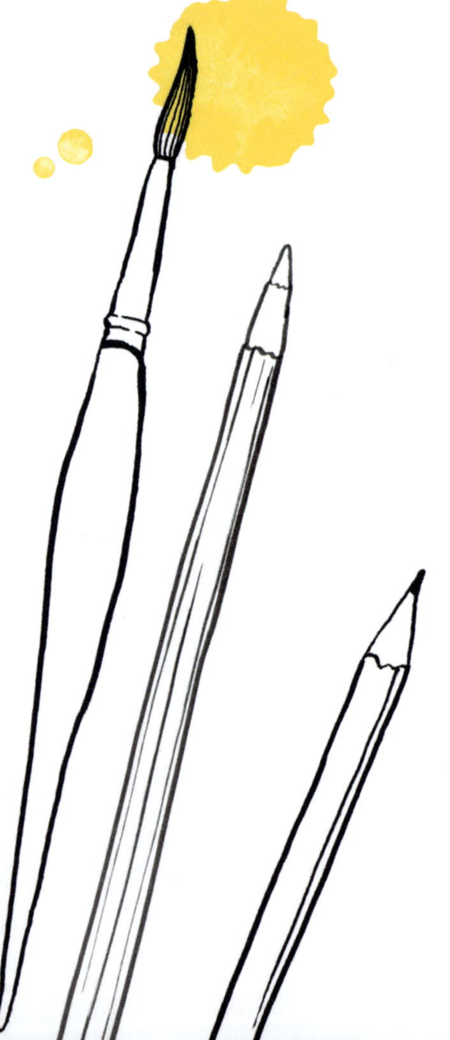

You can use any art materials you like to create colourful art. Complete the activities in this book with tools you already love, or take the opportunity to explore materials that you've always been interested to try. Through exploration, find what works for you, and if that means using something different to what is suggested in the activities, that's no problem at all! This is *your* book.

I like to prepare my art materials before I start creating, laying them out in front of me where I can see them. I find this inspires me to experiment, take more risks and be bolder with my colour choices. You could try this too. Embrace the way of working that feels natural to you and aim to work instinctively, grabbing colours that feel right.

There's no rush or need to spend lots to build your toolkit. I have suggested a few of my favourite art materials here, but I also recommend visiting art shops. Here you can see the vast array of pens, paints and pencils available, and staff can offer advice on different materials to suit your needs. You could also browse online for recommendations, or swap tips and discuss thoughts with friends and fellow creatives.

Ink pens and watery paints can bleed through paper. If you are concerned about this happening you can prime the pages of this book with **clear gesso** before you start an activity. Use a brush to apply the gesso over the page and allow it to dry before you start – you could use bulldog clips to keep your page open.

Pencils

Pencils and coloured pencils are a great addition to your toolkit. There is a huge variety of colours to choose from, they are simple to use and are relatively mess-free. Drawing pencils range in softness, commonly from a 9B, which creates a soft black line, to a 9H, which is very hard and creates a sharp, light line. Coloured pencils also range in softness, so I recommend trying out samples to find what you prefer before buying a full set. Pencils are also sold individually in stores – look out for colours that bring you joy!

Mechanical pencils can be useful for sketching. They contain a pencil lead, but feel more like a pen to hold as the casing is metal or plastic. I enjoy using the **Staedtler Mars Micro 0.5** and the **Pentel P205 0.5**. Mechanical pencils don't need sharpening, but you will need to buy extra lead refills for them. Make sure you choose the correct size refill (the mechanical pencil will give the lead refill size on its side).

I love to mix and match coloured pencil brands based on which colours I am inspired by. I really enjoy the vast array of hues available in the **Faber-Castell Polychromos** range. Some coloured pencils are water soluble, such as the **Caran d'Ache Supracolor** pencils, which have a soft lead and also come in a large range of colours. You can blend them with water and a paintbrush. I also enjoy the **Staedtler Ergosoft** pencils, which have a harder lead and produce very solid, bright colours.

If you are using pencils, it's worth buying a good eraser and sharpener from an art store.

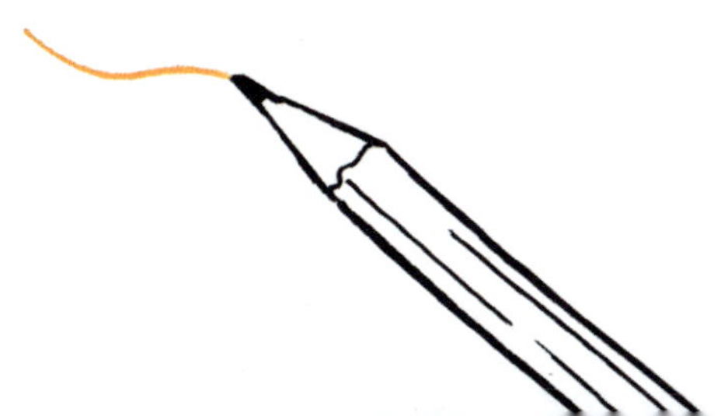

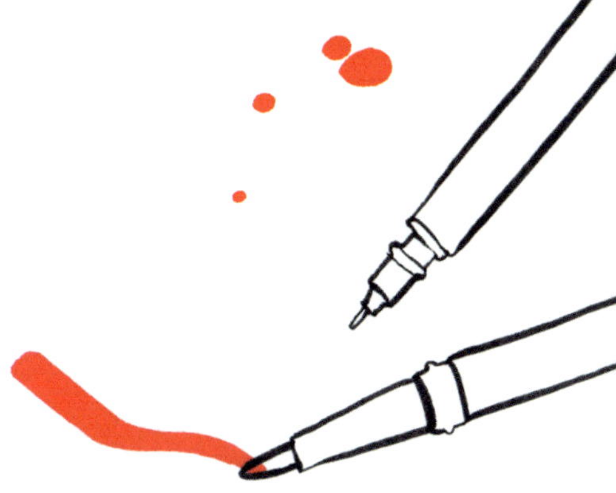

Brush tip pens

These are a great way to add colour to a page quickly. I'd recommend water-based pens for this book – there are fantastic colours available, they are easy to use, and less likely to bleed through the paper. I enjoy using **Tombow ABT Dual Brush Pens**, especially for colouring backgrounds or creating bold shapes and marks.

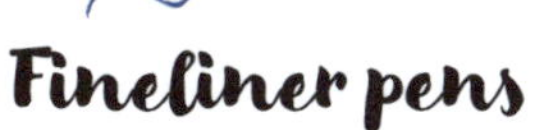

Fineliner pens

It's useful to have a few fineliner pens for jotting down notes and ideas, making quick sketches and adding detail to artwork. There is a wide range of brands, colours and nib sizes to choose from, so I recommend experimenting with the testers in an art store. My favourites include **Uni Pin Fine Line** pens, **Pilot Juice Up** gel pens, **Sakura Pigma Micron** pens and **Derwent Graphik Line Maker** pens.

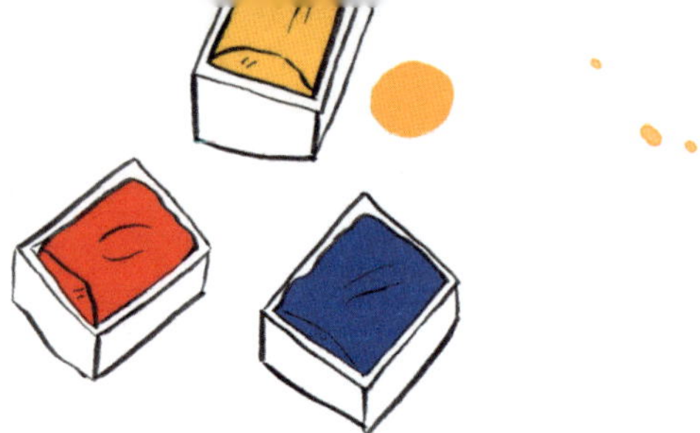

Watercolour paint

Watercolour paint is very versatile – it's not too messy, you can control the intensity of your colour, it dries quickly and colours can be blended easily.

Daler-Rowney and **Winsor & Newton** both produce wonderfully vibrant colours in palettes or 'trays'. When you run out of a particular colour (called a 'pan') you can purchase individual replacements so your tray of watercolours can last forever. For particularly rich colours, I enjoy using **Kuretake Gansai Tambi** paints. I like to use **Pentel Aquash Water Brushes**. These brushes come in a few sizes and can be filled with water, providing a useful alternative to a pot of water and paintbrush when painting with watercolours.

Paintbrushes vary greatly, and it's useful to have a range of brush sizes and shapes. Brush tips can be pointed, round or have a square-end, and each produces a different effect. Experiment with different types and see what you prefer. You'll also need a container for your water, and this can be anything from an old mug to an empty yoghurt pot, and some paper towel for blotting water off your brush. You'll need a wet brush in order to pick up paint from the pan, and it can be a good idea to rinse brushes in water before changing colour to keep colours clean.

Most watercolour palettes come with a space inside the lid to mix colours – a mixing palette. These can be revisited even when the paint has dried out, just by applying a bit of water from your brush.

Acrylic paint

Acrylic paint comes in an extensive range of vivid, pre-mixed colours that are highly pigmented. If you can't find a tube of the colour you are looking for, you can also mix colours yourself. Acrylic paint dries quickly and can be watered down to make the consistency thinner or more transparent. I like to use **Daler-Rowney System 3 Acrylics** and **Liquitex Heavy Body Acrylic**.

As with watercolour, you'll also need brushes, a pot of water, some paper towel for blotting and a mixing palette. Be sure to wash your brushes once you've finished using them, as once the paint dries it can be harder to get off. You can use mixing palettes from art stores, or an old ceramic plate does a great job too. Paint will also dry quickly on the palette when exposed to air, but you can keep your colours from drying out so fast by sealing the whole palette in a zip lock bag.

Pastels

Wax and oil pastels are a fun material to use as they slide easily over paper, and you can cover large areas quickly when using them on their sides. Colours can be bought individually or in sets, and they can get a little messy. I like **Caran d'Ache Neocolor II Aquarelle** pastels, which are water-soluble. Just use a brush or sponge to add a little water to your wax pastel drawing for an interesting effect. **Sennelier Oil Pastels** are also lovely and creamy.

Coloured paper

Keep aside any interesting coloured, patterned and textured paper – you can even use gift wrap or brown paper bags in your art. They are great materials to have in your kit for collage. You can build your own library of coloured paper over time, and also paint your own sheets of coloured paper to use. Origami paper is great as it is thin, easy to tear and cut, and often comes in a range of exciting colours and patterns.

Here are some other materials you may like to have in your art kit:

- **Sketchbooks:** Use these to continue your creative journey. They are a great place to experiment and record your ideas, and come in many different sizes and styles.
- **Watercolour paper:** Useful when using watery paint. You could choose to work onto sheets of watercolour paper for some activities, and then stick your artwork in your sketchbook.
- **Clear gesso:** A primer to apply with a clean brush to paper or board to prevent materials from bleeding through. Acts as a barrier between the paper and the art material.
- **Gouache:** These are water-based paints, similar to watercolour, but can provide a more intense colour as they are more opaque. They dry quickly and are great if you're interested in layering colours.

- **Scissors:** Useful for collages and cutting paper.
- **Glue:** PVA or a glue stick can be used to stick down collages. Water down PVA to make it less gloopy, and apply with a scrap of hard cardboard or an old paintbrush.
- **Masking tape (low-tack sticky tape):** Handy for sticking things quickly, and easy to remove and draw on. Can also be used for straight lines; stick it down before you start painting, then peel off once finished to reveal a straight edge.
- **Tracing paper:** Use masking tape to stick this over drawings that are a bit messy, so marks don't transfer to the opposite page.
- **Fixative spray:** Apply on top of completed artwork to prevent smudging.
- **Bulldog clips:** Useful for holding back other pages while you work on an activity.

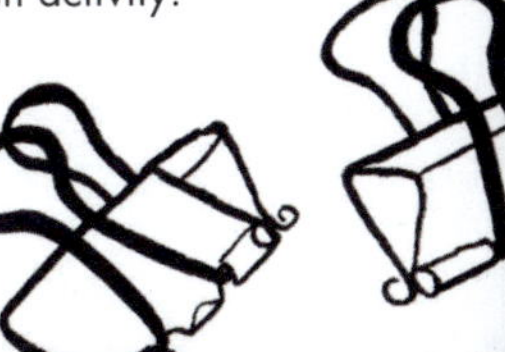

1

Referring to a colour wheel whilst creating art can be really helpful – you can see the relationship between colours and also use it to decide which colours to use in your designs.

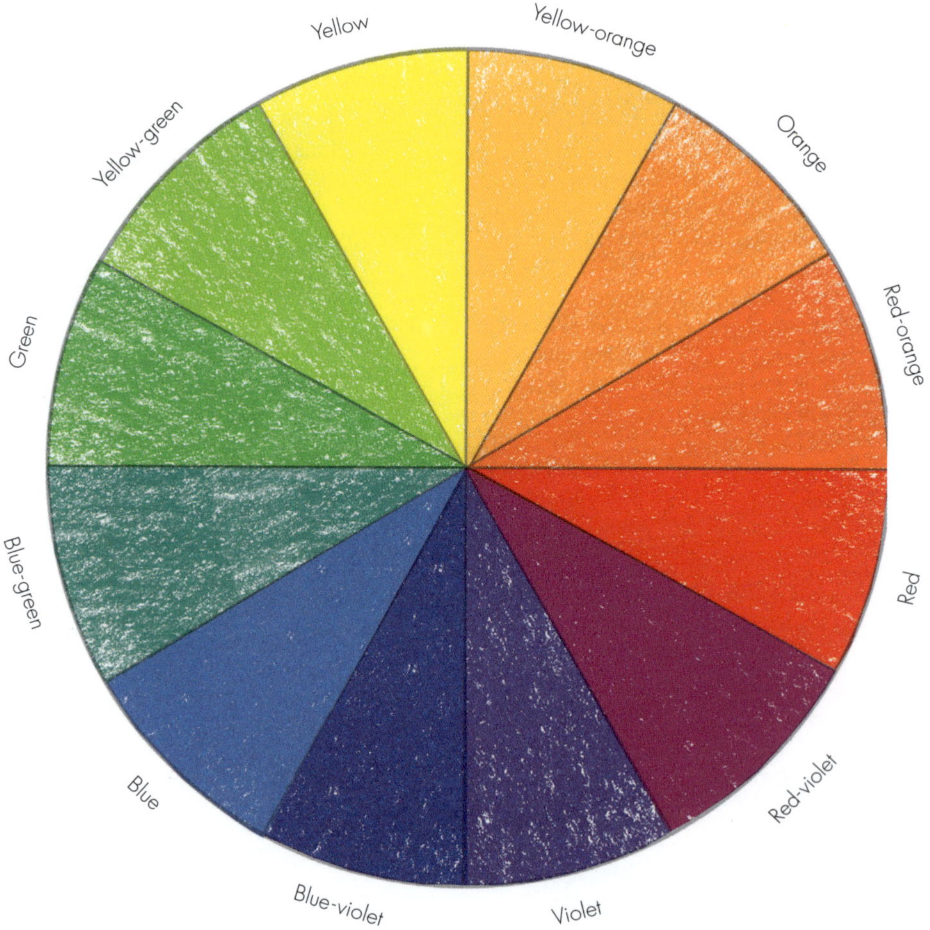

Yellow
Yellow-orange
Orange
Red-orange
Red
Red-violet
Violet
Blue-violet
Blue
Blue-green
Green
Yellow-green

Analogous colours are groups of three or more colours next to each other on the wheel. These often form a harmonious palette. →

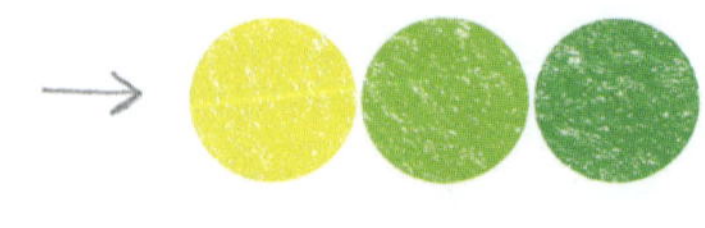

Complementary colours can be found opposite each other on the wheel, and these pairs will create striking contrasts within your work. →

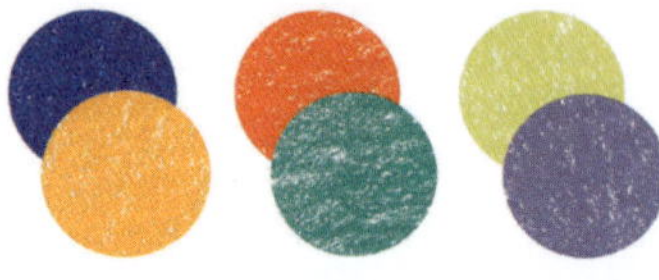

Create your own colour wheel by adding colours to the segments below. You can use any material you like.

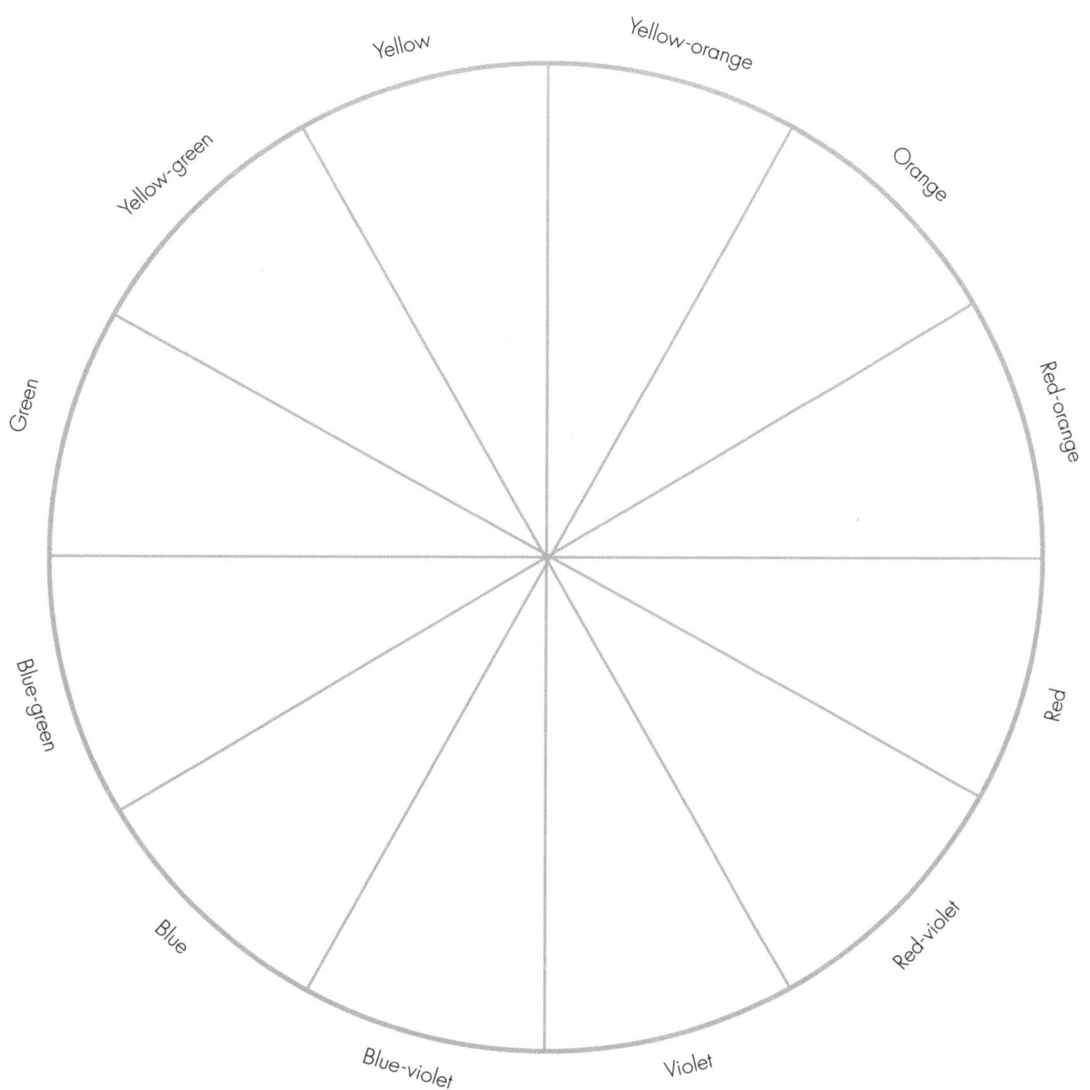

Tip: *You may find it helpful to refer back to this colour wheel when you are completing other activities. You could photocopy it, or create a separate one on a piece of paper and keep it with your art materials.*

2

Allow yourself to be bold and confident with your colour choices. Create a lively page of colour using any that appeal to you from your collection of art materials.

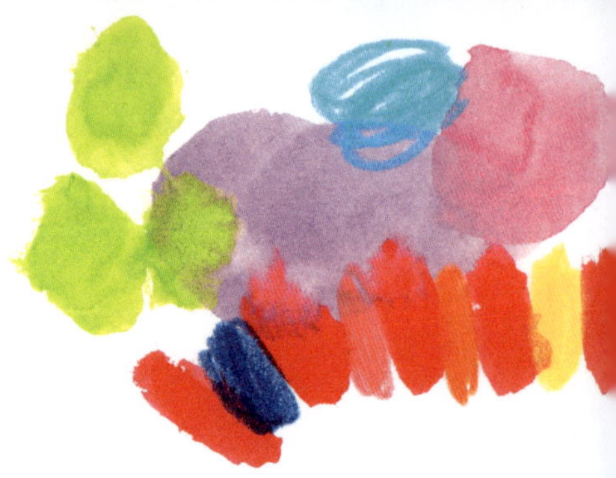

Tip: *Enjoy the process of creation and the chance to be playful and messy. Get those colours on the page!*

3

You can help turn a simple sketch into a colourful painting by taking colour notes when you make the sketch. Look at a scene and make a quick drawing, noting down the colours you'd like to paint each area.

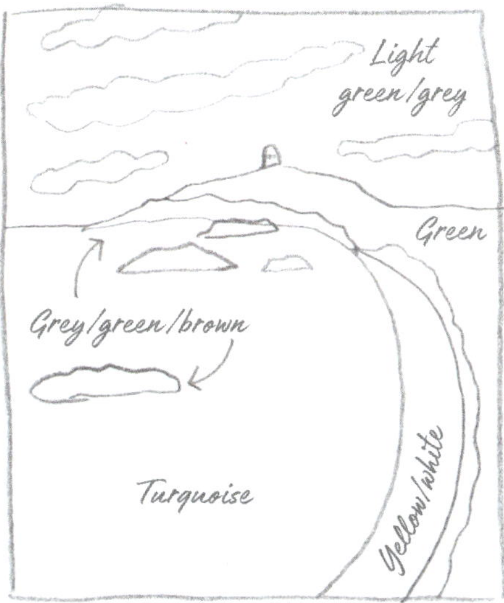

Then make a new colour sketch, roughly mapping out each area of colour based on your notes. If you feel inspired to create a painting based on your sketch, go for it!

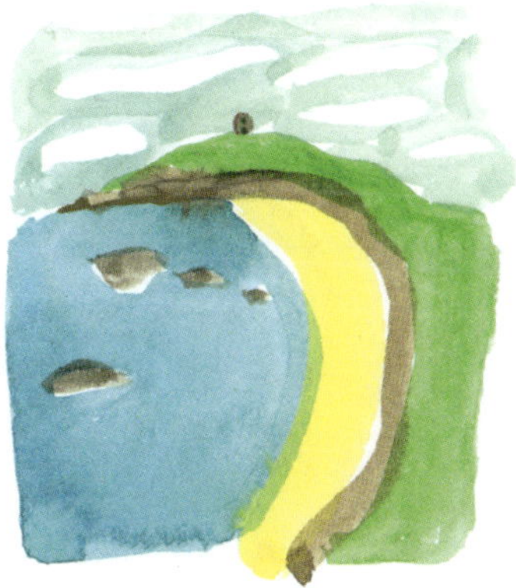

Tip: *The image can evolve! Perhaps you discover you'd like to try alternative colours, or change the composition of your sketch – that's great! Go with whatever feels right to you.*

Different colours can make us feel different things, and this can be a useful tool in art. Add splodges of many colours and consider the mood they evoke. Describe how each colour makes you feel.

Tip: *There is no wrong answer – it will be entirely personal to you.*

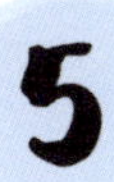

5

The primary colours are red, blue and yellow, and they cannot be made by mixing other colours. Broadly speaking, all other colours can be made by mixing different combinations and quantities of primary colours. The vast array of colours available to us can be overwhelming, so it can be a useful reminder that they all come from this starting point!

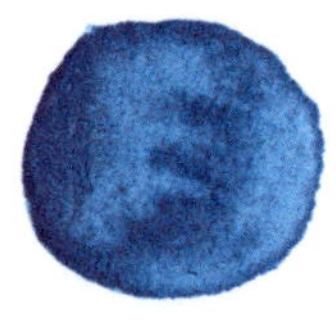

For this activity you'll need paint. Add the three primary colours to a mixing palette (or you can use a plate). Mix as many different colours as you can on the palette, using different amounts of the primary colours (and also the new colours you've mixed from them). Record all the colours you create as swatches below them.

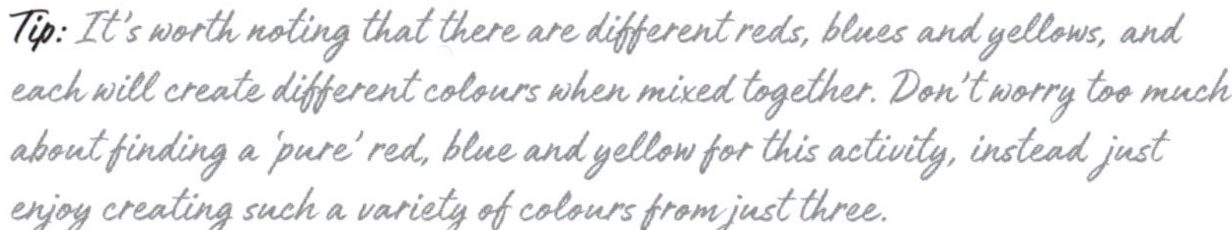

Tip: It's worth noting that there are different reds, blues and yellows, and each will create different colours when mixed together. Don't worry too much about finding a 'pure' red, blue and yellow for this activity, instead just enjoy creating such a variety of colours from just three.

6

Add colour to these vessels. Consider showing textures and reflections. Are they glass? Metal? Ceramic?

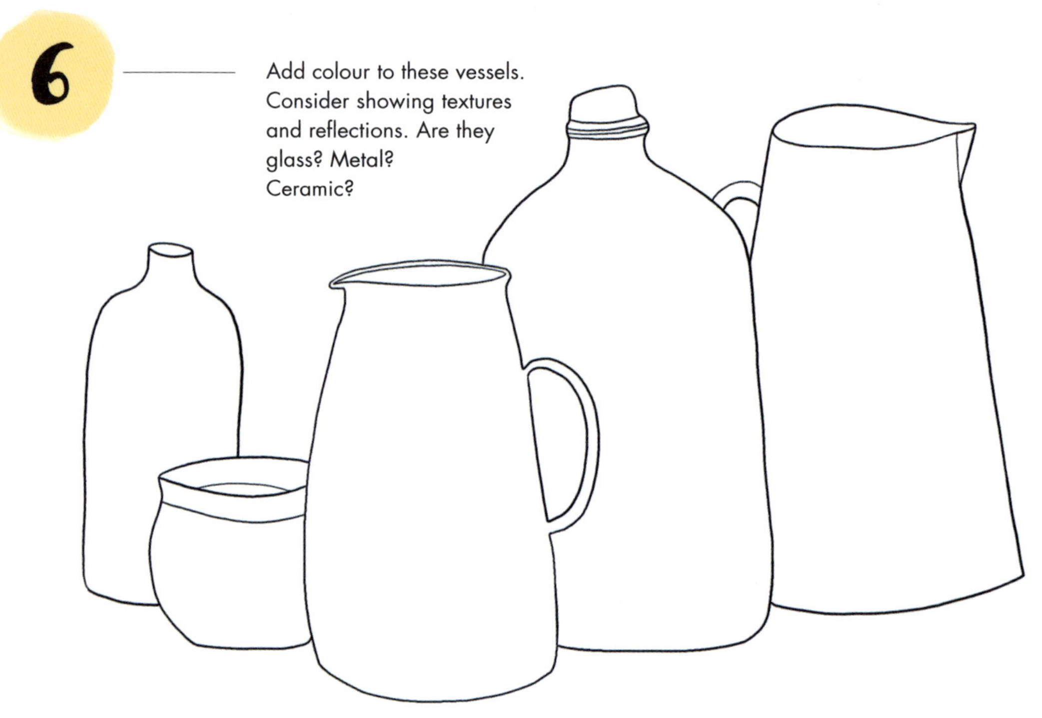

7

Never feel afraid to use bold colours in your art. Make a drawing of an object from your home using bright, bold colours. Don't worry about making a mistake ... there's no such thing!

8

Oil or wax pastels are a brilliant material for making colourful artwork because the colours are often rich and vibrant. You can also get a lot of coverage, quickly. Explore using them by creating an abstract, colourful design.

Tip: As these can get messy, you could use a fixative spray once you've finished your artwork to seal the pastels and prevent smudging. Or tape a sheet of tracing paper over the top of the page.

9

Continue adding lines of colour to the page. Use a variety of art materials and choose colours you rarely use as well as those you enjoy.

The colour red can suggest anger, danger, confidence, heat and love. Be inspired by how red makes *you* feel and turn this shape into an image.

Create a chequerboard pattern using pinks, reds and purples.

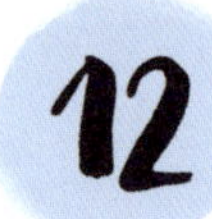

Part of learning to enjoy colour is realising the huge variety of colours and materials available to us which we can use in our art. Add swatches of as many colours as you can find, or mix colours yourself.

Tip: You could use found bits of coloured paper, or fabric too.

Grass green	Dark green	Coral red	Turquoise	Mustard	Burgundy	Navy blue

13

Complementary colours are those found opposite each other on the colour wheel. When used together, they can create striking images because they are contrasting.

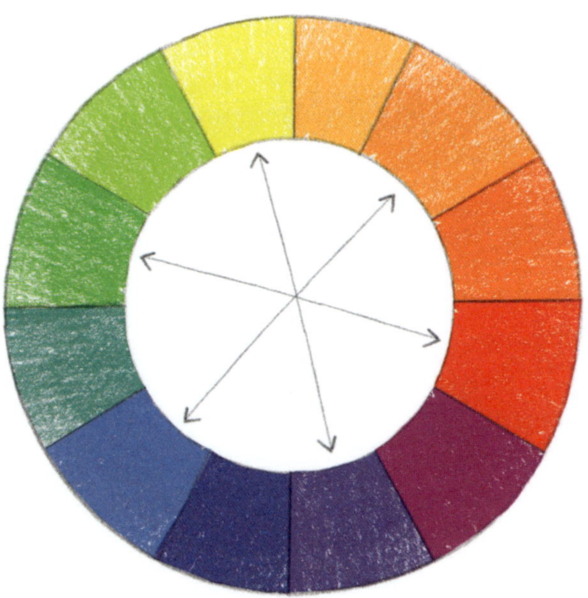

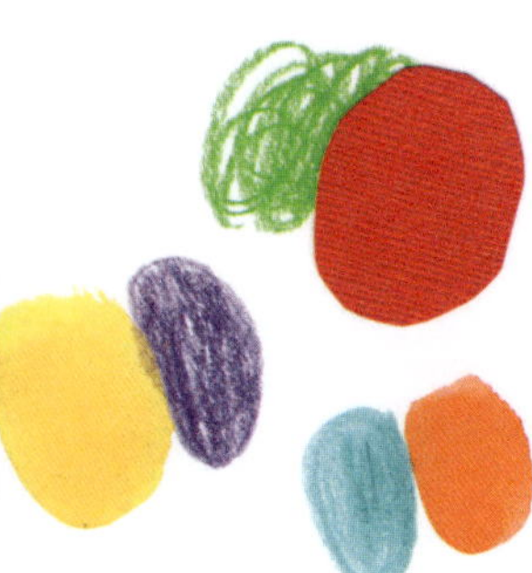

Fill the space with pairs of complementary colours using different art materials. Are there any pairings you particularly enjoy?

14

Make a drawing of a person using a confident blue line to create a loose, joyful image.

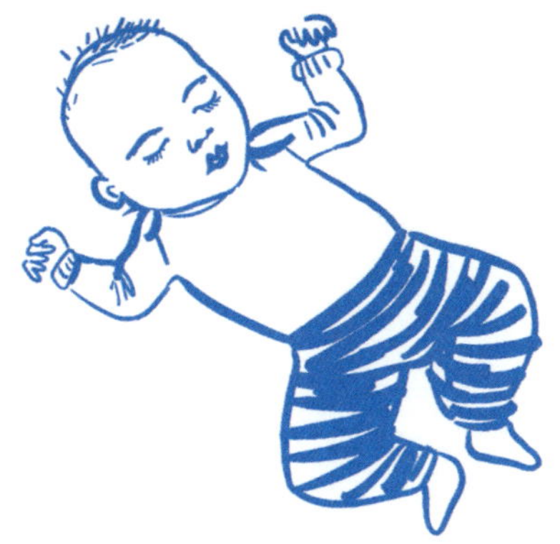

15

You can blend paint to create colourful artworks. Add colours here or create your own sheets of blended colours. You could then use these painted sheets for collages, or enjoy them as they are.

Tip: *Blending is when you merge colours together when they are wet, but don't fully mix them. Watercolour works well to make blends.*

16

Draw around your hand using a coloured pencil, and create a piece of art inspired by this colourful outline. You could also draw around the hands of other family members or friends too.

Tip: You don't have to fit your whole hand on the page, you may choose to draw around your fingers, and create an abstract piece.

17

A 'tint' is a lighter version of a colour, and a 'shade' is a darker version. Use the space on the right to explore mixing paints to create tints and shades of your colours. You can use any paints – you'll just need some colours, plus black and white, and you might find it easiest to mix your paints in a palette or on an old plate.

Tip: Using tints and shades can be especially useful when painting the light and shadow of an object – the 'tone' – because you can capture colours more effectively compared with using pure black or white.

To create a 'tint', add white to a colour.

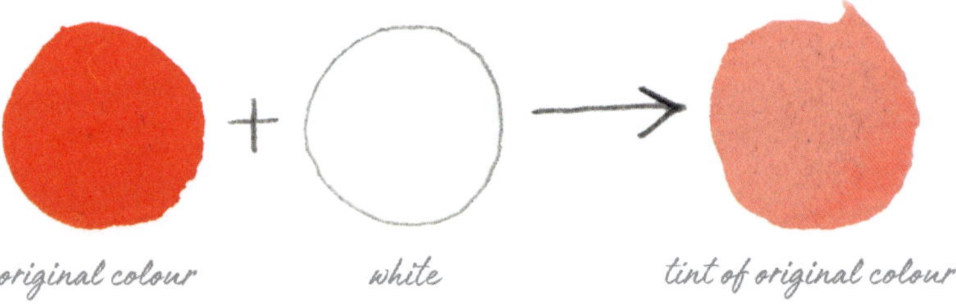

To create a 'shade', add a small amount of black to a colour.

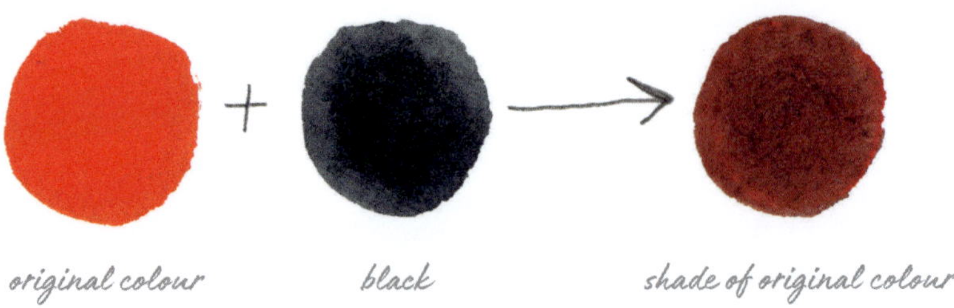

Tip: You could try adding different amounts of black to get different shades of the same original colour.

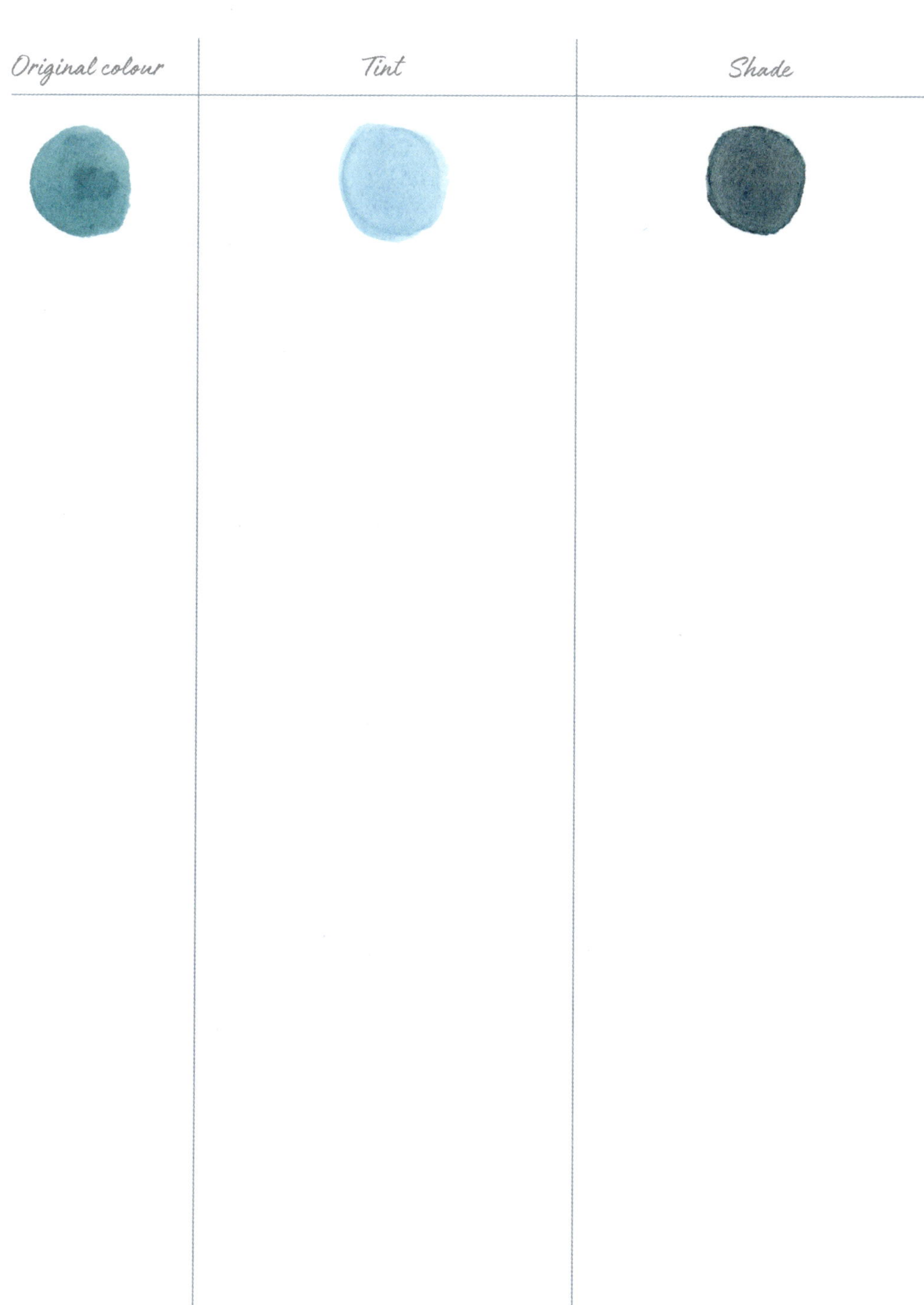
Original colour
Tint
Shade

18

Drawing using a continuous line is a great way to practise looking at a scene in front of you, rather than just drawing what you *think* you can see. Choose a scene and three or four coloured pencils that will help capture it. Each time you start a new colour, keep the pencil on the page until you are ready for the next colour. Try not to be tempted to lift the pencil from the page – embrace the challenge!

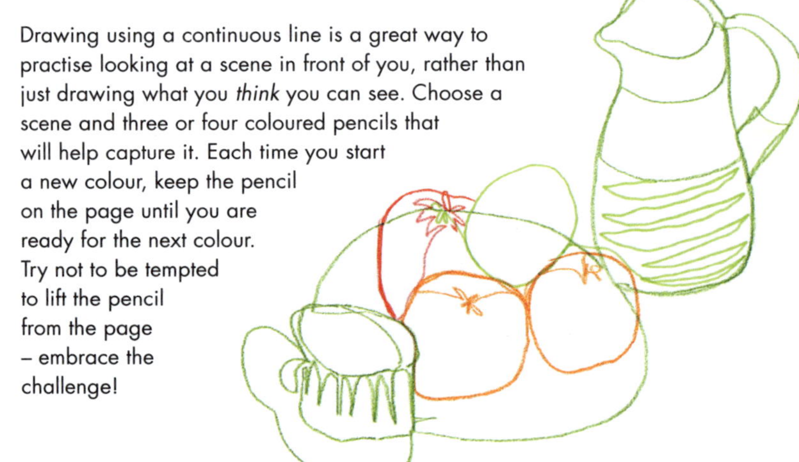

19

A colour gradient is when a colour gradually blends into another colour. Make a gradient using watercolour paint; it doesn't need to be perfect. Start by selecting two colours that you'd like to blend.

Add a colour at each end, cleaning your brush in between so the colour stays pure.

Add a little more water to your brush and apply more of each colour.
It's alright if a little of the colour from each end is left on your brush at this stage.

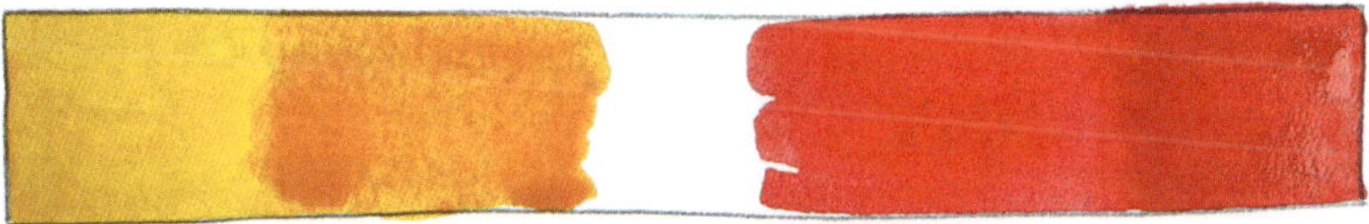

Then drag the paint from each side to fill in the middle section. You'll notice the colours start to run into each other and begin to blend.

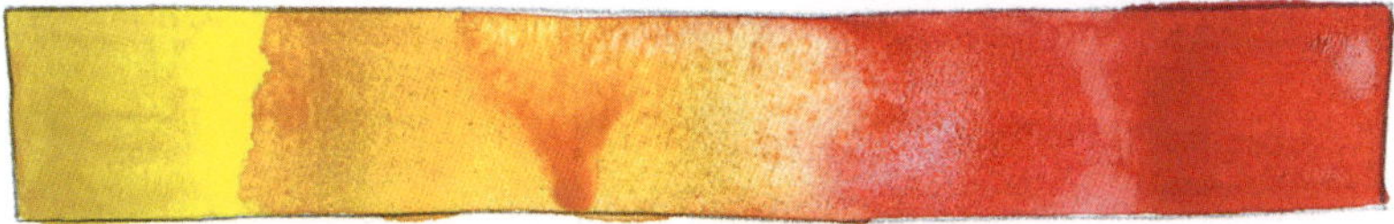

Continue blending the colours yourself, using gentle movements with your brush. It doesn't need to be perfectly smooth to still look effective.

***Tip:** If you are worried about the water bleeding through the page, you can prime the page first using clear or white gesso.*

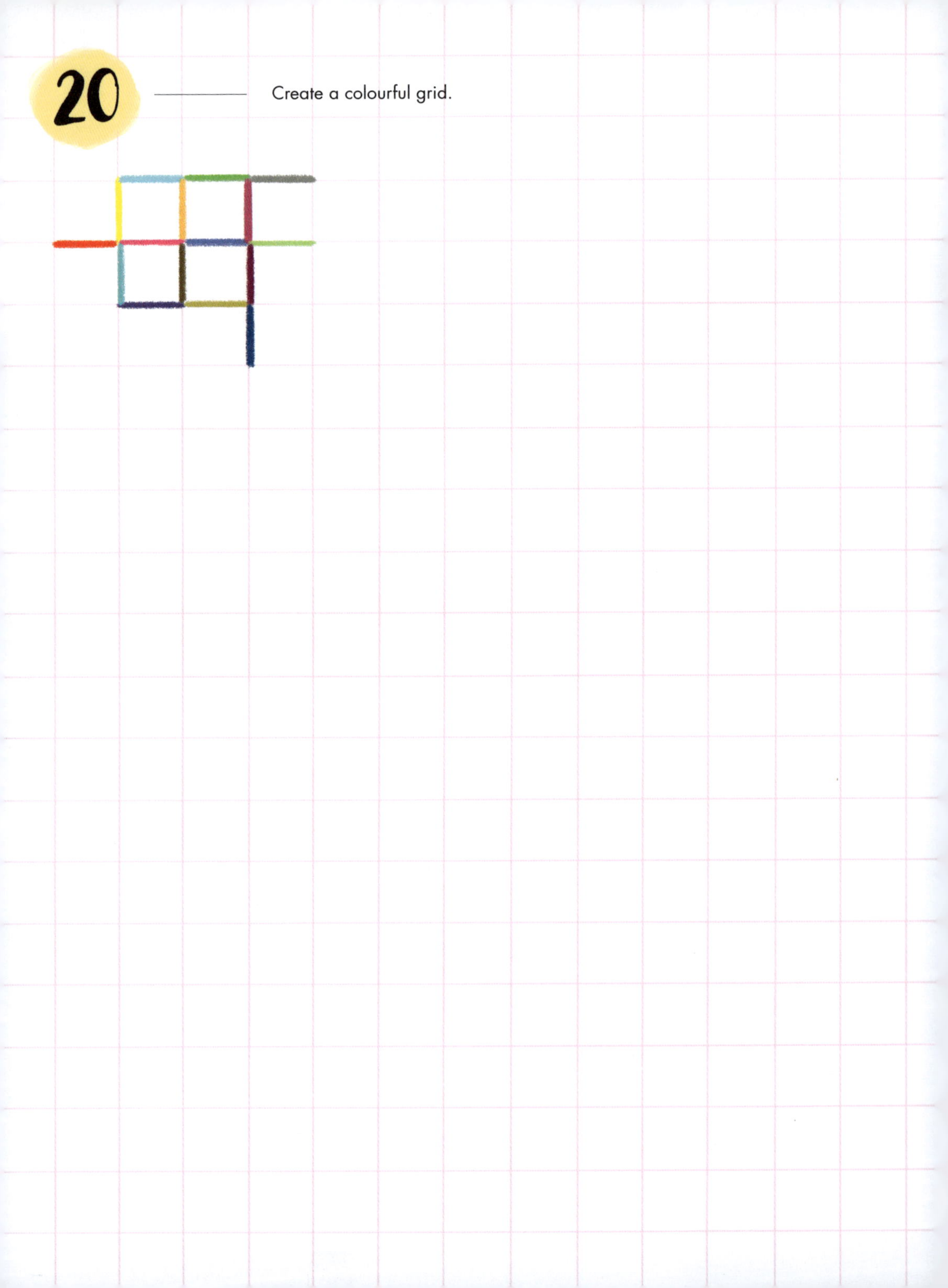

20

Create a colourful grid.

21

Practise blending colours together to create new hues.Use dry materials here, such as coloured pencils, chalks or pastels.

Tip: The colours can't be completely mixed like a wet material such as paint can be, so the effect can be quite beautiful as both colours show through!

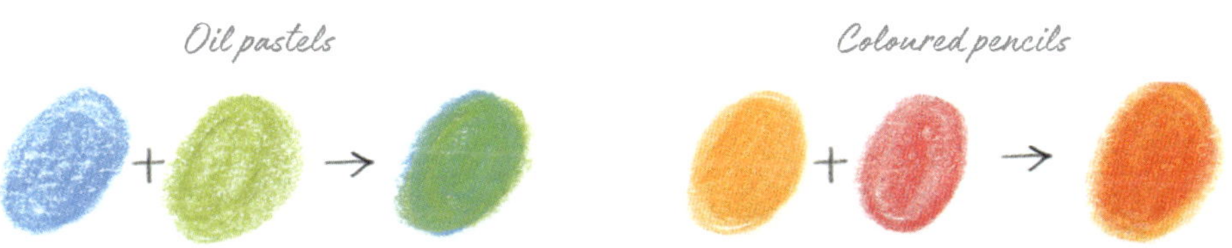

Tip: Try applying just a light amount of pressure to make your swatch, and alternate layers of colour, e.g. a thin layer of green, then a thin layer of blue, then green again, then a bit more blue, until you are happy with the result.

22

Colour palettes are collections of colours, which you can then use within your artwork and designs. Inspiration for colour palettes can come from anywhere! You may see an outfit someone is wearing and think the colours look great together. Or perhaps some pink flowers look gorgeous next to a particular green. Spend time looking out for groups of colours you like, and create your own colour palettes.

You could create grids and fill the boxes with your collection of colours – this can help you see how each colour interacts with the others. Or you can just create swatches of colour, loosely assembled in a group.

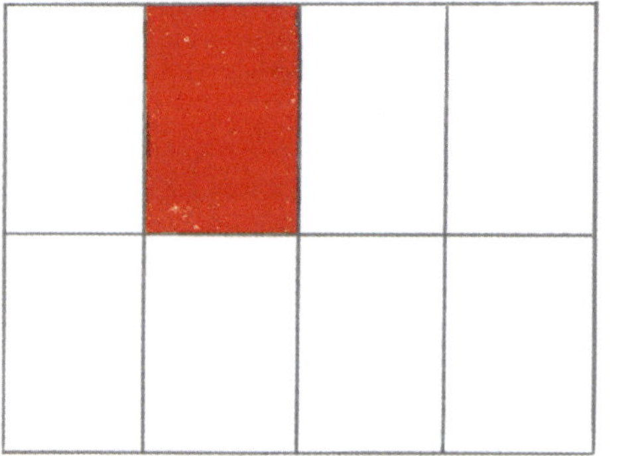

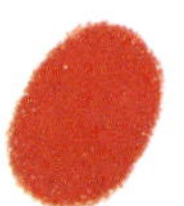

Select one colour initially and build your palette around it. For a balanced palette, you can also include tints and shades of some of your selected colours, and perhaps consider introducing a complementary colour too.

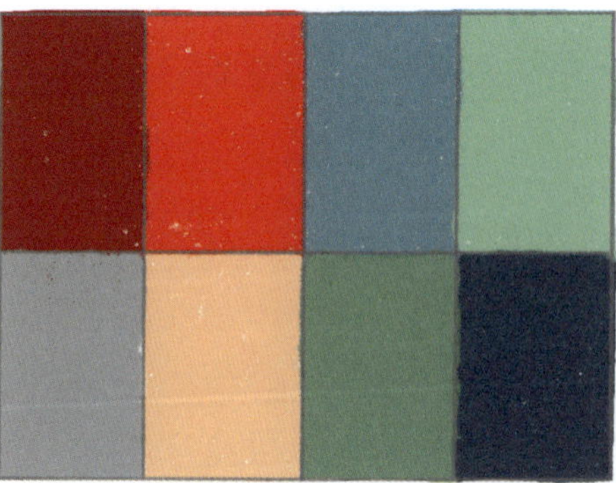

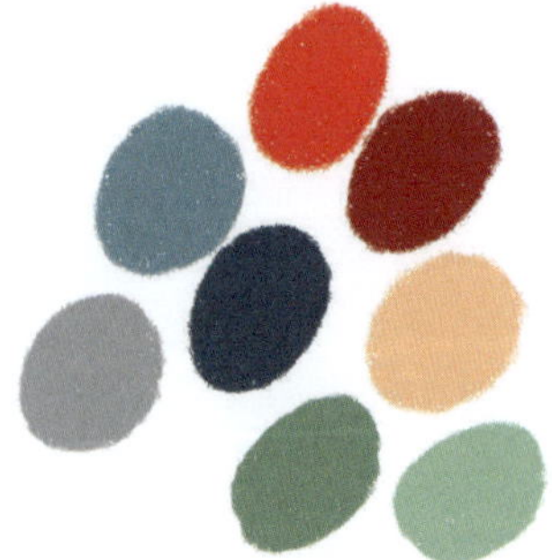

As well as including bright primary and secondary colours, think about which muted, neutral and darker colours would look good in your palette too. Or just go wild and choose any colours you think look fun together!

23

Practise using a small amount of bright, vibrant colour on muted or dark backgrounds. Create little backgrounds using paint or cut paper. Once dry, add a flash of bright colour, perhaps using wax pastel, coloured pencil or cut paper.

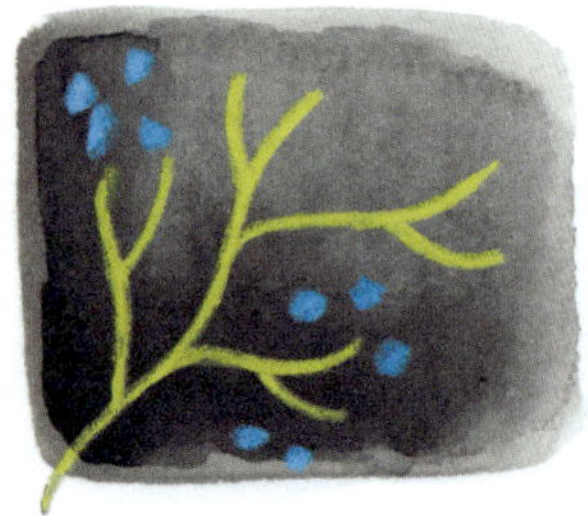

Tip: You don't need to draw anything specific, just explore the effect of using bright colours alongside muted colours.

24

Describe your feelings today using colour. Perhaps the way you create the marks help express your feelings too – a calm mood might prompt you to make slow, sweeping marks, and any agitation might inspire you to make quick marks.

25

Draw a colourful piece of clothing.

26

Colours described as 'pastel' are pale, soft colours that appear creamy and subdued. They are often associated with tranquillity, and you can use them deliberately in your art to convey serenity. Make some swatches using pastel colours.

27

Analogous colours are found next to each other on the colour wheel and can be used to create images that are satisfying to look at. For example, orange, yellow and green are analogous and would produce a pleasing, fresh palette. Using your colour wheel as a guide, create an abstract image using three analogous colours.

28

Continue drawing the pattern, and then add colour to your design using only those in this palette plus one additional colour of your choice.

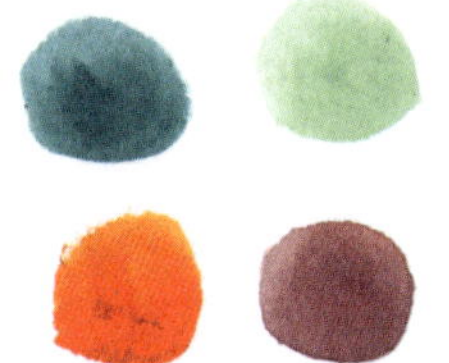

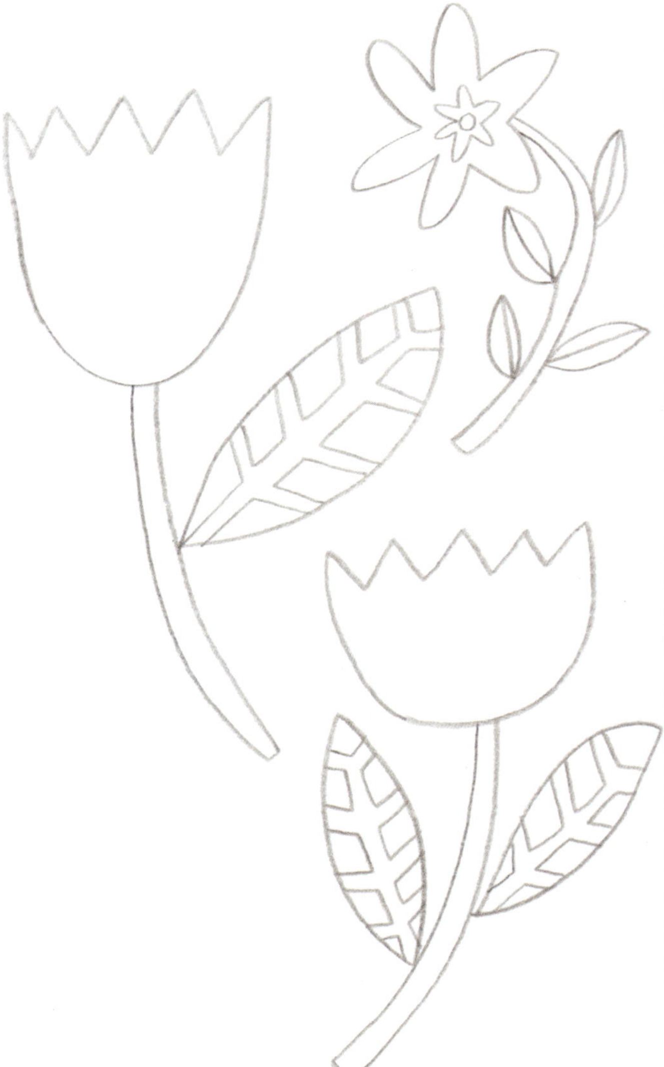

29

Paint pieces of paper using colours inspired by different moods you feel. Use a separate sheet of paper for each mood. Once the paper has dried, cut out bird shapes and collage them here to create a flock of colourful birds.

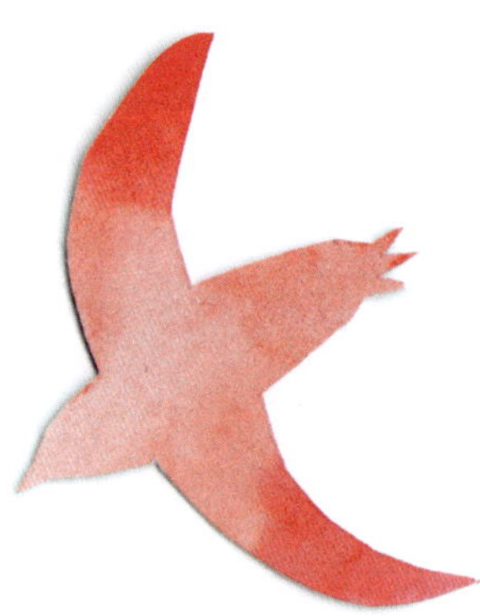

Tip: You can keep any coloured paper you don't use for future collages.

30

Creating a colour palette can be a really useful starting point for pieces of art. Choose an image (perhaps a photo, or image from a magazine), and create swatches of the main colours that you can see. Once you've identified the colours, you could use your palette to create a drawing of your image or to inspire different artwork.

Tip: To make the swatches, try to find colours in your art materials that match those you see, or mix them yourself using paint.

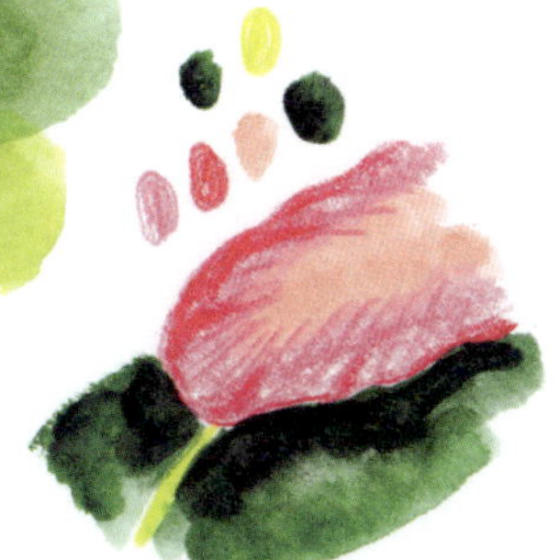

31

Look back at your colour wheel and identify which colours are complementary (they will be opposite each other in the colour wheel). Create different combinations of complementary colours, for example greens and reds or oranges and blues, using different materials. Are there any pairs you find particularly striking or appealing?

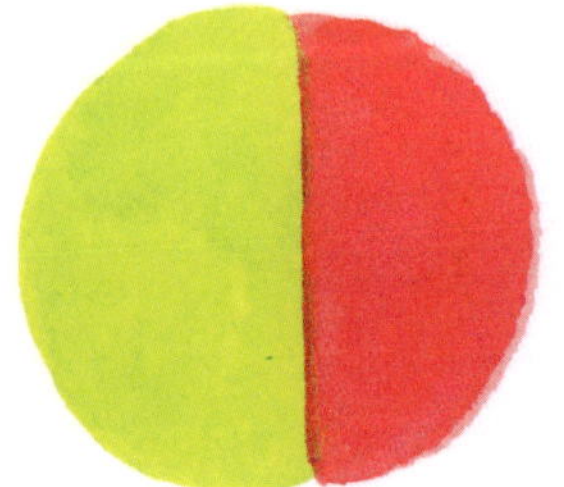
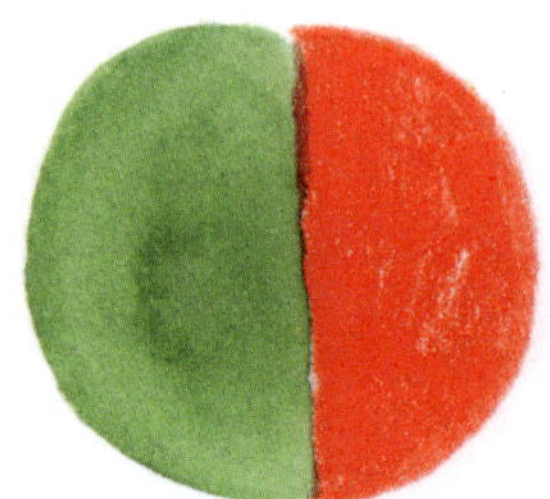
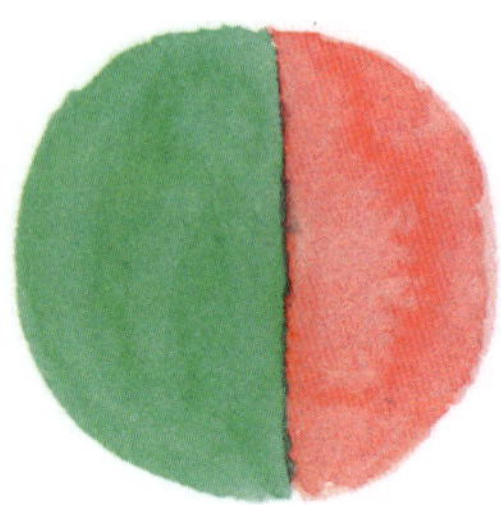

32

The sky isn't always bright blue, and grass isn't always green! Create a postcard of somewhere you love, but really think about what colours you can see in the landscape. Are there purples? Pinks? Yellows?

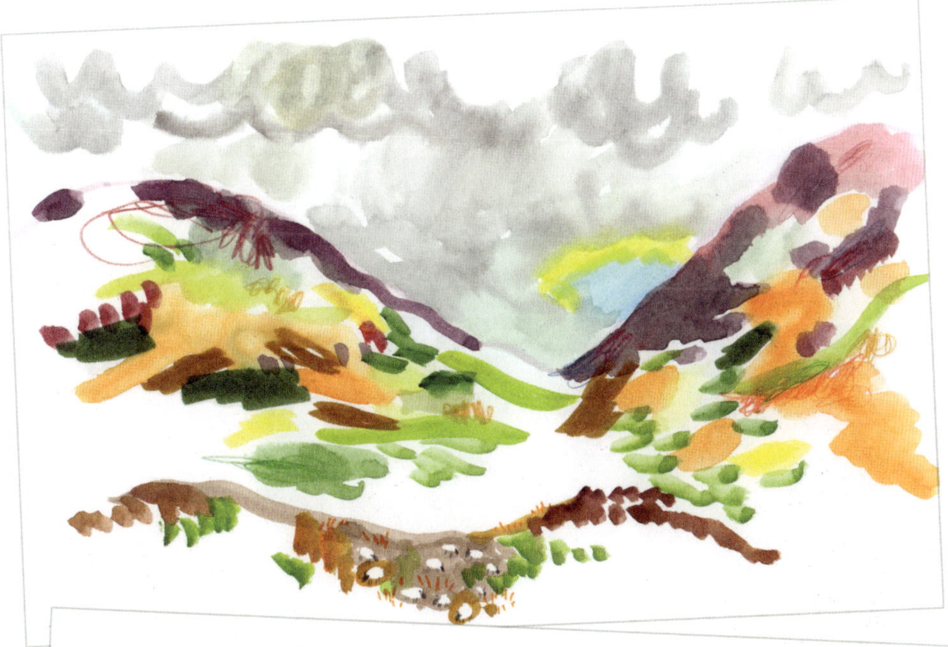

33

It can be fun to use a dark background as a starting point for observational drawing – it helps you take a fresh approach to your art, and light subtle colours suddenly pop! Create a drawing from observation on black paper. You could use pastels or colouring pencils.

Tip: Think about how the black can be used to make your image stand out – what object and colours will make for a good contrasting image?

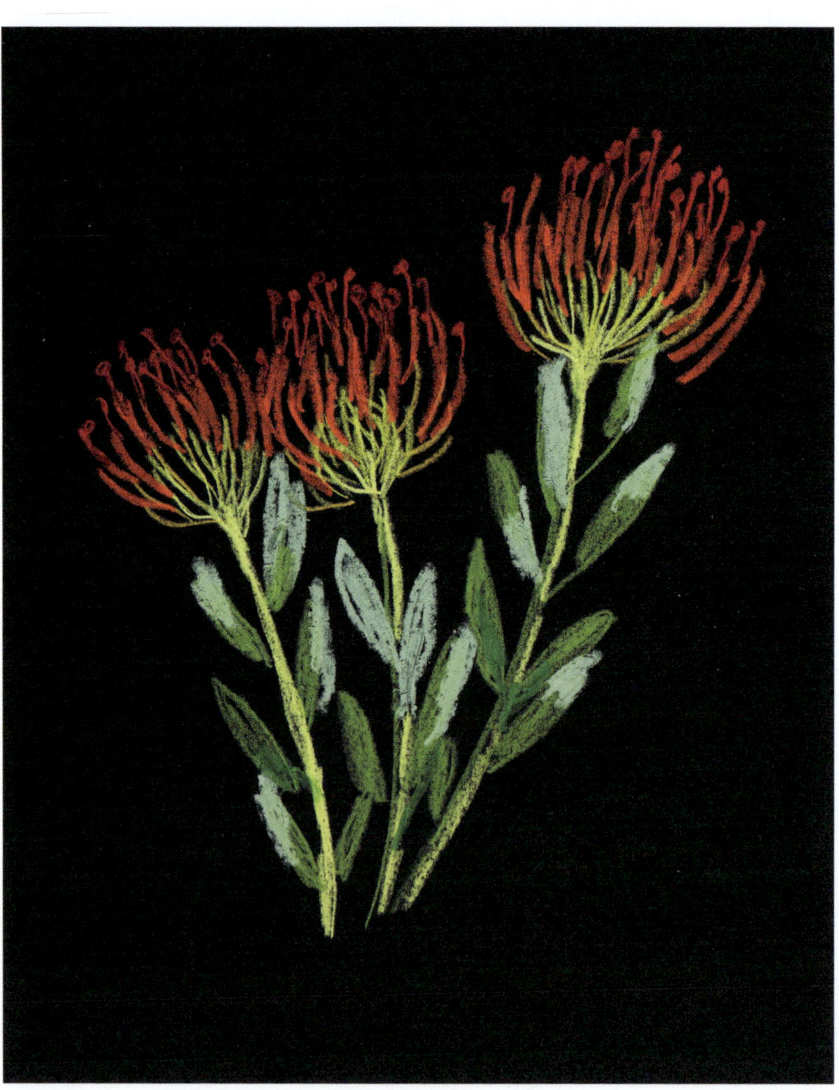

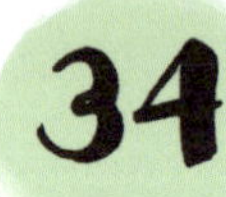

Find a piece of fruit and draw or paint it, seeing if you can avoid using outlines. Start by capturing the lighter colours in blocks, and then add the darker colours in blocks on top.

Tip: You could put your fruit on a brightly coloured plate or piece of paper to make the colours stand out.

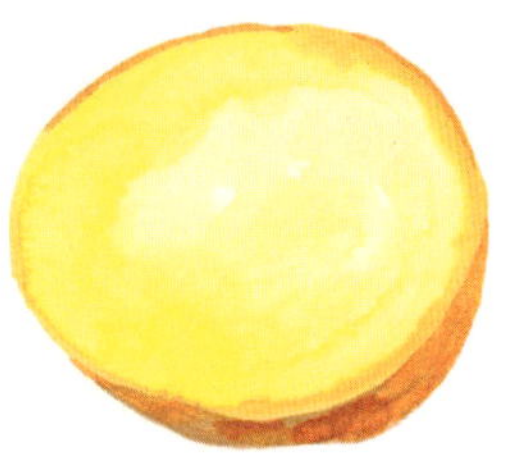

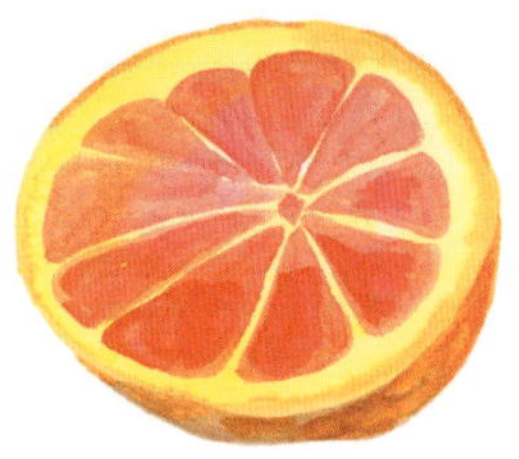

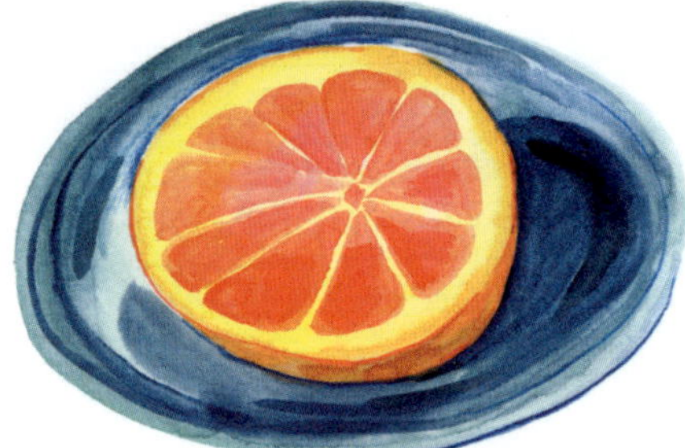

35

Write down ideas for potential colourful subjects in your artwork. For example: people, pets, things you enjoy looking at around your home or perhaps things in nature that inspire you. Refer to this list in later activities, if you are needing a suggestion for a subject.

Tip: A 'subject' is the object or scene being represented in your art.

36

Which colours do you avoid using in your art? Encourage yourself to use them here, and consider why you avoid them.

37

Fill the page with calming pastel shapes. Relax and enjoy the peaceful nature of the colours.

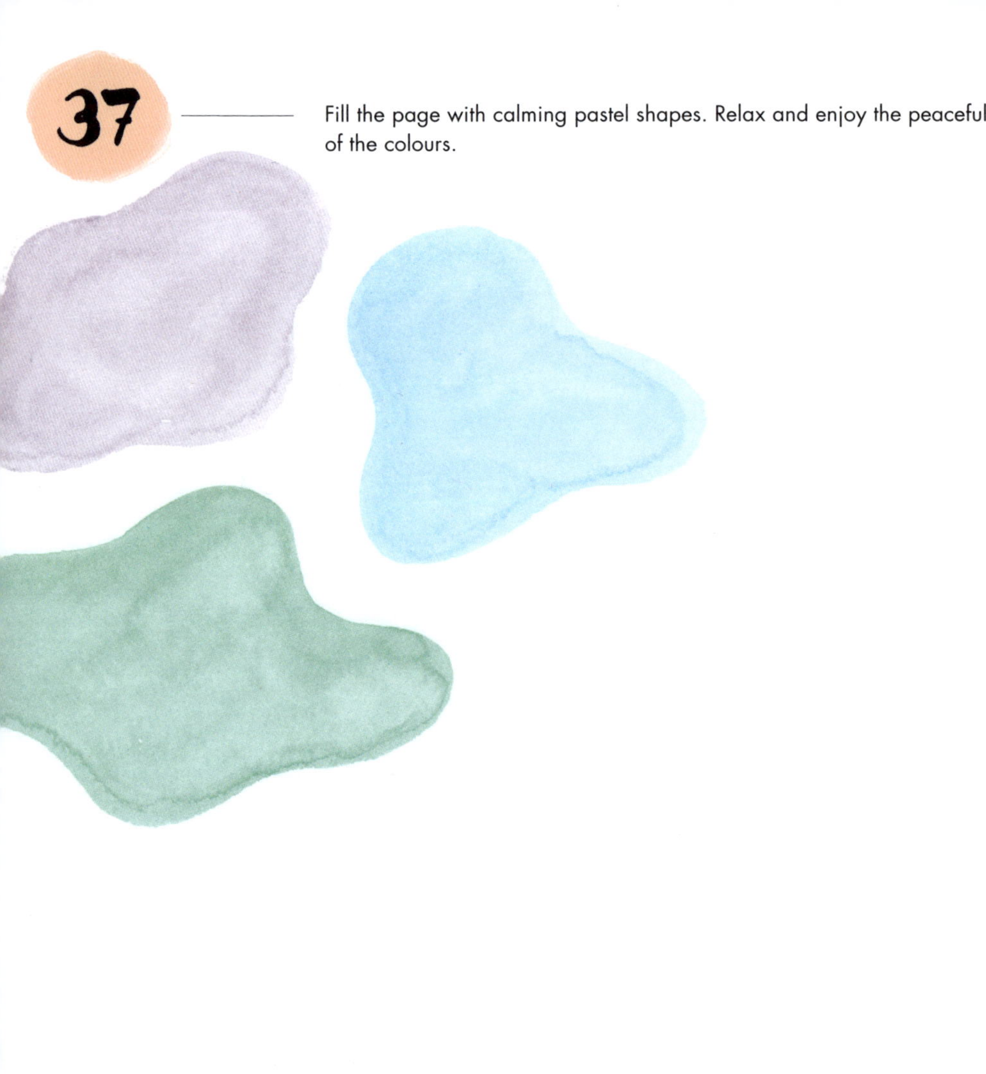

38

The secondary colours are orange, green and violet, and are made by mixing two primary colours together. Slightly different reds, yellows and blues will produce different hues of secondary colours. Using paint and a palette to mix, create secondary colours here, noticing how varied the results can be depending on which red, blue and yellow you use.

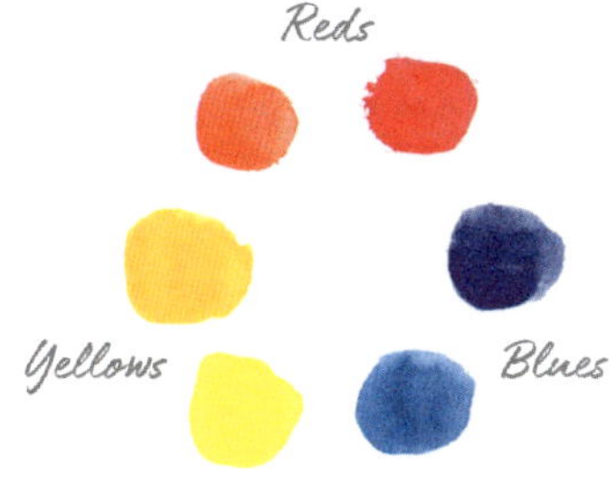

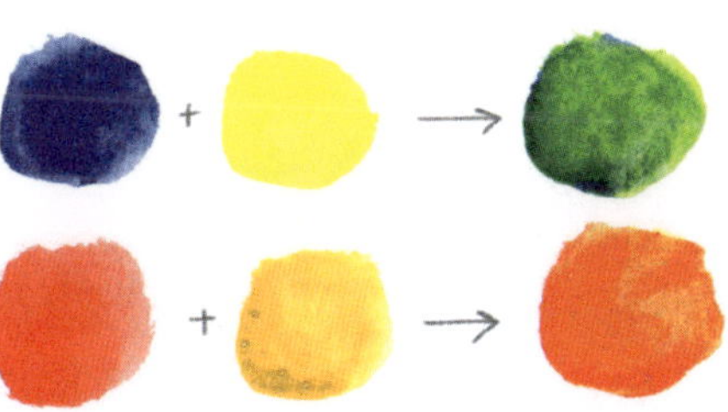

39

Add colourful scenes or designs to each coloured background.

40

Draw some of your art materials and then colour them in.

41

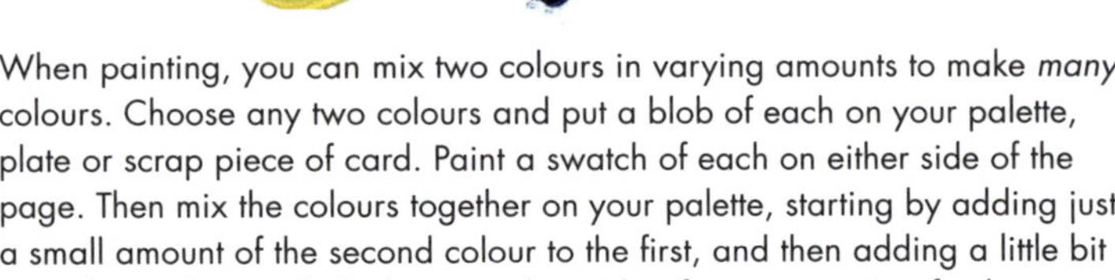

When painting, you can mix two colours in varying amounts to make *many* colours. Choose any two colours and put a blob of each on your palette, plate or scrap piece of card. Paint a swatch of each on either side of the page. Then mix the colours together on your palette, starting by adding just a small amount of the second colour to the first, and then adding a little bit more for each swatch. Perhaps try this with a few more pairs of colours.

Tip: Some of your swatches will only be subtly different!

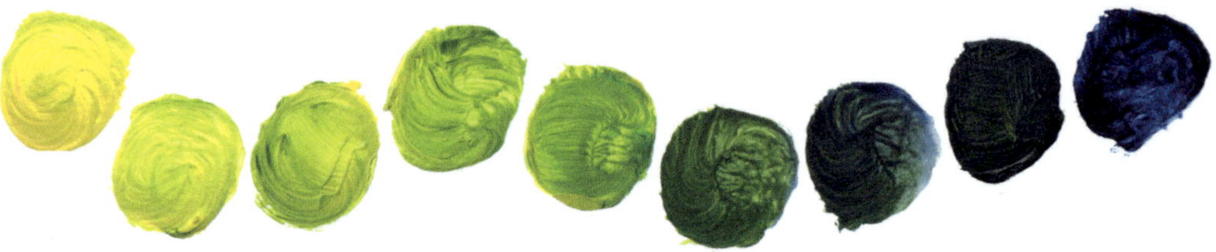

42

Find an object that is your favourite colour and draw it.

Blue can evoke feelings of calm, healing, security and consistency. Consider how blue makes *you* feel and create an image using this shape as a starting point.

44

Find an object in your house which is comprised of complementary colours and draw it. You can work quite quickly, not worrying too much about accuracy, just enjoying the shapes you see.

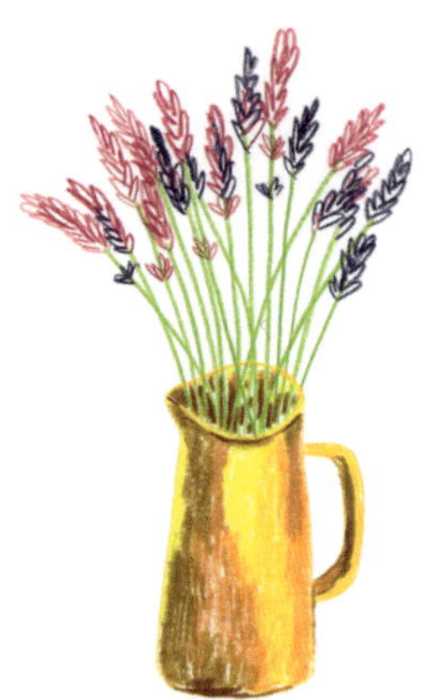

45

Add to the pattern to fill the page.

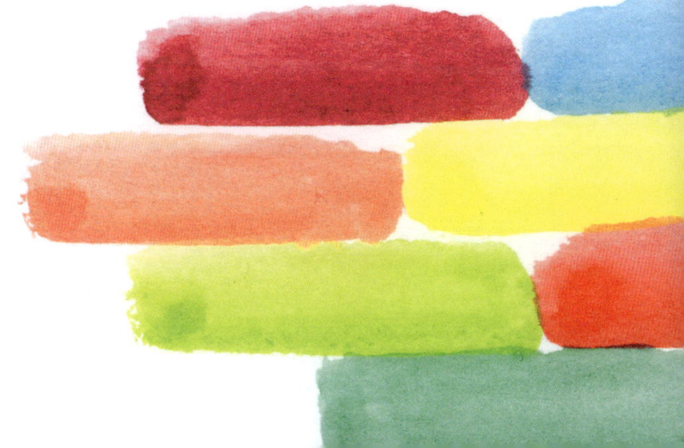

46

Choose six things that you enjoy looking at. Using any material, create palettes made from the colours you see.

A mug

A flower and leaves

47

Design a pair of colourful trainers.

48

Colour this design.

49

Create a portrait or self-portrait using collage. Use coloured paper, cut-out magazines or wrapping paper, or anything else you'd like.

Tip: *The colours can be very abstract and bold, or you might try to match colours more closely to what you truly see – it's up to you!*

50

Get messy! Put some paint in a mixing palette, or on a piece of card, dip your fingers in and make some fingerprints on the page! Once your prints are dry, turn the shapes into objects or little scenes.

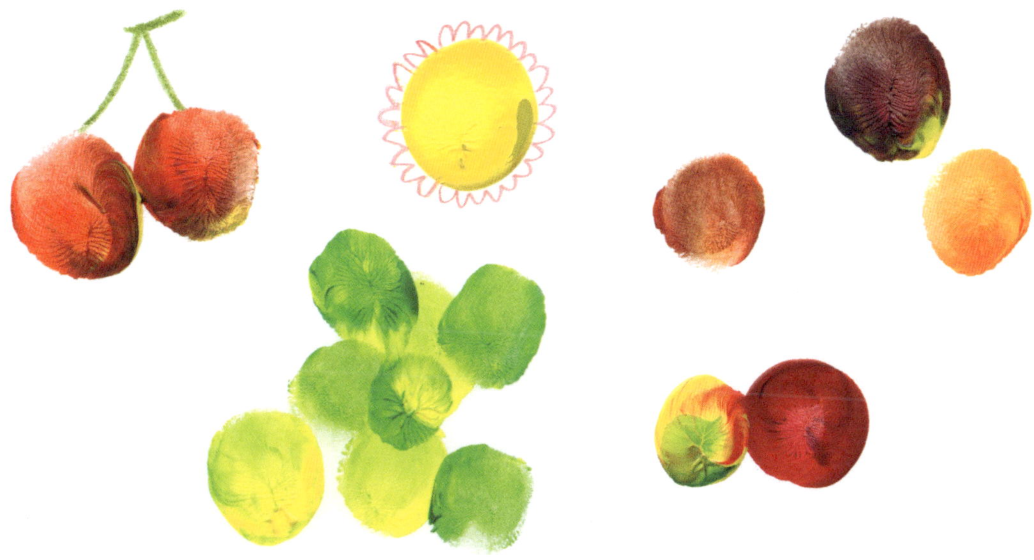

51

Make three drawings of a human figure using three different colours. Ask a friend or family member to model for you, and give yourself just one minute to draw them in three different poses! Work fast, trying to capture as much of the figure on the page as possible. You can layer the drawings on top of each other or draw them separately.

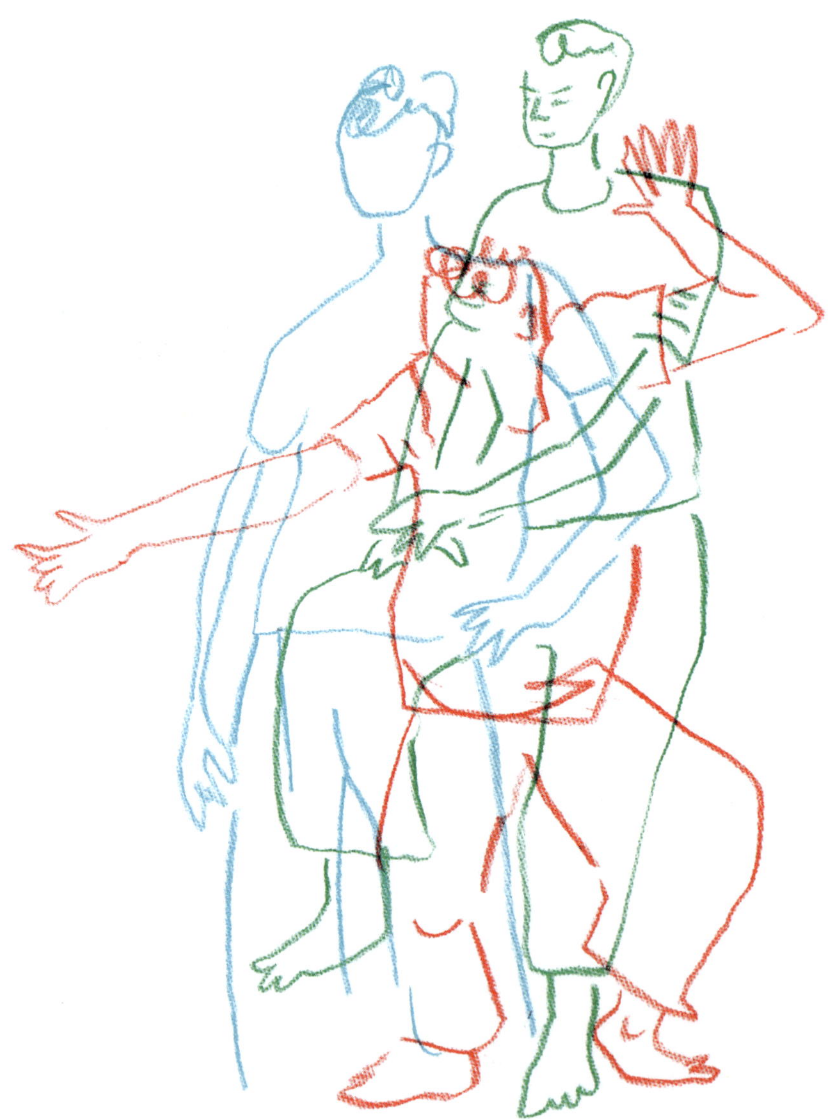

Tip: Using three random pre-selected colours means you will focus on the form of the figure, rather than worrying about choosing colours.

52

Gather some coloured paints, a paintbrush, water, paper towels and a clean mixing palette (or a clean, smooth plate), and use this space to practise combining paints to make specific colours. Try to match the colours below.

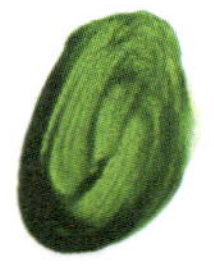 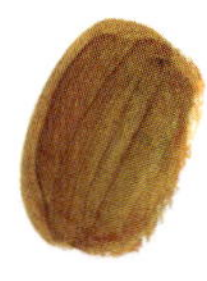 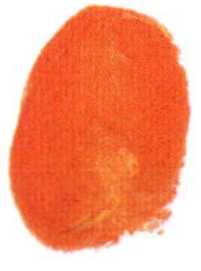 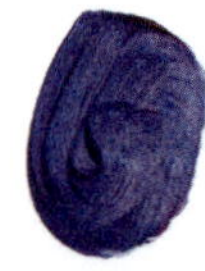 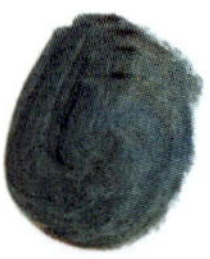

Tip: Start by guessing which colours might be in each colour, then mix small amounts of paint together on your palette to see if it feels right.

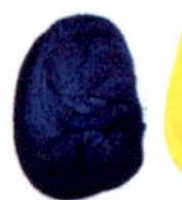  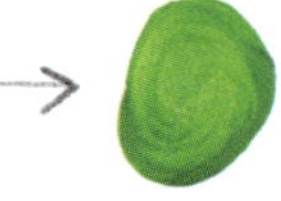

Mix blue and yellow to make green. Different blues and yellows will make different hues of green.

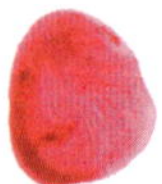 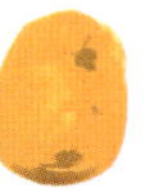 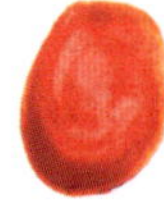

Mixing a small amount of magenta with yellow will make a cherry red.

Tip: Don't worry if you don't make an exact match for these colours – it's more about getting used to mixing colours and learning what results you can create.

53

Fill the page with colourful squares. Enjoy choosing which colours look good alongside each other.

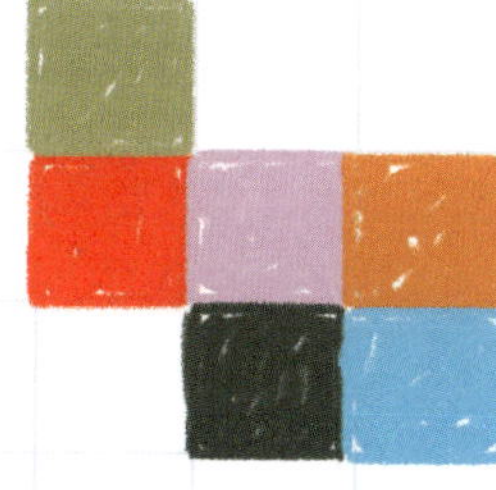

54

You can blend two or more colouring pencils to create new colours. These blended colours aren't truly mixed, as they are when you combine paints, and so they have a rich, textural appearance. Colour each circle using a coloured pencil to create blends where the circles meet.

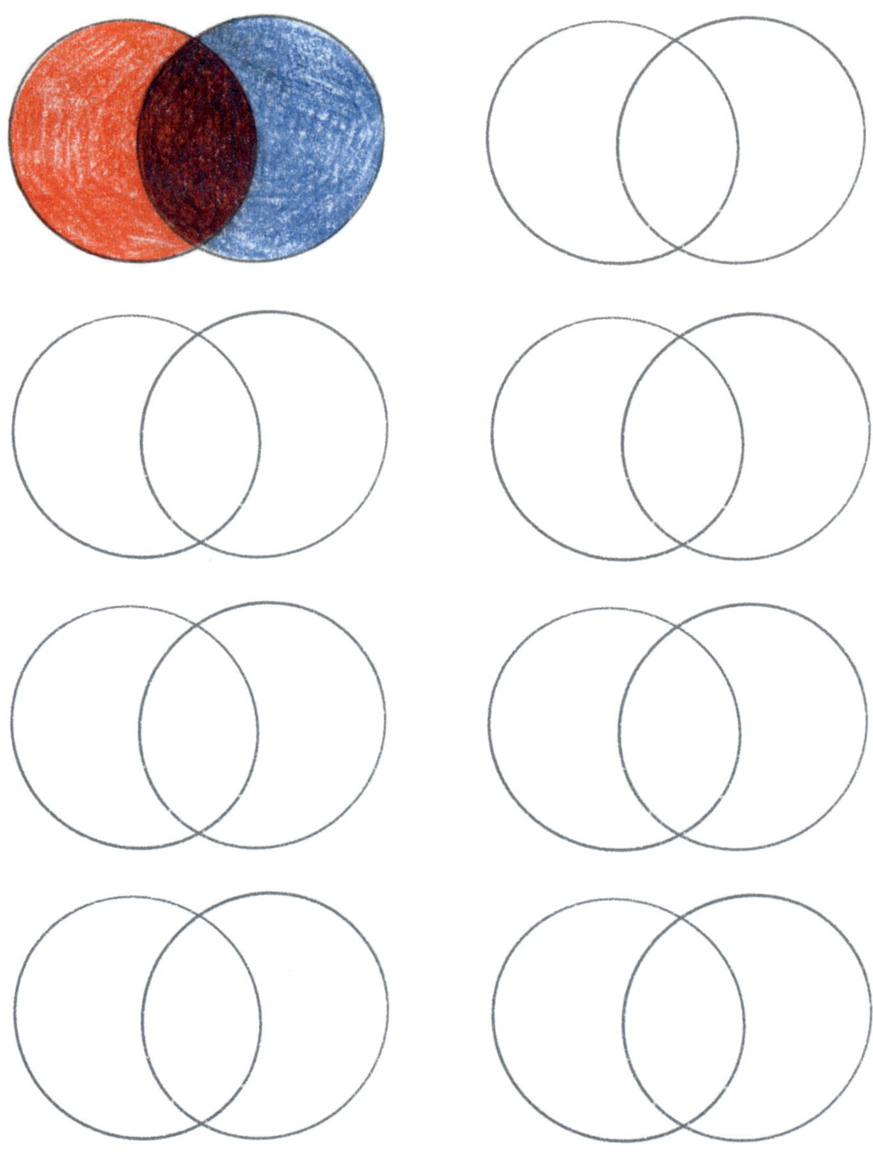

Tip: For a smoother, richer blend, add multiple layers of each colour, alternating between the two different hues.

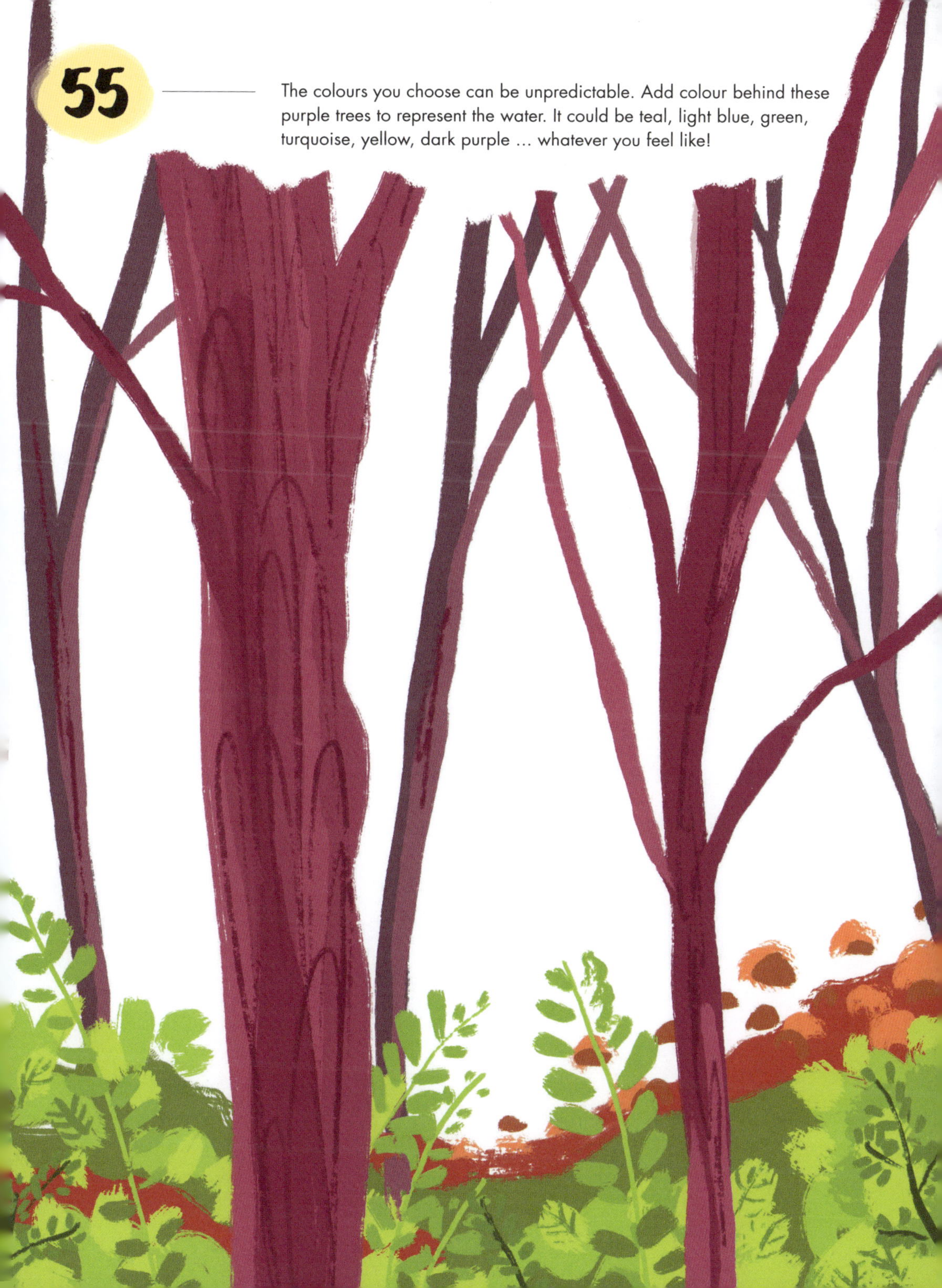

55

The colours you choose can be unpredictable. Add colour behind these purple trees to represent the water. It could be teal, light blue, green, turquoise, yellow, dark purple ... whatever you feel like!

56

Off-white is a colour too! There are so many variations of 'almost' white that you can use in your art. Paint lots of swatches of off-white too. Consider how some have 'cool' undertones and some have 'warm' undertones, depending on how you make the white.

Tip: Mix very small amounts of colour with white to create your off-whites. Try green, blue, red, yellow ... any colours you have to hand.

57

Oranges and yellows can evoke feelings of warmth and joy. Create an abstract drawing using these two colours.

58

Create a painting around this image. Consider which colours will complement the orange.

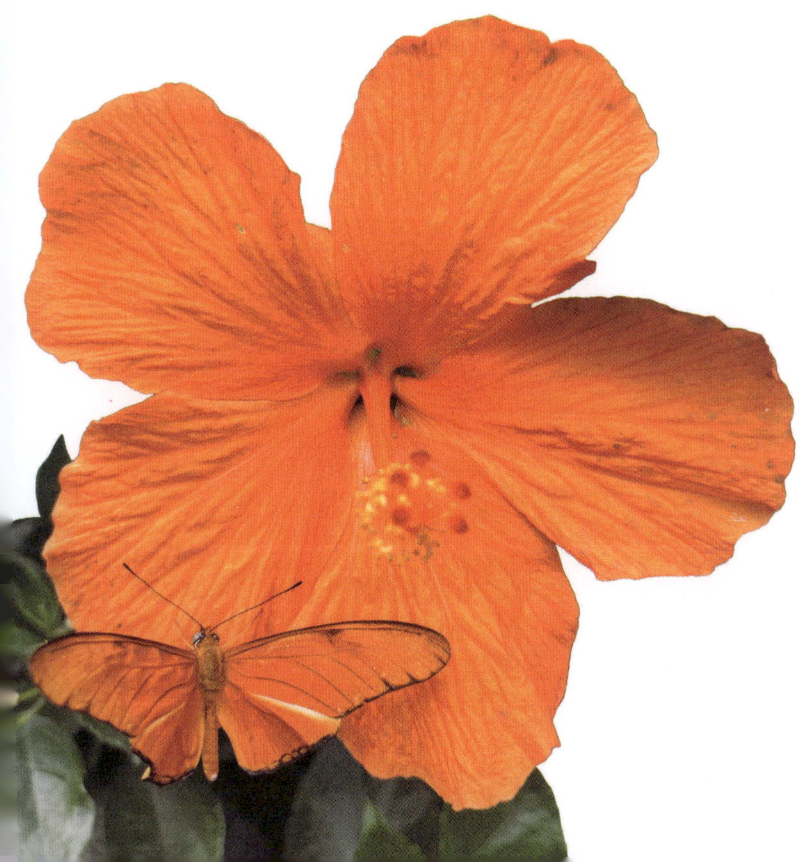

59

Neutral colours are earthy, natural colours – light tans, browns, olives, greys and creams – and can be very calming.

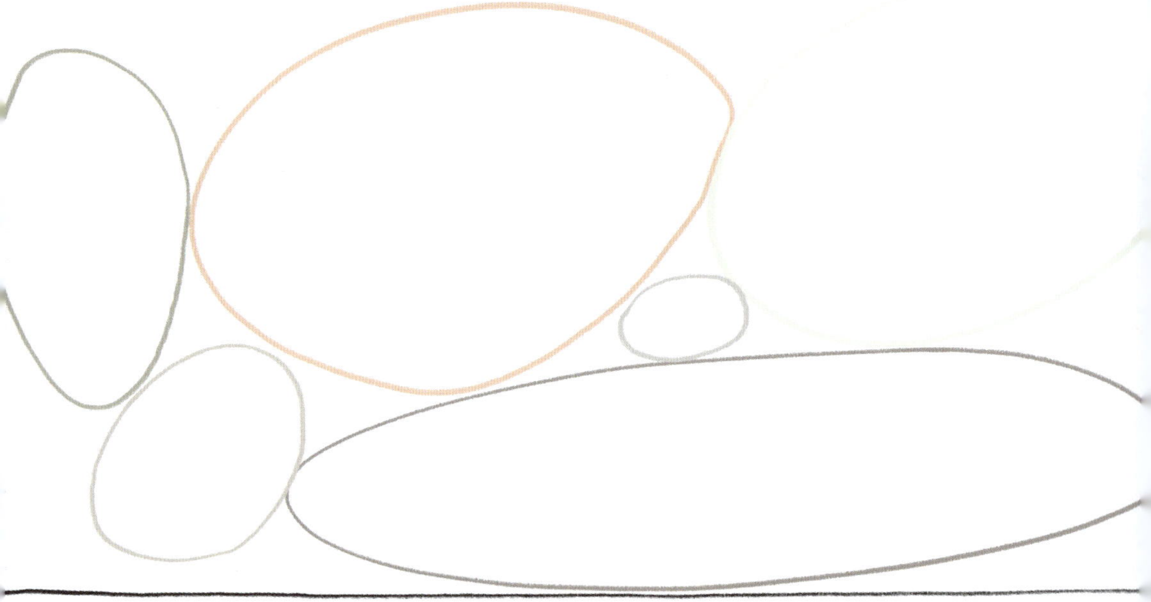

60

'Hue' is a word sometimes used interchangeably with the word 'colour', although it specifically refers to *where* a colour can be found on the colour wheel in its purest form. A colour's hue is a bit like the 'family' the colour belongs to. Decide the hue of each of these collections of colours. (In your view, which family would the colours live with on the colour wheel?)

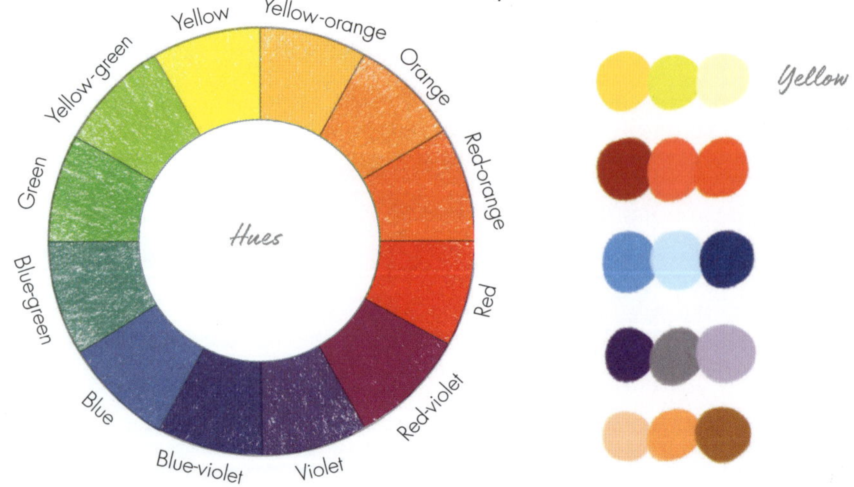

61

Put on relaxing music and create some abstract art, allowing yourself to be inspired by the music and how it makes you feel.

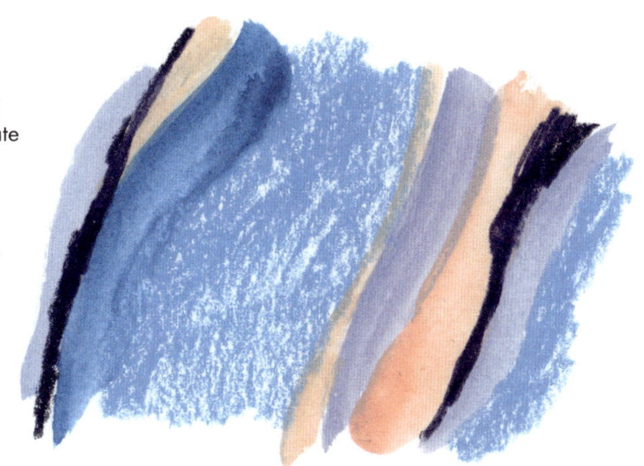

62

Draw some colourful houses.

63

Complementary colours, such as violet and yellow, are found opposite each other on the colour wheel. By gradually mixing complementary colours you can make a complementary colour scale. This scale can then become a harmonious palette to use in your art – any colours you choose from the scale will look good together. Mix a complementary colour scale below using acrylic, watercolour or gouache paint.

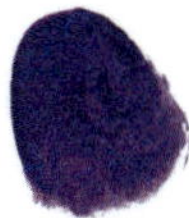

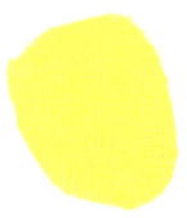

Choose two complementary colours from your colour wheel and create swatches of them at either side of the page. Gradually mix a little of one colour into the other and create a swatch below. Then add a bit more of the other colour for your next swatch, and so on. Continue until your mixed colour looks similar to your original complementary colour. You may want to mix the colours in a clean mixing palette, and start by adding the darker colour to the brighter one.

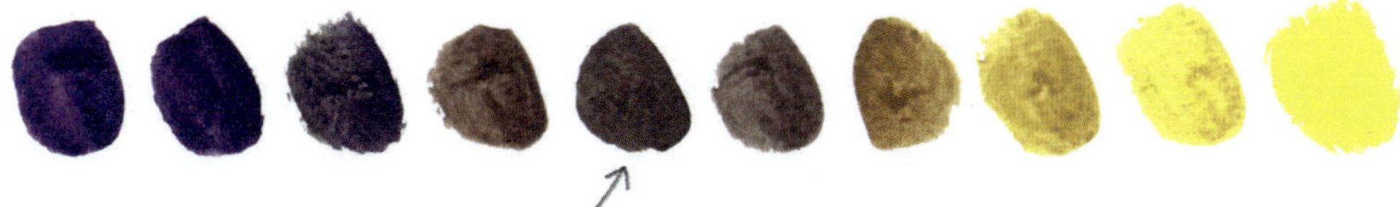

Tip: You can make browns and blacks by mixing complementary colours. All the colours on the scale are called 'neutrals' and when used alongside the pure complementary colours they originate from, the neutrals can form a calming background to help brighter colours stand out.

64

You can use the white of the page to add separation between colours in your art, and to help objects stand out. This is especially useful when the colours next to each other are similar. Make a piece of art, leaving a bit of white space between objects and the background.

Tip: Have a go at drawing the shapes you see as blocks of colour rather than drawing the outlines. This will make it easier to leave a white outline around objects.

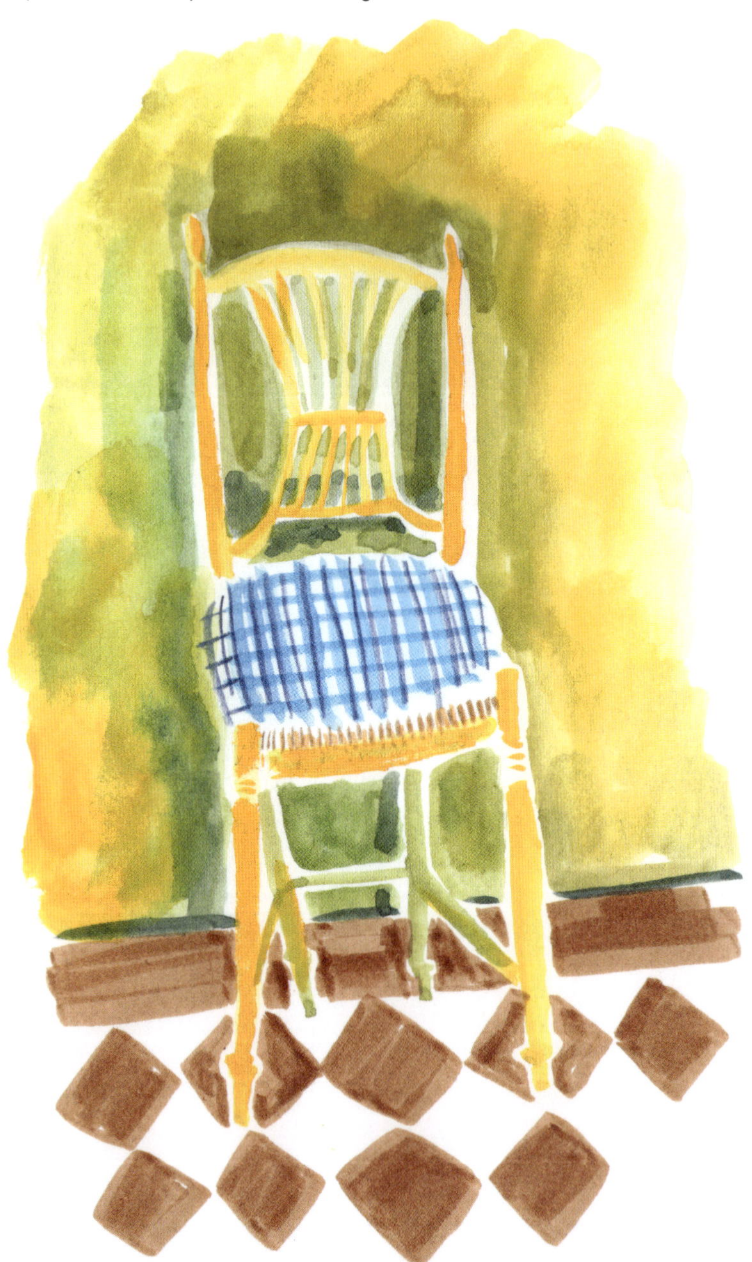

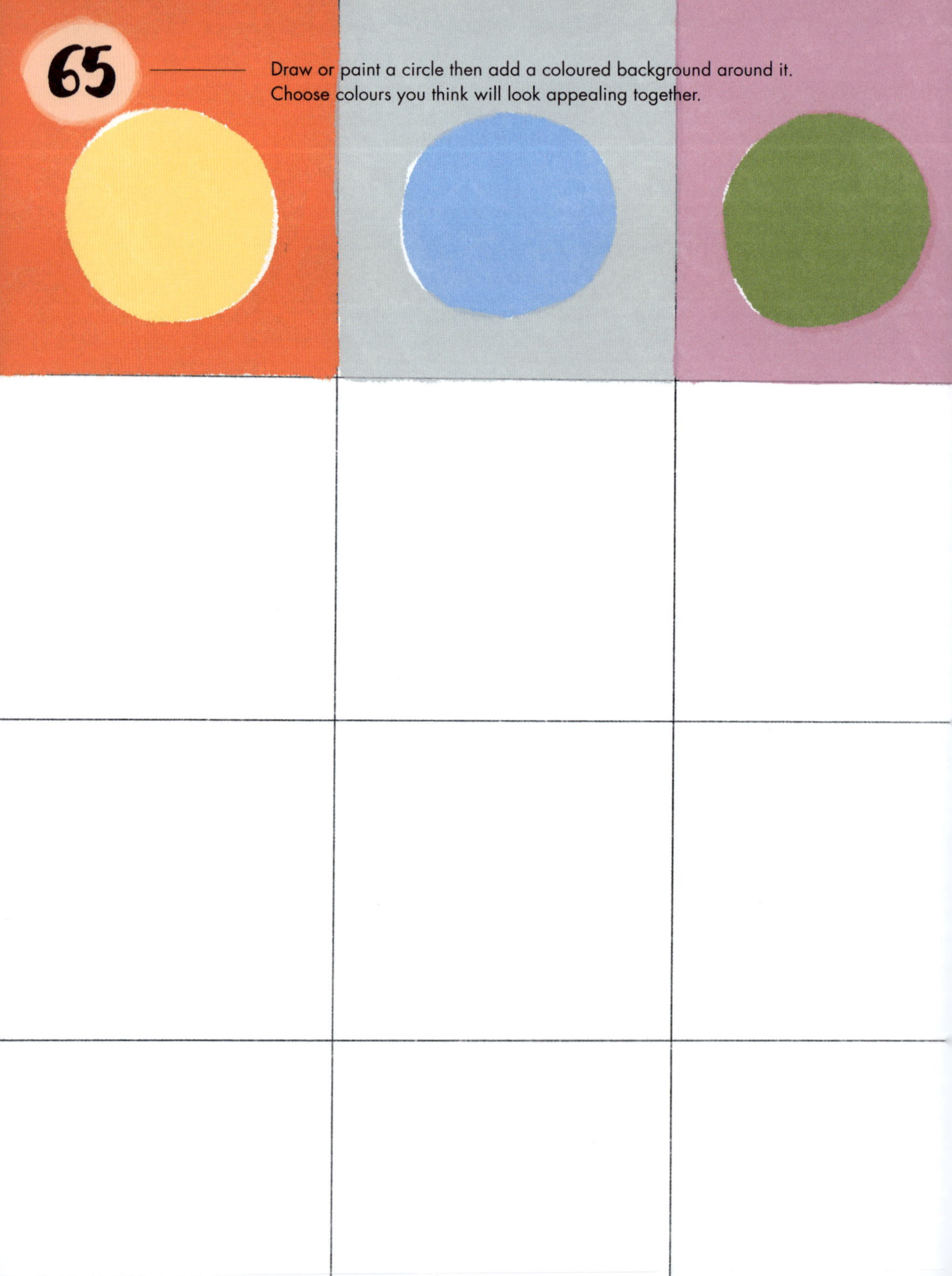

65

Draw or paint a circle then add a coloured background around it.
Choose colours you think will look appealing together.

We can describe colours as having a 'temperature'. They can appear warm or cool depending on their position in the colour wheel, and also their context (which other colours are near).

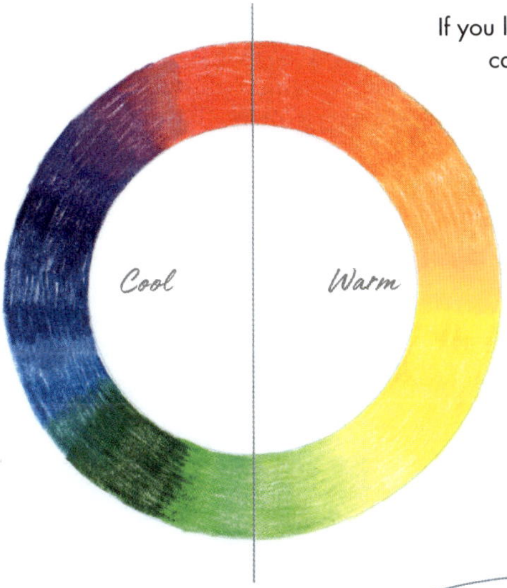

If you look at a colour wheel, colours from red to green can be perceived as warm, and colours green to red can be seen as cool. Create your own colour wheel and identify which colours feel cool and which feel warm. Have a go at blending hues.

Cool

Warm

Tip: *This can be subjective. Perhaps you'll feel that some colours in the warm area look cool – such as a yellowy green. It's useful to know roughly which colours seem which temperatures, but you can make your own decisions about how you use them in your art.*

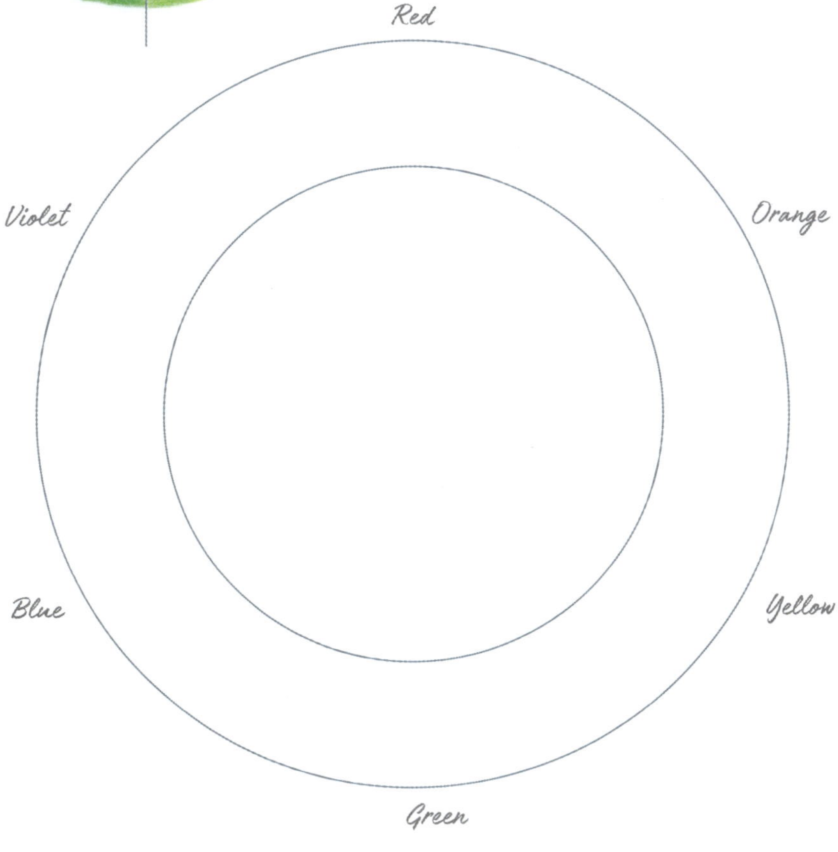

Red

Violet

Orange

Blue

Yellow

Green

67

A colour that appears very rich and pure is described as being saturated. A colour that is more faded, as if some of the intensity of the colour has been removed, is less saturated. We can make colours appear muted by mixing them with a little bit of their complementary colour. Complete this diagram using paint to show pure colours, less saturated-colours and even further less-saturated colours!

Tip: Using a paint palette, mix a small amount of complementary colour with the original colour to make it less saturated.

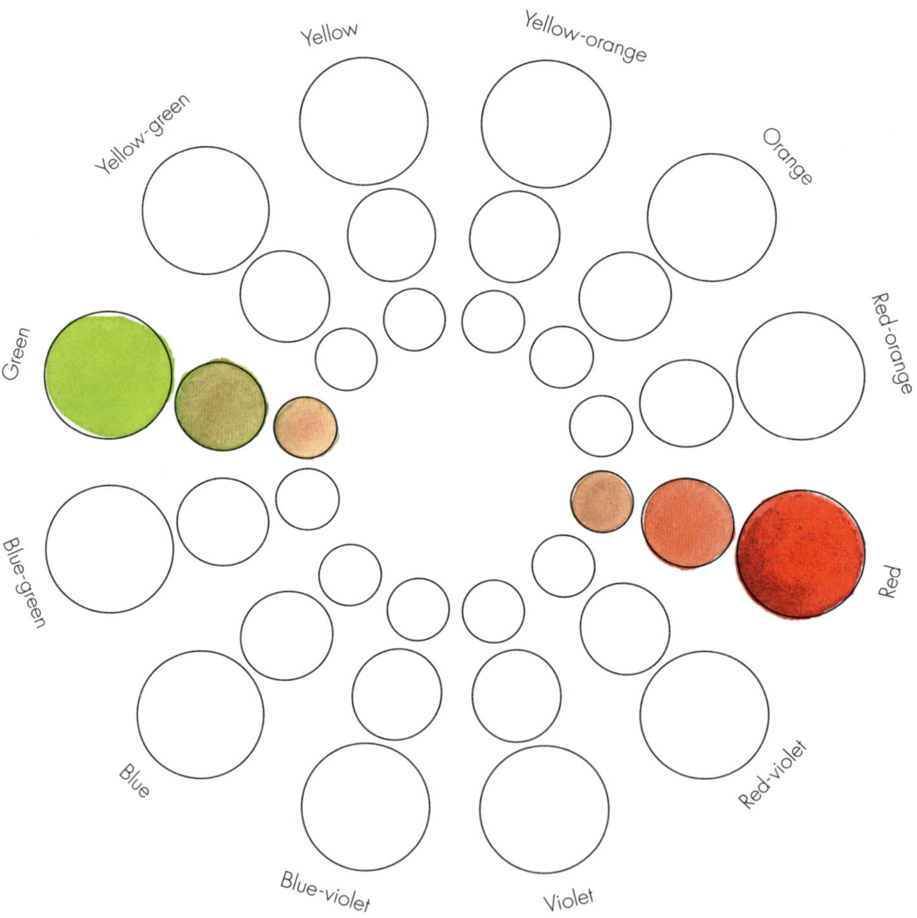

Tip: It's useful to know how to make colours less saturated as often, when looking at an object, you can see the pure, intense colours but also less saturated colours as a result of the light conditions around it.

68

Use different browns to create the form of a tree. You could add leaves in a variety of greens, or more trees to make a forest.

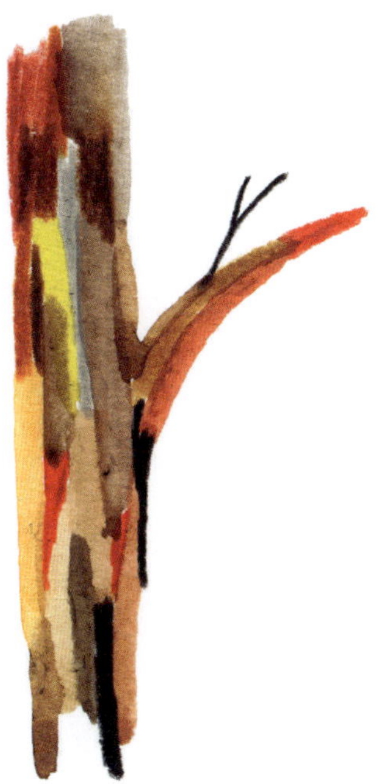

69 Paint a rainbow.

70

Take some time to look for colour around your home. Choose a corner and paint it, paying particular attention to the vibrant colours you can see, to create an energetic image.

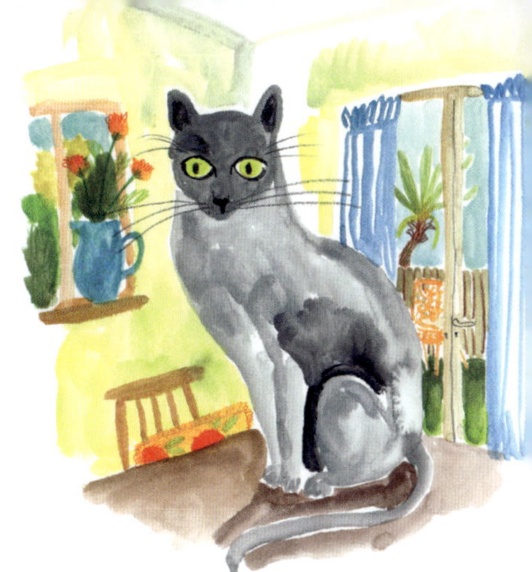

71

Frames don't have to be plain! Create some mini abstract artworks and then design colourful frames.

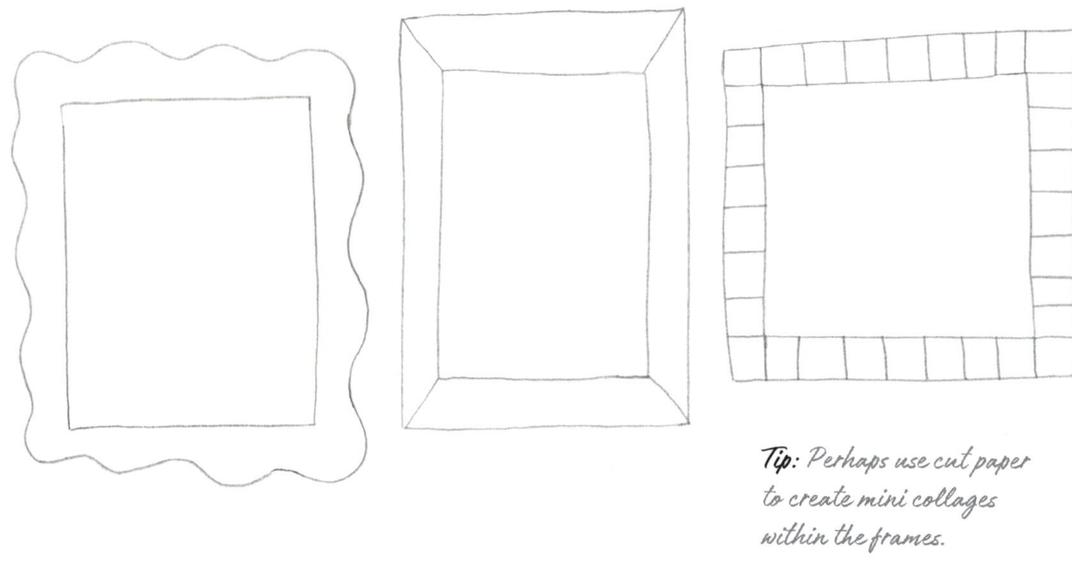

Tip: Perhaps use cut paper to create mini collages within the frames.

72

Paint or draw the sky you can see today, capturing all the colours you notice.

73

Different colours can suggest different emotions – and there's no right or wrong answer as it depends on how *you* perceive them. Consider the emotion each of these colours could be representing, and draw an expression to match.

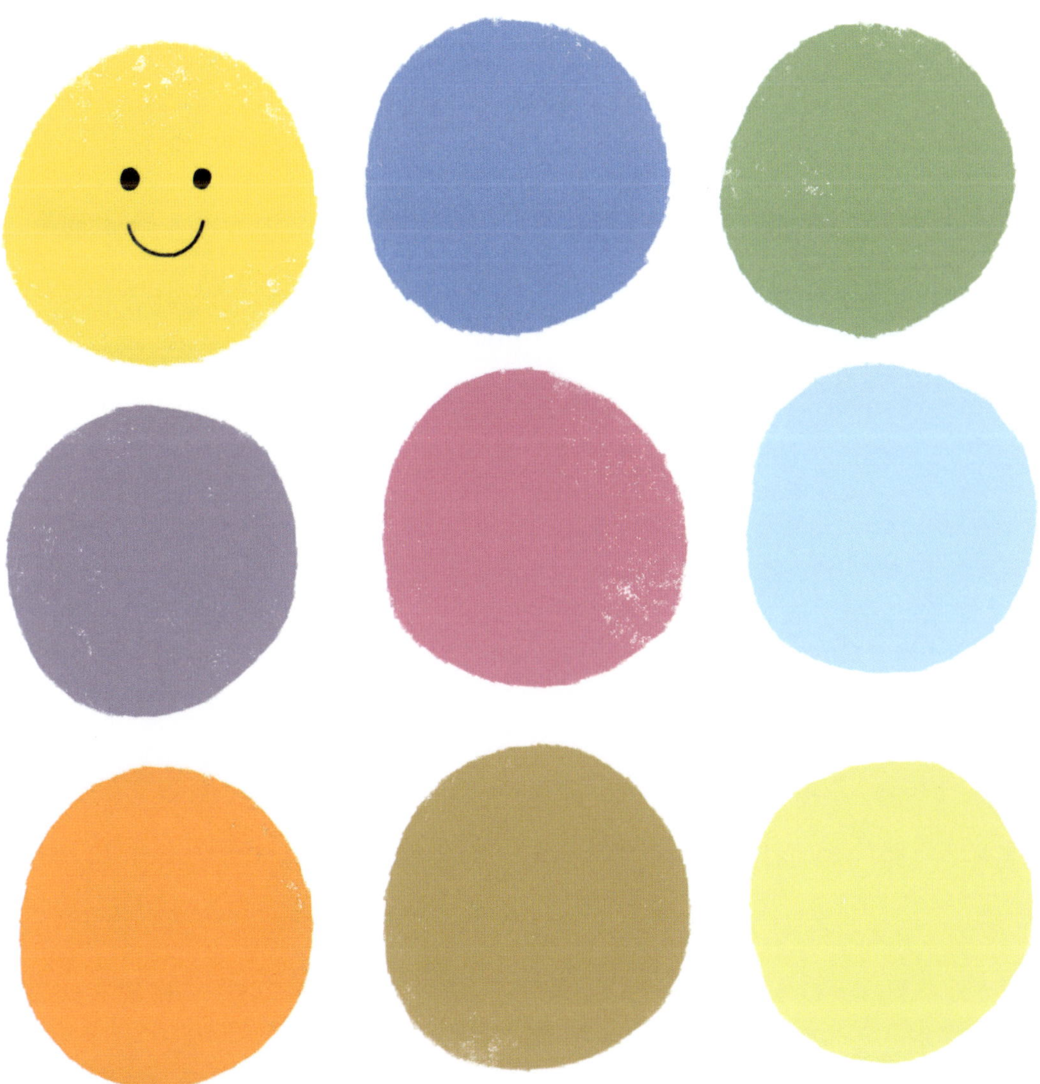

74

Create a painting of an object using three colours. Combine your three colours in a mixing palette to create new hues.

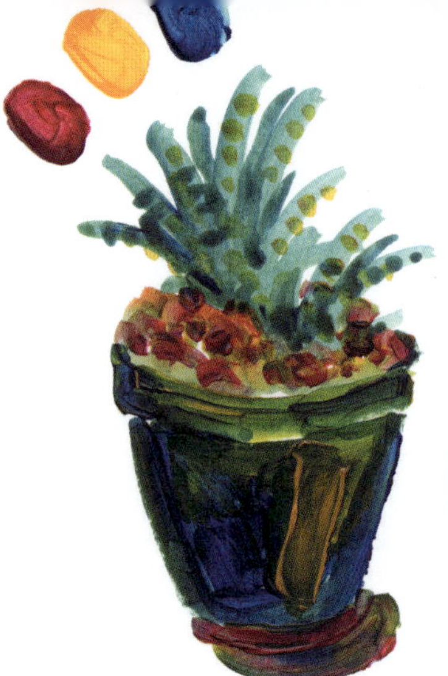

75

'Clean' colours are those that look fresh and pure, and 'dirty' colours are muddy, muted colours. It can be useful to identify and use clean *and* dirty colours in art. They can be used alongside each other to create balance, and using dirty colours around a clean colour will make it stand out. Decide whether the colours you have are clean or dirty, and add them to the grid.

Clean colours	*Dirty colours*
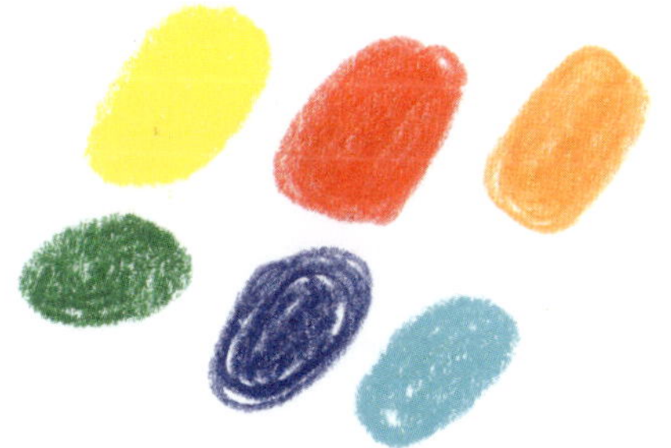	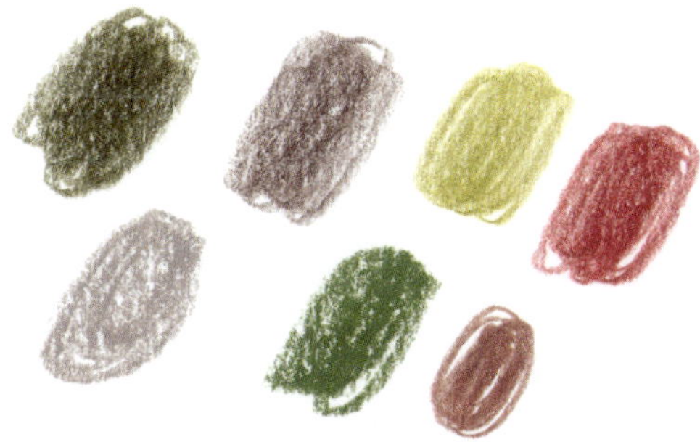

Tip: *Whether a colour is clean or dirty is subjective – there's no wrong answer.*

76

Paint a portrait using patches of bold colour as your starting point. You could look at a photograph or observe from life.

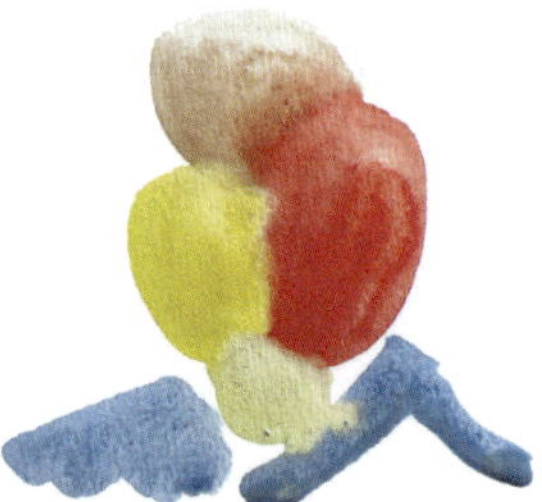

Begin by drawing blobs of colour, roughly marking out the areas of the face. Choose darker colours for areas of the face that are in shadow.

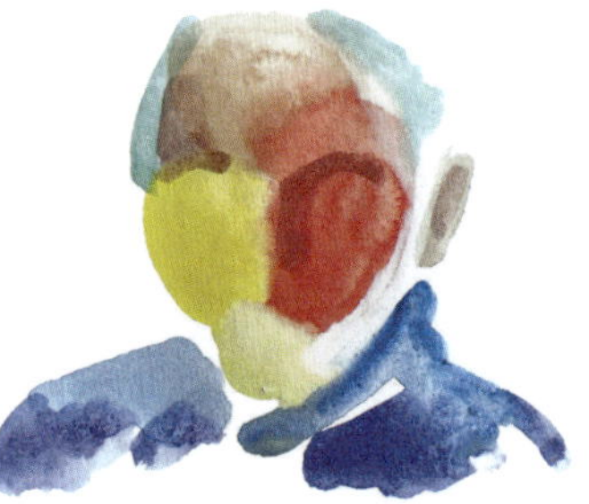

Then add more definition to the face with coloured marks – map out the key features and some areas of tone.

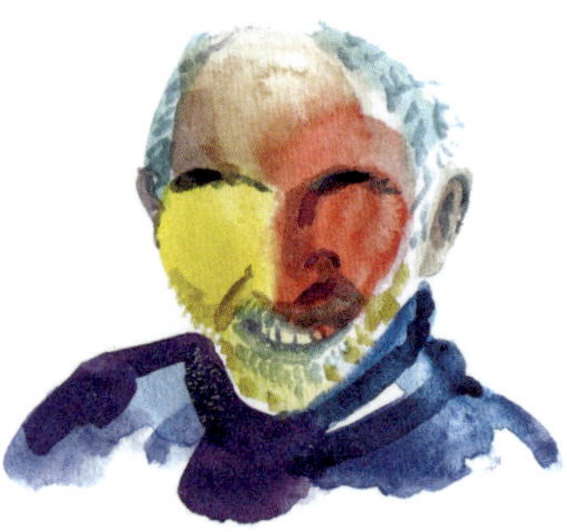

Continue adding detail, perhaps in a material that allows you more precision – a coloured pencil or pen.

Tip: *Use a white pencil or white paint to add highlights, but see if you can avoid using any pure black!*

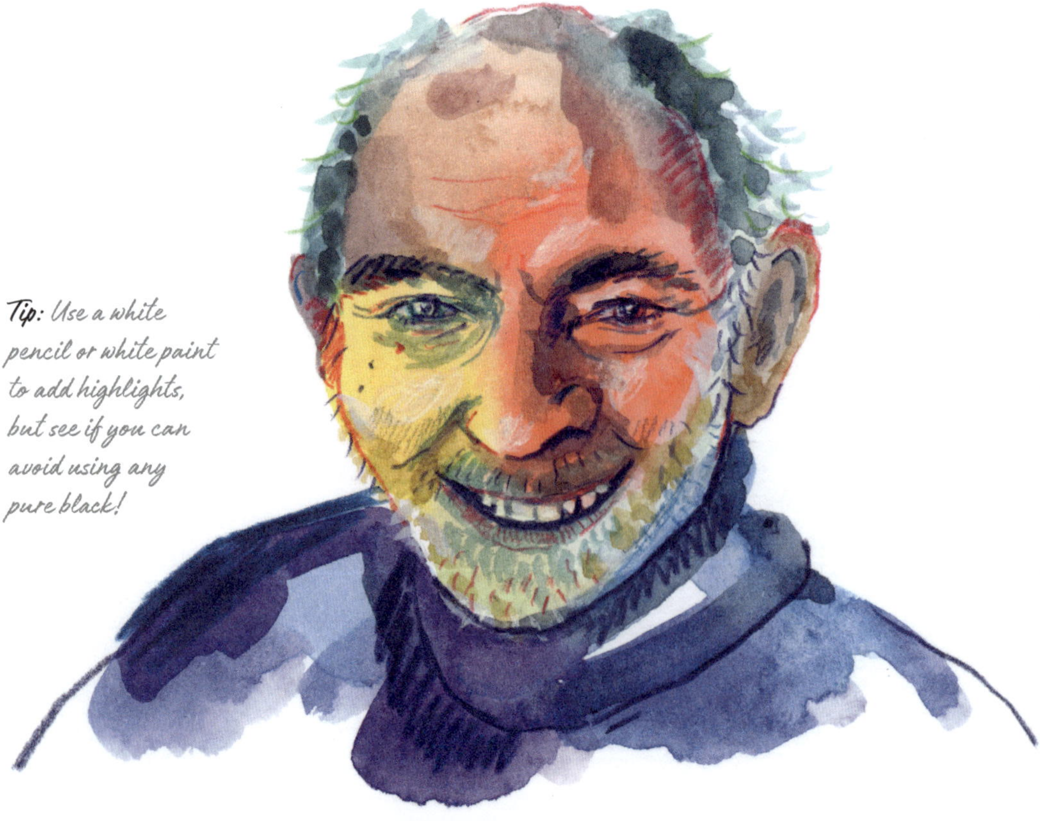

77

Create a wallpaper design using three to five colours.

78

Think about how you could introduce more colour into a room in your home. Perhaps a small glass or vase of flowers, or putting a colourful postcard in a clipframe. Write down some ideas here.

79 — Use this swipe of blue paint to inspire a picture.

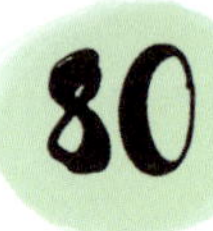

Paint a beautiful view, enjoying and exaggerating the variety of colours you can see. Paint the colours in blocks to create a tapestry of colour.

Tip: You could use an image from the internet, draw from life or from a photo.

81

Notice how the shadow on an object usually isn't just grey or black, but a darker, less-saturated tone of the colour of the object. Choose a simple object such as a cup, and make a tonal drawing of the colours you see.

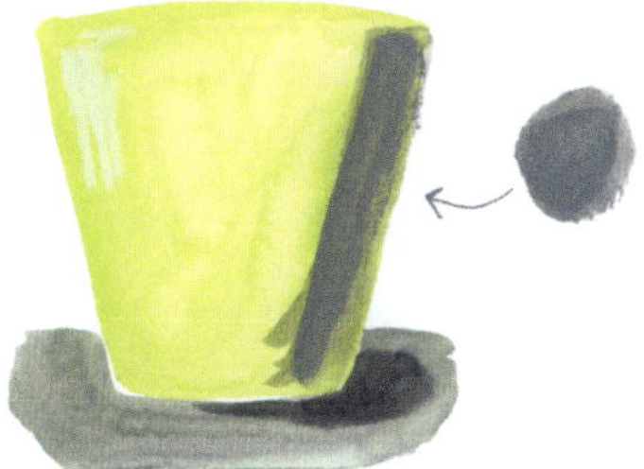

If the object is coloured, using grey or black for the shadow will make the image appear flat and lifeless.

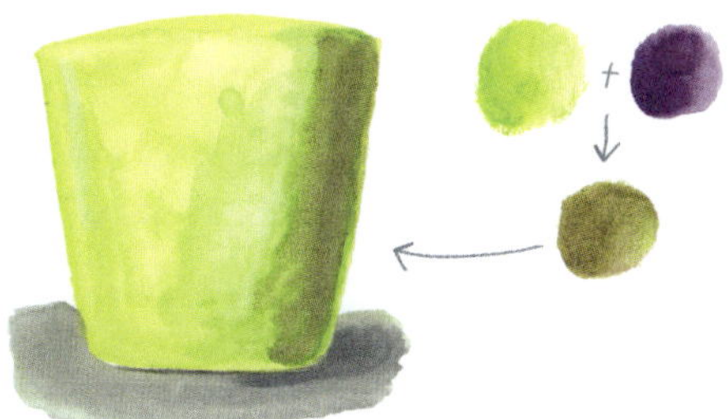

So instead, mix the brightest colour you see with its complementary colour and use this tone for the shadow. It will create a more harmonious image, as well as being a more accurate colour.

82

Design some colourful mugs based on different moods.

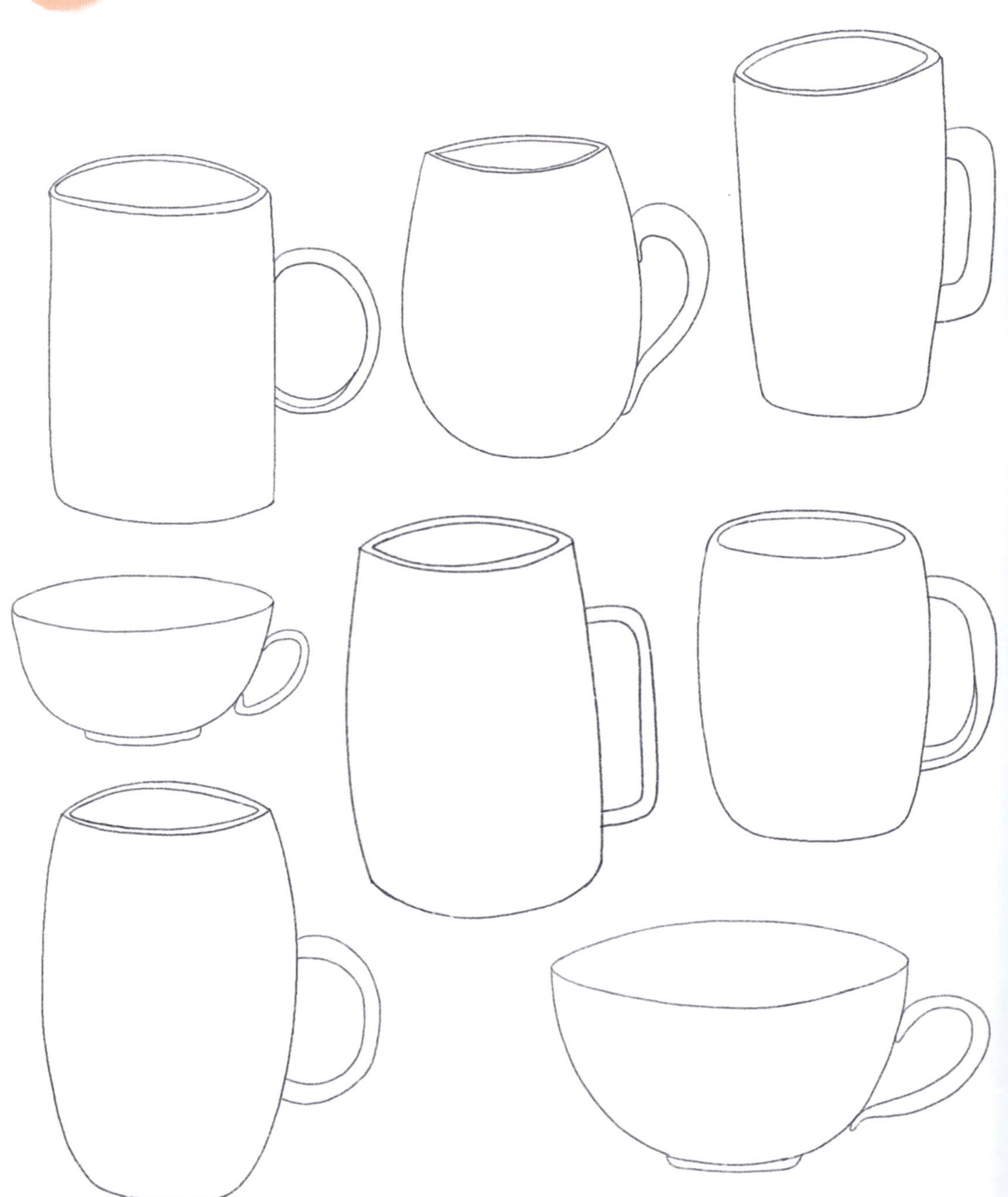

83

Colour and print can be used as a disguise. Draw an animal hiding in foliage of a similar colour and pattern, so it appears camouflaged.

84

Paint the weather that you experienced today.

85

All of these colours could be described as having a green hue.

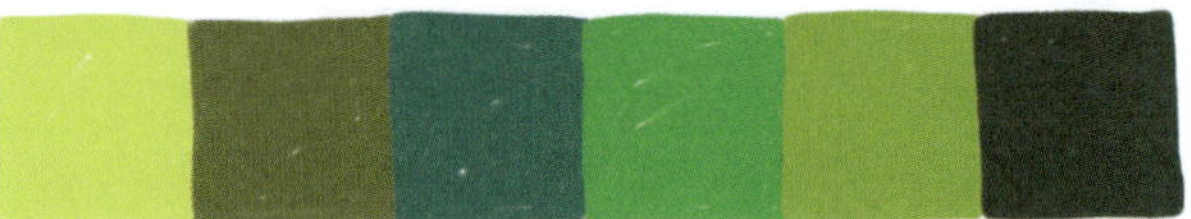

Choose a hue from the colour wheel and enjoy recording as many different colours as you can. You could make a pattern.

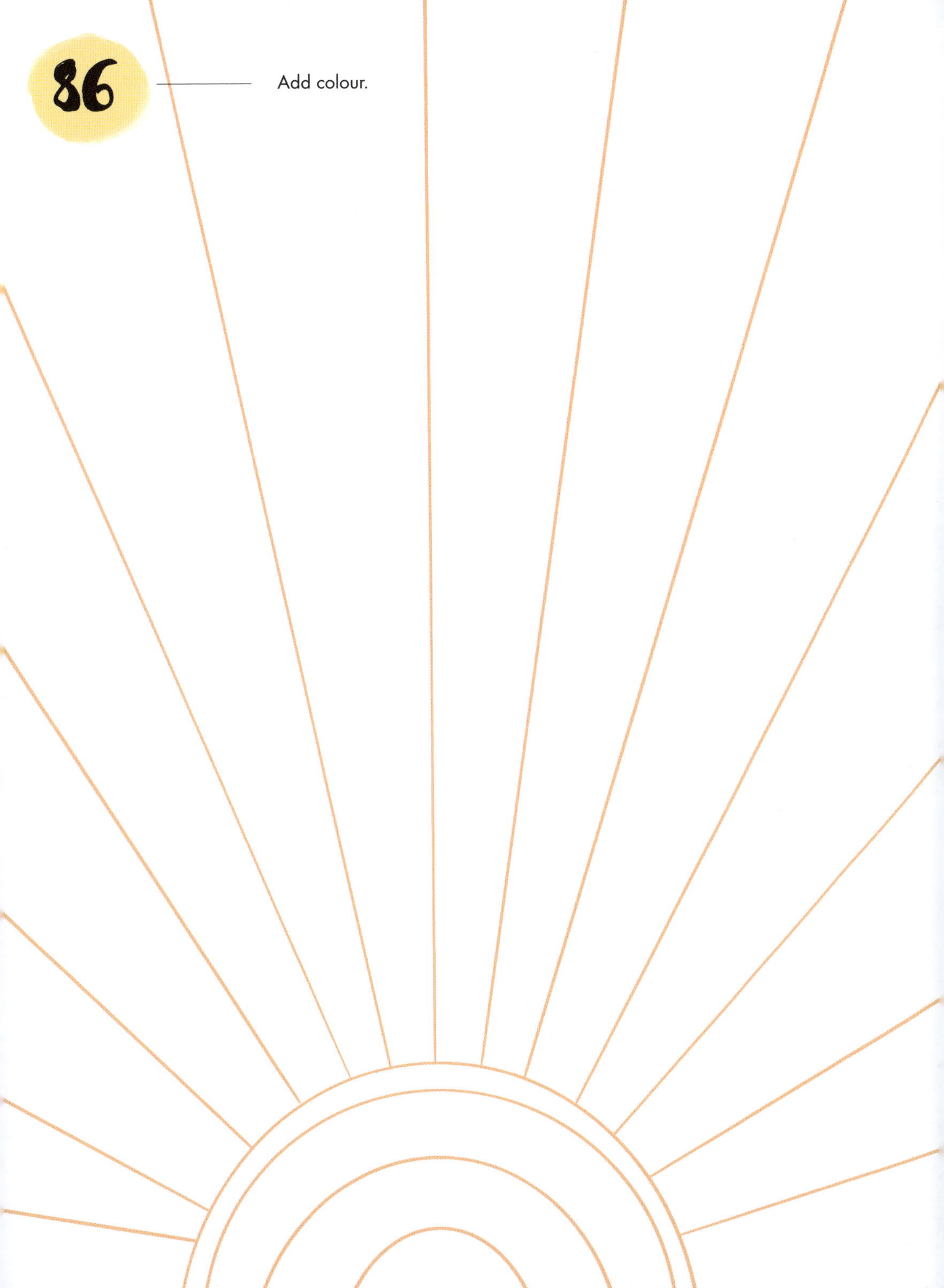
86
Add colour.

87

Fill the page with painted circles, allowing colours to blend into each other.

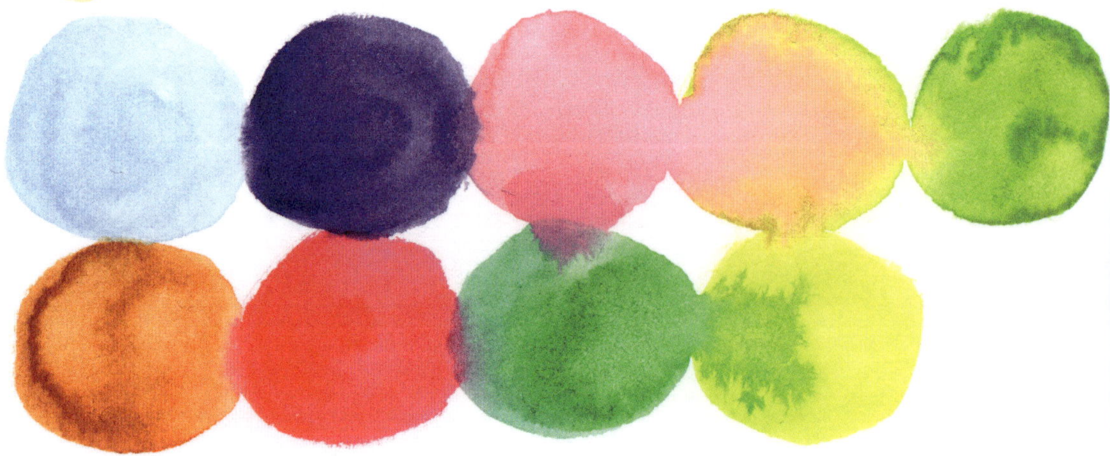

88

Place a simple object and some coloured pencils in front of you. Look carefully at your subject – it's not just one colour, but made up of lots of colours depending on the lighting in the room and the colours of the object. Make a drawing of it carefully including all the colours you can see.

89

Make an image where you explore complementary colours. Perhaps a violet tree against a yellow sky, a person wearing a blue outfit on a red chair, or a blue-green car on a red-orange road.

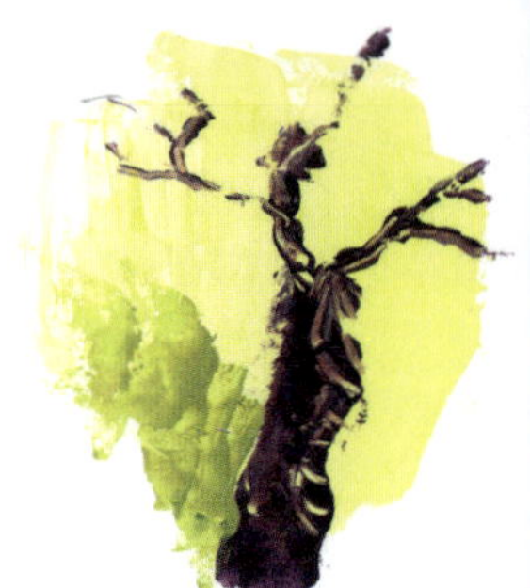

90

Refer back to your colour wheel in activity 66.
Create a winter scene using cool colours.

Tip: An absence of colour can also appear cool. You may like to use neutral colours too, or try using tints of white.

91

Colours like orange, red, bright pink and bright blue can be used to create bold, eye-catching imagery that feels positive and energetic. Use colours that you find positive to design a graphic or poster. You could choose a phrase you like, and illustrate that in colour.

Tip: Use black and white alongside these colours for more graphic imagery.

92

Paint some coloured shapes, then, once these have dried, draw a pattern on each shape using contrasting colours.

Tip: These patterns could be inspired by ones you see around you, or completely made up. They can be as simple or complex as you like – have fun and enjoy being creative.

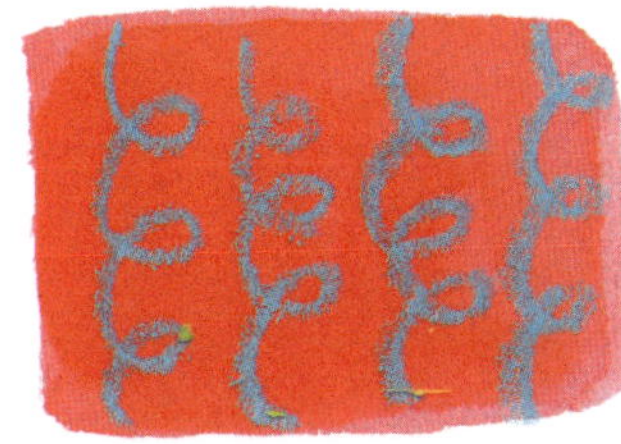

93

The 'negative space' refers to the empty area around or between objects. If you have a light-coloured object, you may choose to fill the negative space with colour rather than the object itself. The paper can become the white of your object. Choose a white or light-coloured object and add colour to the negative space to create a striking, contrasting image.

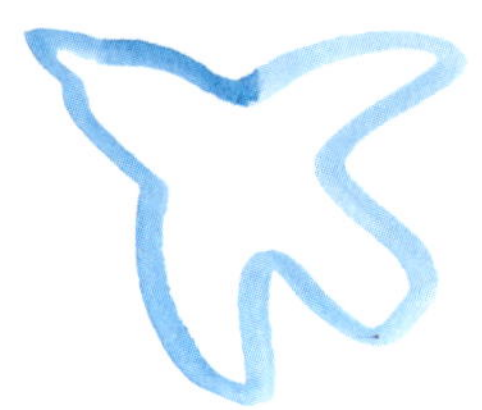

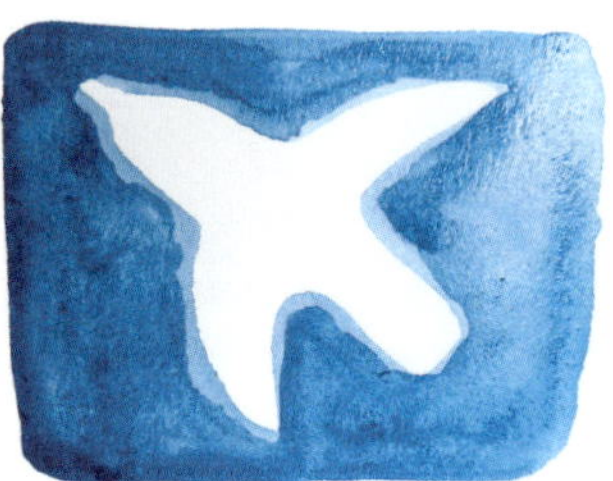

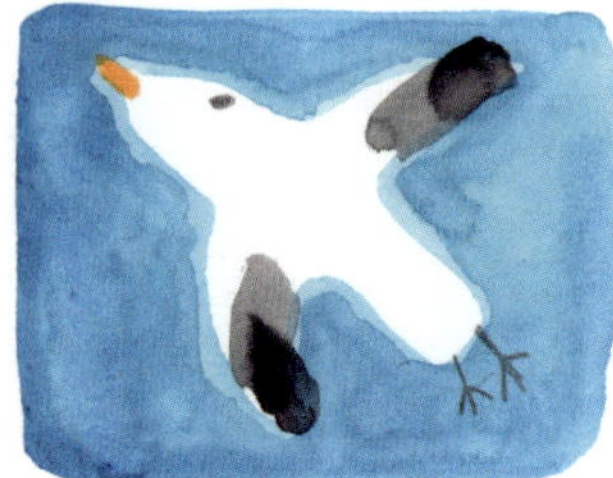

94

Triadic colour schemes are those that use three colours found evenly spaced on the colour wheel, for example yellow-green, red-orange and blue-violet. You can use triadic colour schemes to create appealing combinations. Make some triadic colour schemes below. You don't have to use the colours at their full intensity – you could use tints of the colours too.

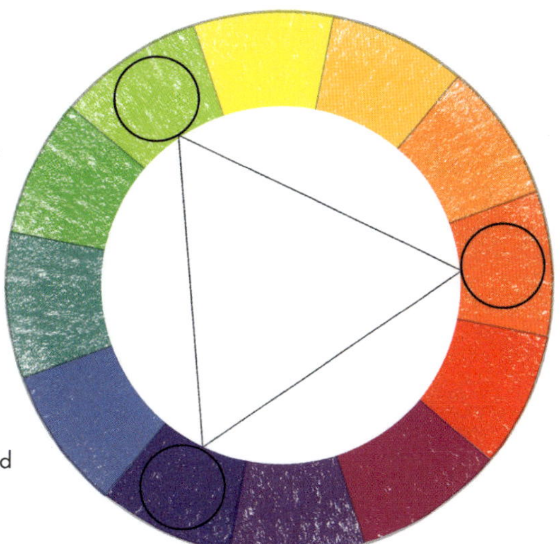

Tip: Refer to activity 17 as a reminder of how to mix tints.

Tip: When using a triadic colour scheme, you don't have to use all three colours equally. Perhaps make one colour more dominant than the other two.

95

Yellow can suggest joy, energy, warmth and ease. Be inspired by how yellow makes *you* feel and turn this shape into an image.

96

Add colour to the shapes.

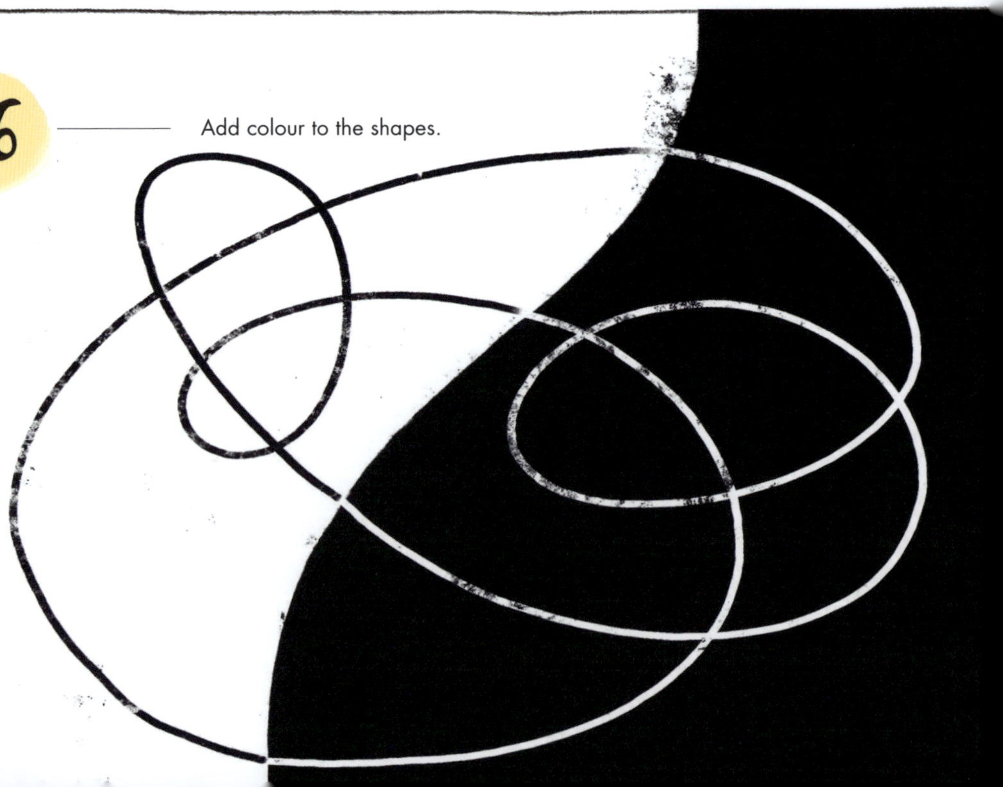

97

Mix as many colours as you can from three paint colours. Once you've mixed two together, what happens if you mix this with another of your colours? You should find that all of these mixed colours form a cohesive palette and would go together beautifully in a piece of art.

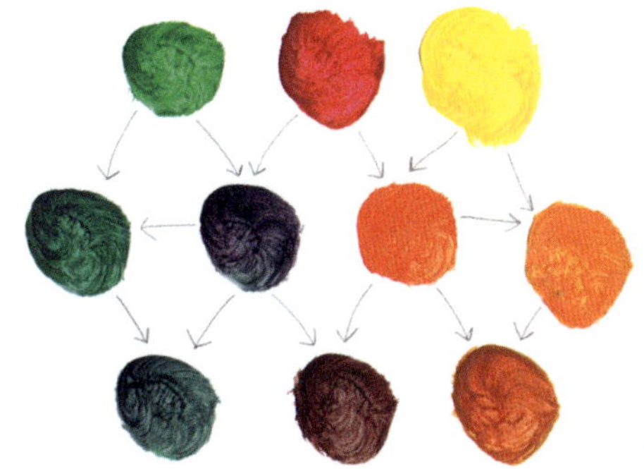

98

Draw a vivid fire using yellows, reds, oranges and any other colours that evoke warmth and cosiness.

99

Layer oil pastel shapes over each other and enjoy the colour blends you create.

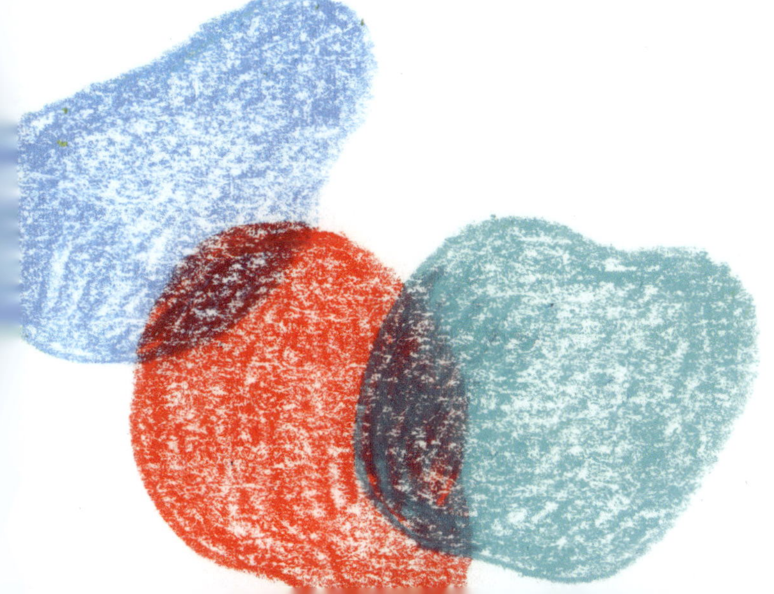

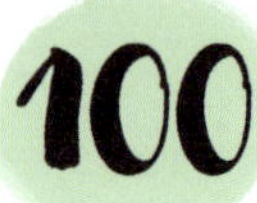

Create a colourful drawing of a location you experience today. There's no need to match the colours exactly as you see them, just enjoy getting lots of colour down onto the page and exploring different materials to capture the moment.

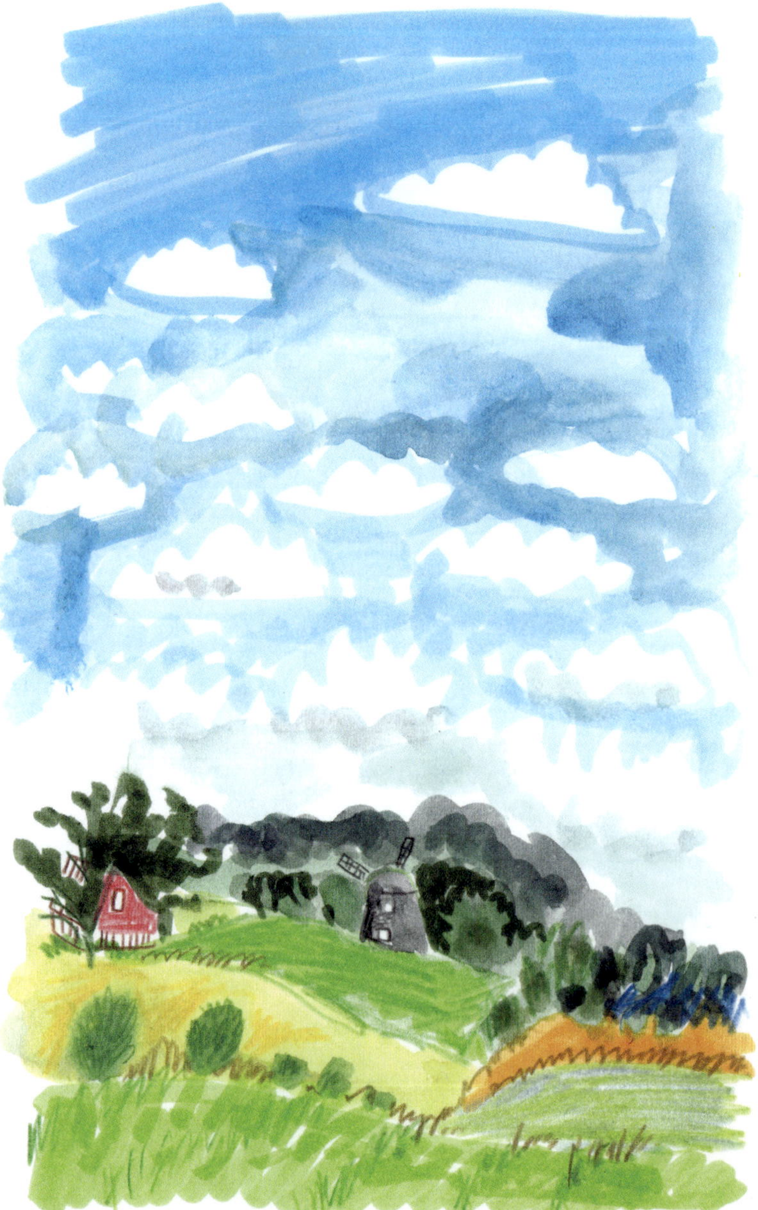

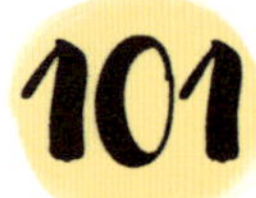

Continue adding circles of colour to the page, enjoying the effect of all the colours together. The many small parts form one cohesive whole, whichever colours you choose!

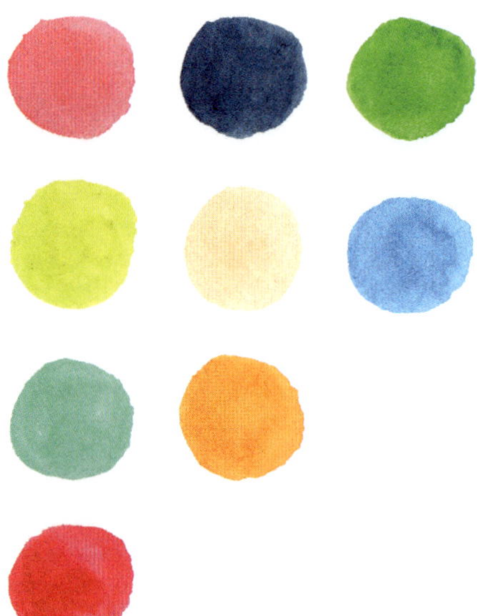

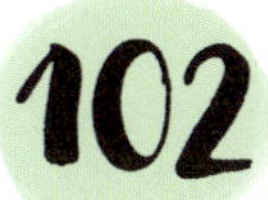

When looking at a landscape, there are sometimes so many colours that the thought of painting them all can feel overwhelming. It can be useful to start by breaking down the image into just a few colours and see the scene in sections. Perhaps there is a large bright green section at the front, or you notice big areas that look ochre. Look at a landscape (your local park, a garden, some fields or even buildings) and map out the colours you see in big, simple areas.

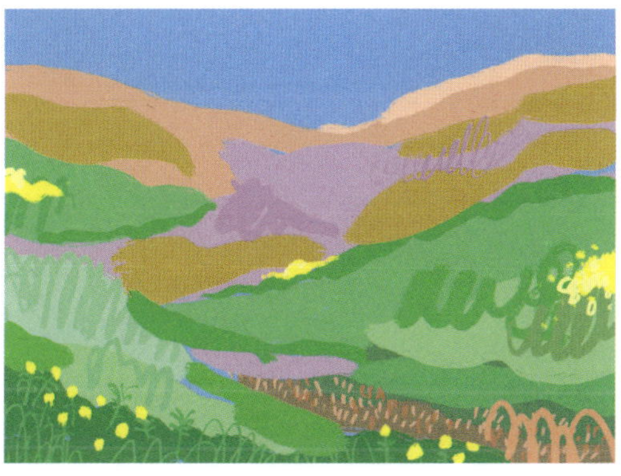

Add details afterwards if you like, and perhaps some pops of bright colour using paint or collaged paper.

103

Explore using clean colours alongside dirty colours to create interesting combinations. Remember – whether the colour appears clean or dirty is your own personal interpretation, there is no right or wrong.

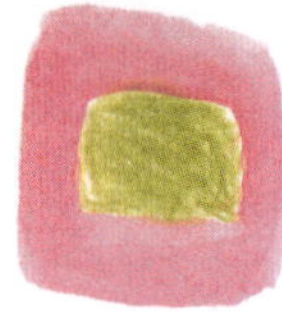

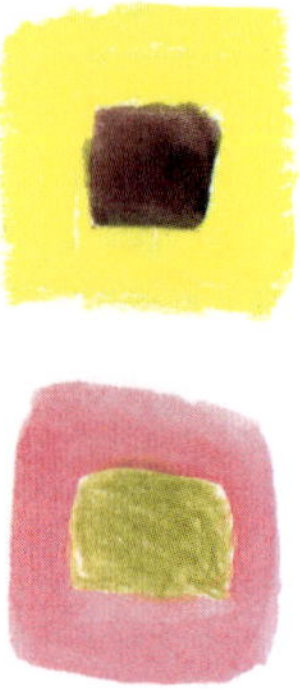

104

Add colour to this design.

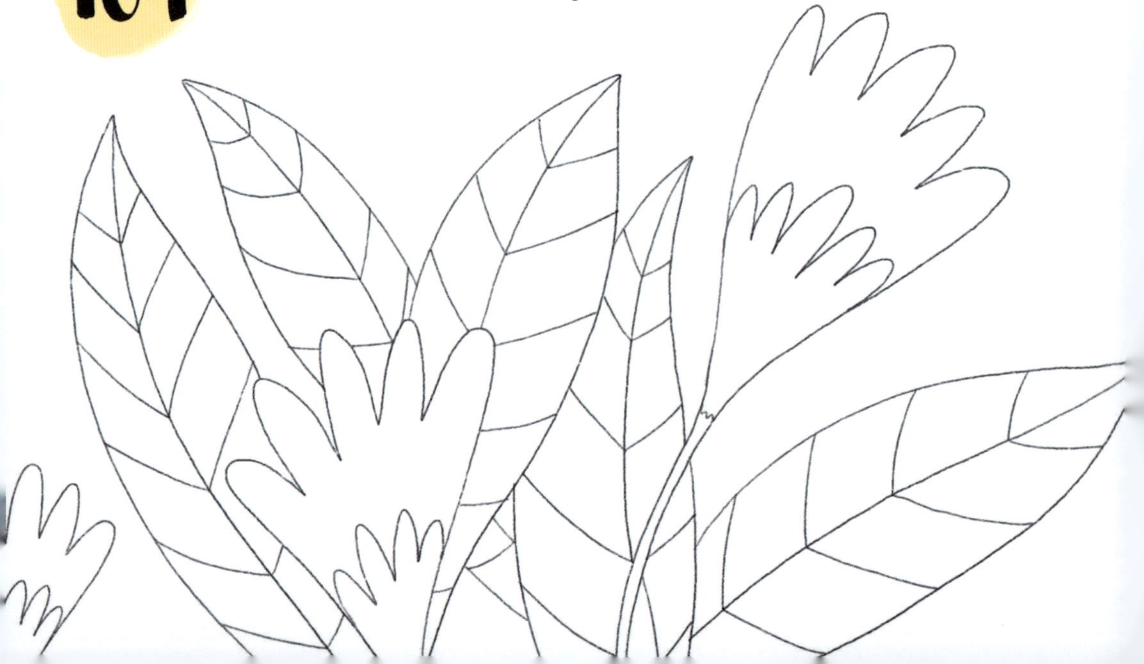

Red can be seen as an aggressive colour. It can evoke passion, fire or strong emotion, and can be used in a deliberate way in your art. Create two or three abstract designs where you use red with lots of energy and confidence. What is the atmosphere of the pictures you have created?

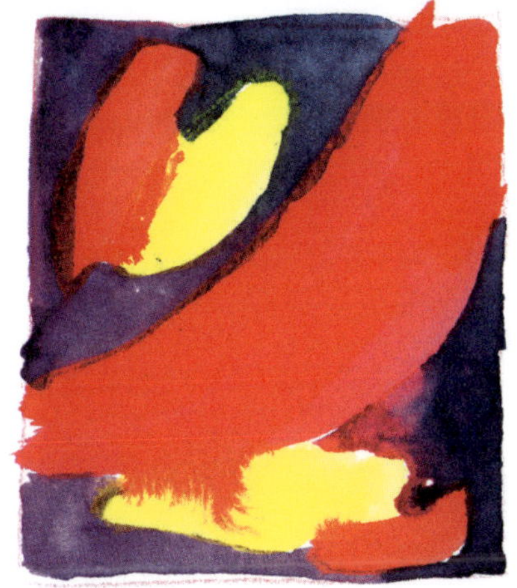

Create a collage using bold semicircle shapes. You could add lots of the same colour paper to each semicircle, or approach the activity in any way that inspires you.

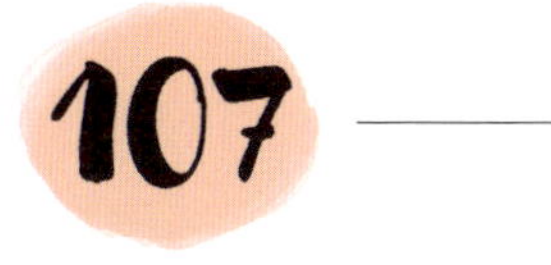

Create a scene using a few analogous colours. This will result in a soothing, relaxed image.

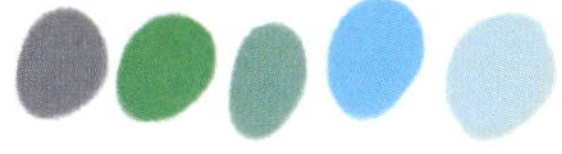

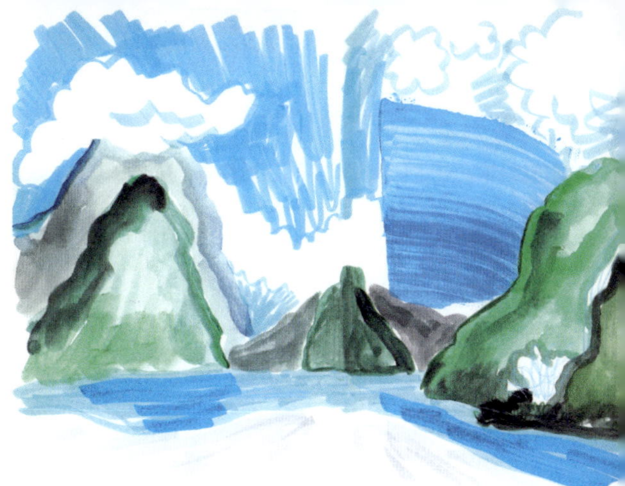

Tip: Analogous colours are those that appear next to each other on the colour wheel.

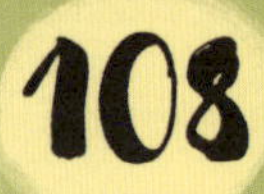

Add more colours to this design to create a harmonious abstract. Consider how big you make each shape – perhaps you use a very bright or very dark colour in small amounts.

109

Draw a leaf, noticing the variety of colours you see. Perhaps add a coloured background.

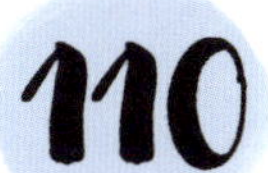

If you are finding the idea of drawing in colour daunting, you can simplify it. Start by creating a simple drawing in pencil. You only need to think about the forms. Then draw it again in colour ... just using colours you love.

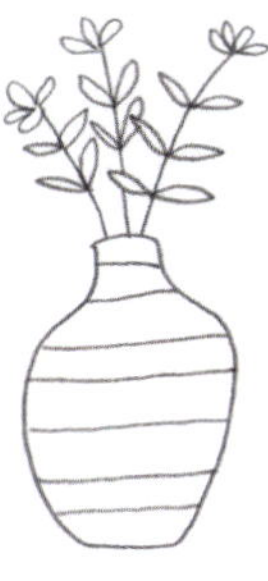

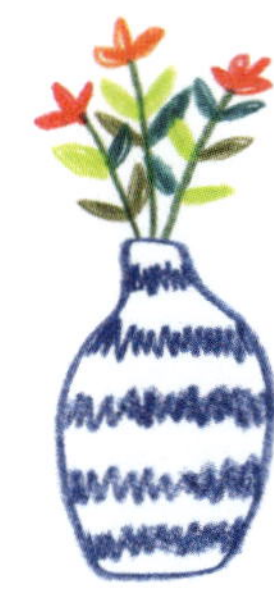

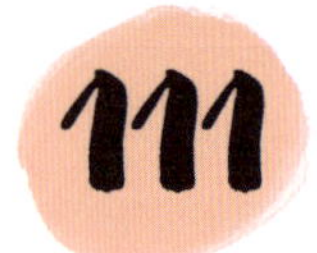

Draw a portrait of yourself using only warm colours.
How does the image make you feel?

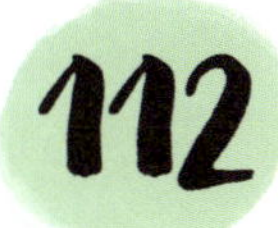

Draw a landscape using lines of colour.

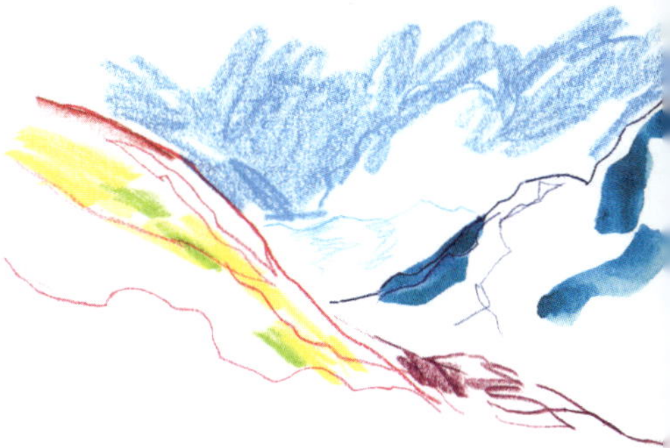

113

Mixing clean colours together can create interesting dirty colours. Create your own dirty colours here, and then make a pattern using your favourites plus one clean, bright colour.

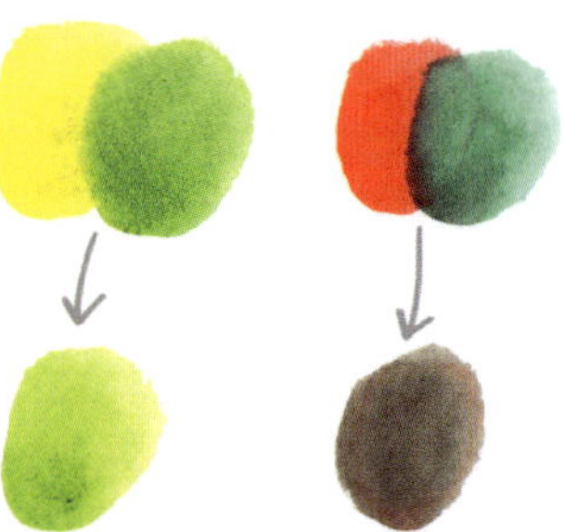

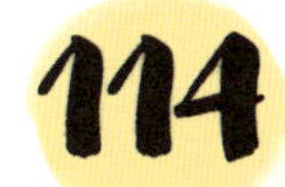

Continue adding colour to the page to produce an undulating patchwork.

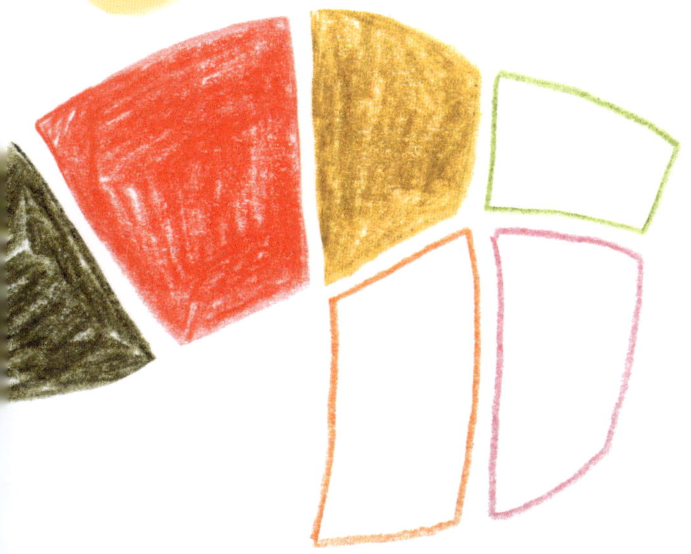

Using a lot of blue in a piece of art can make for a peaceful image. Paint a scene where blue is the predominate colour. You could start by painting a blue background, or perhaps using a blue piece of paper.

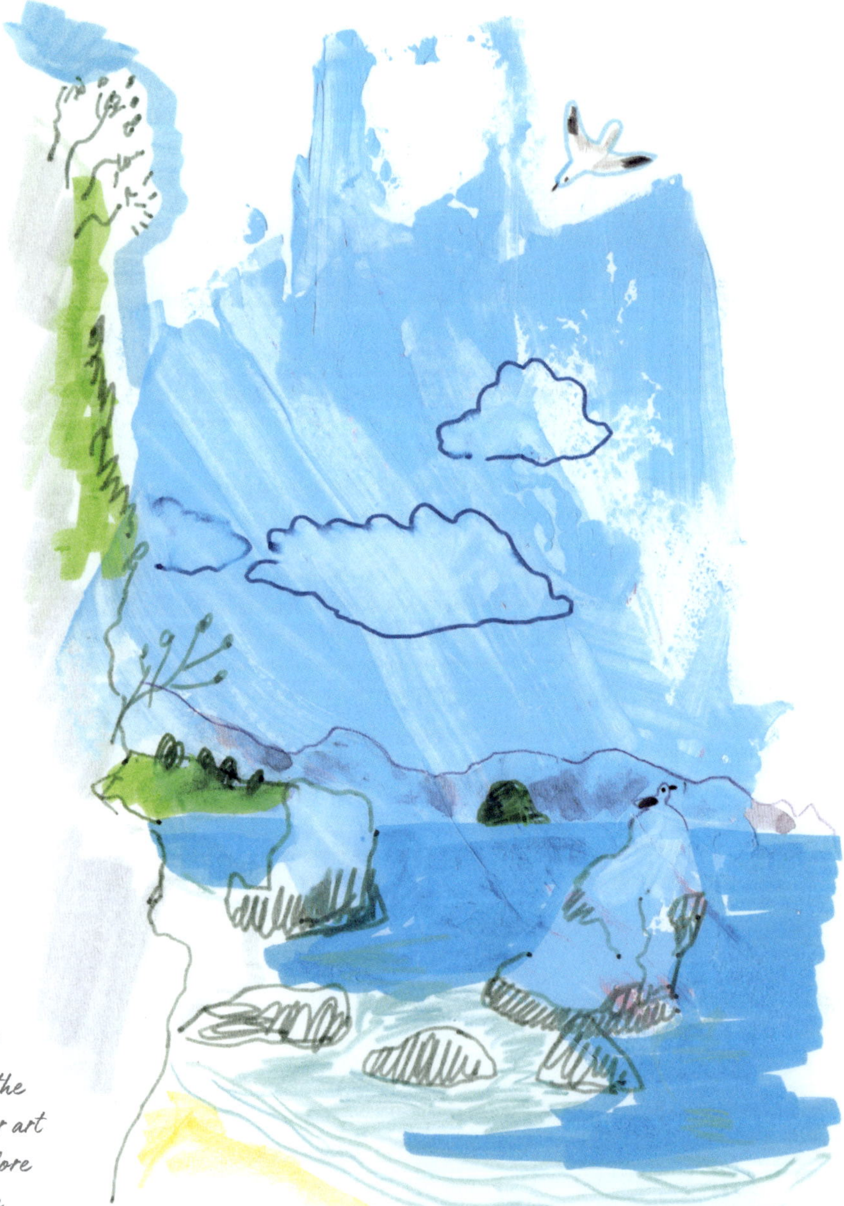

Tip: *You don't have to make the colours in your art accurate. Explore making all the colours bluer than they really are.*

116

Draw an object using only four colours.

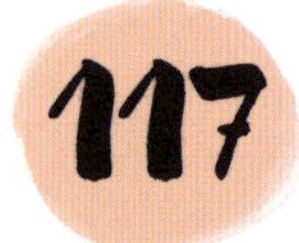

Put on some energetic music and create an abstract design based on how the music makes you feel.

118

Create patterns using blue.

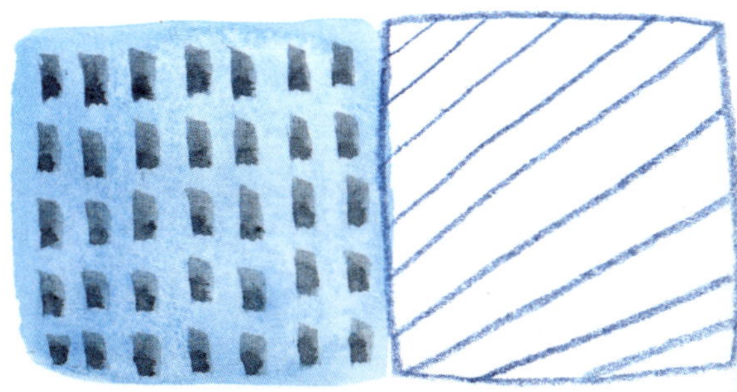

119

Draw dots using as many different colours as you can. You could mix colours too.

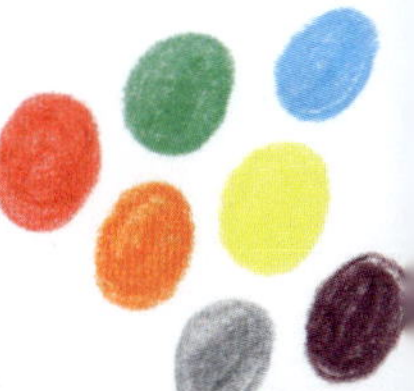

120

Start by painting a shape of colour using watercolour. Then paint another shape of colour next to it, watching as the colours bleed together in the middle. Repeat as many times as you like, perhaps filling the page. Notice how each pair of colours blends differently – and enjoy how wonderfully unpredictable paint can be!

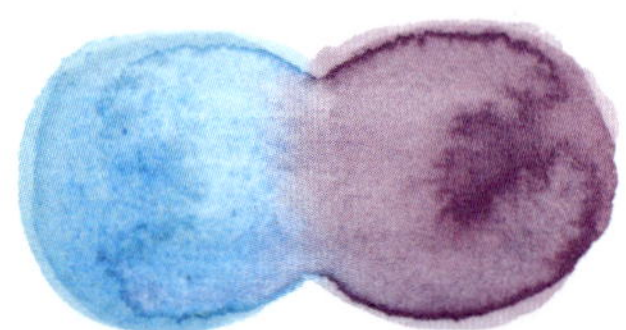

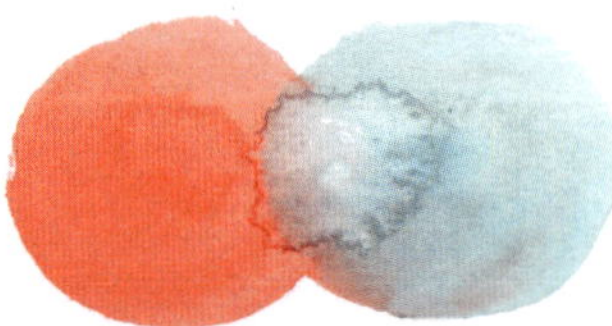

121

Paint or draw a view from observation using the most vibrant colours you have.

Tip: You could start by creating a brightly coloured background on the page. Consider using neon colours.

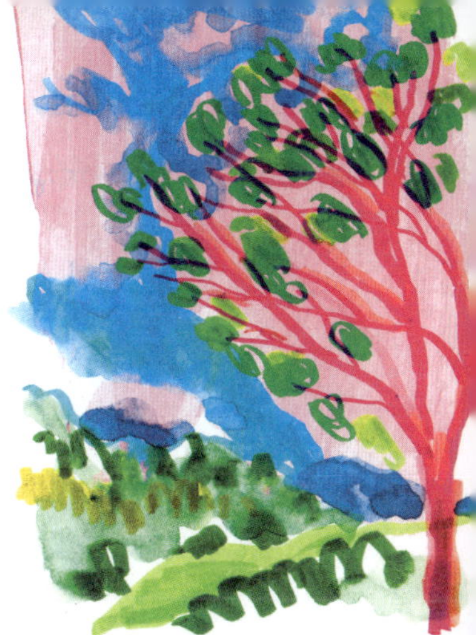

122

Create an abstract piece of art using colours that represent a specific feeling. This can be totally personal to you.

123

Enjoy creating some colour palettes. Consider including clean and dirty colours, and think about how you might use these palettes in future pieces of art.

Tip: *It can be useful to keep a colour palette sketchbook – a book entirely dedicated to your collections of colours.*

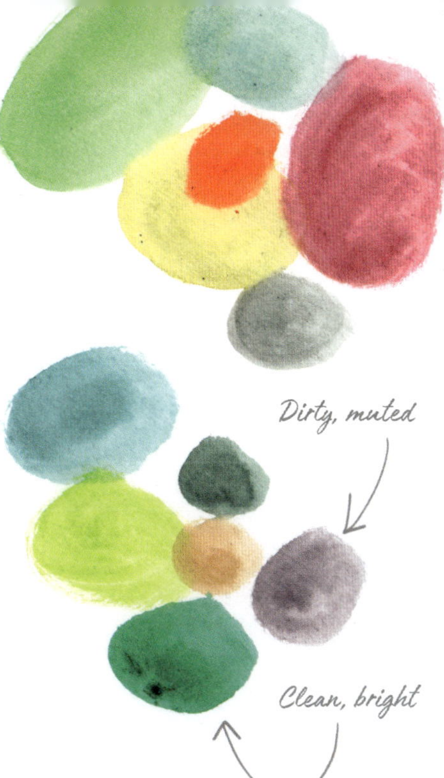

124

Be inspired by the energy and colour of this paint mark, and use it as a background for a piece of art. It could be a scene, a portrait, an abstract ... anything you like.

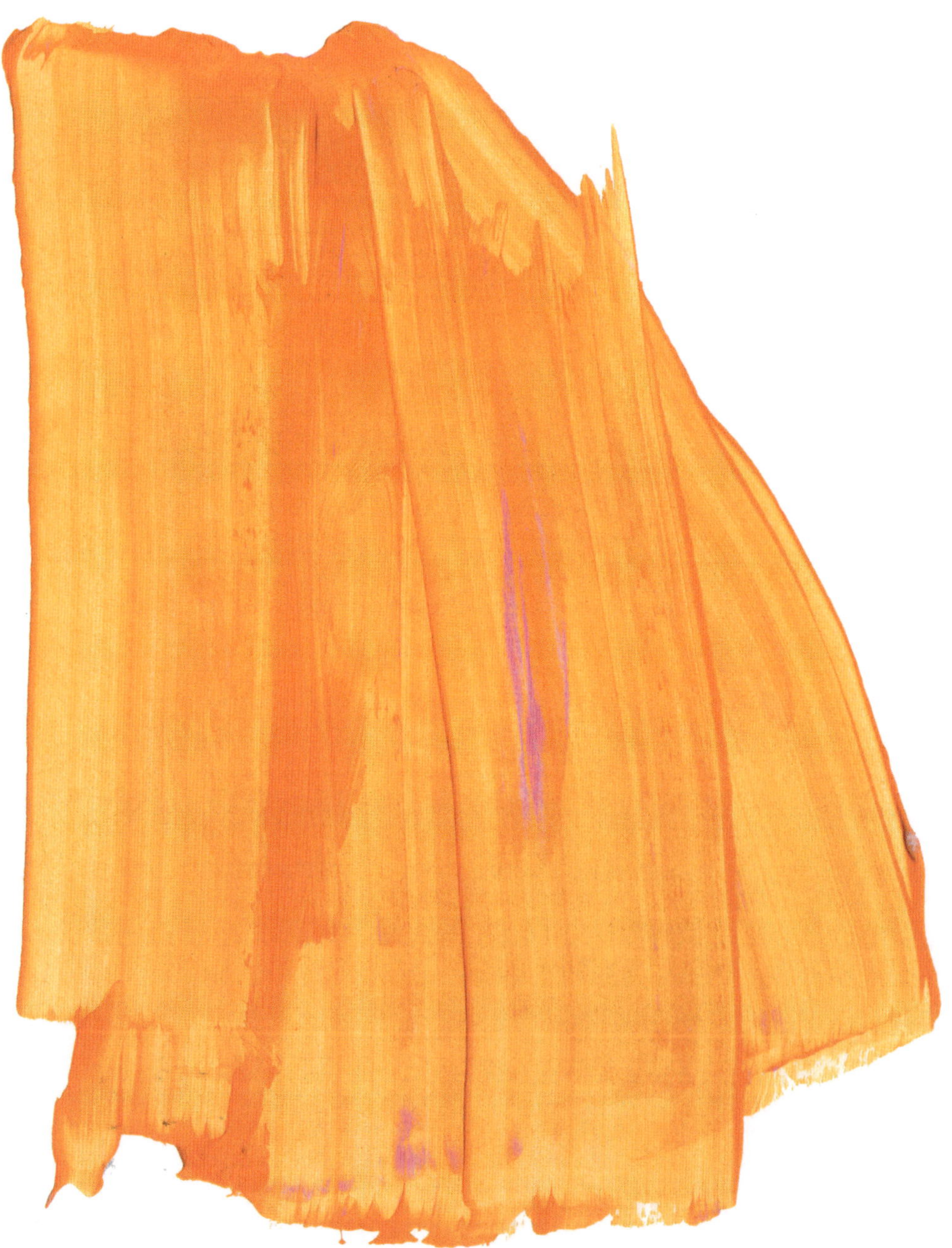

125 — Design a colourful blanket pattern that you could use in your home.

126

Create thumbnail colour studies of the land and sky, starting with colours you expect to see, and then exploring more unusual colour combinations. These could be colours that you've seen or imaginary combinations.

Tip: Exploring colour palettes beyond what we expect can encourage us to be braver about using colour in a more daring way generally. Perhaps one of your thumbnails will inspire you to create a larger piece of art.

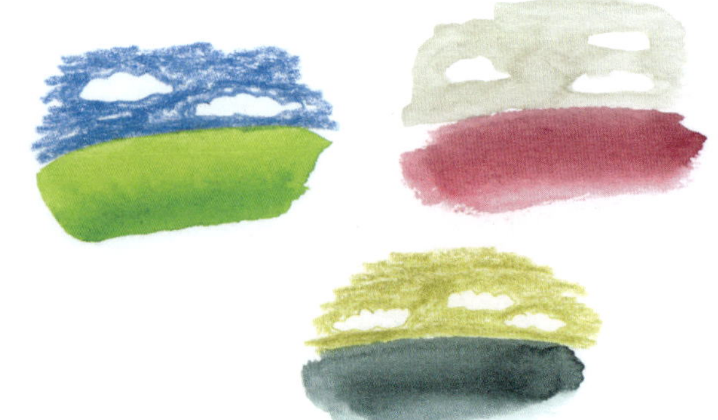

127

Draw nature-inspired shapes using calming, neutral colours.

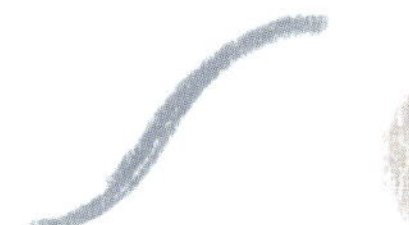  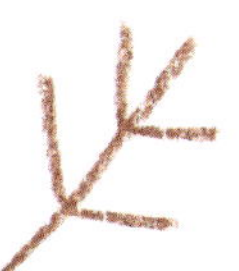 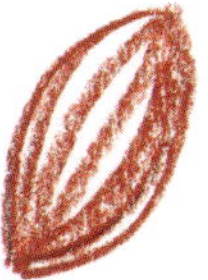 

128

Make some small paper collages of everyday objects. The nature of collage means your art can be bold and graphic, so enjoy this and exaggerate the shapes you see. Consider what the elements would look like in their simplest forms, and enjoy being playful with the colour choices and shapes.

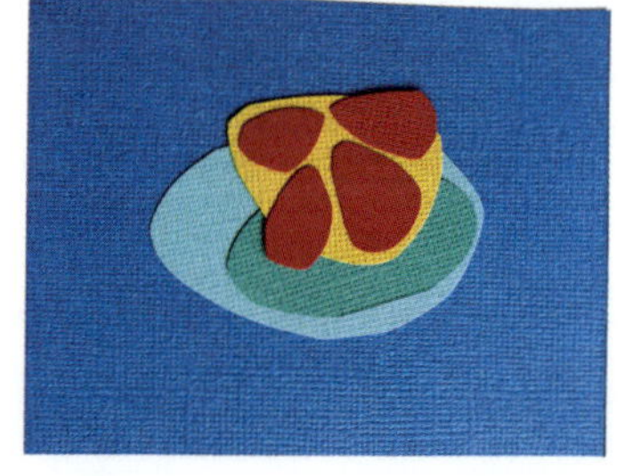

Tip: If you don't have paper in the colours you need, you can paint paper and cut this up once dry.

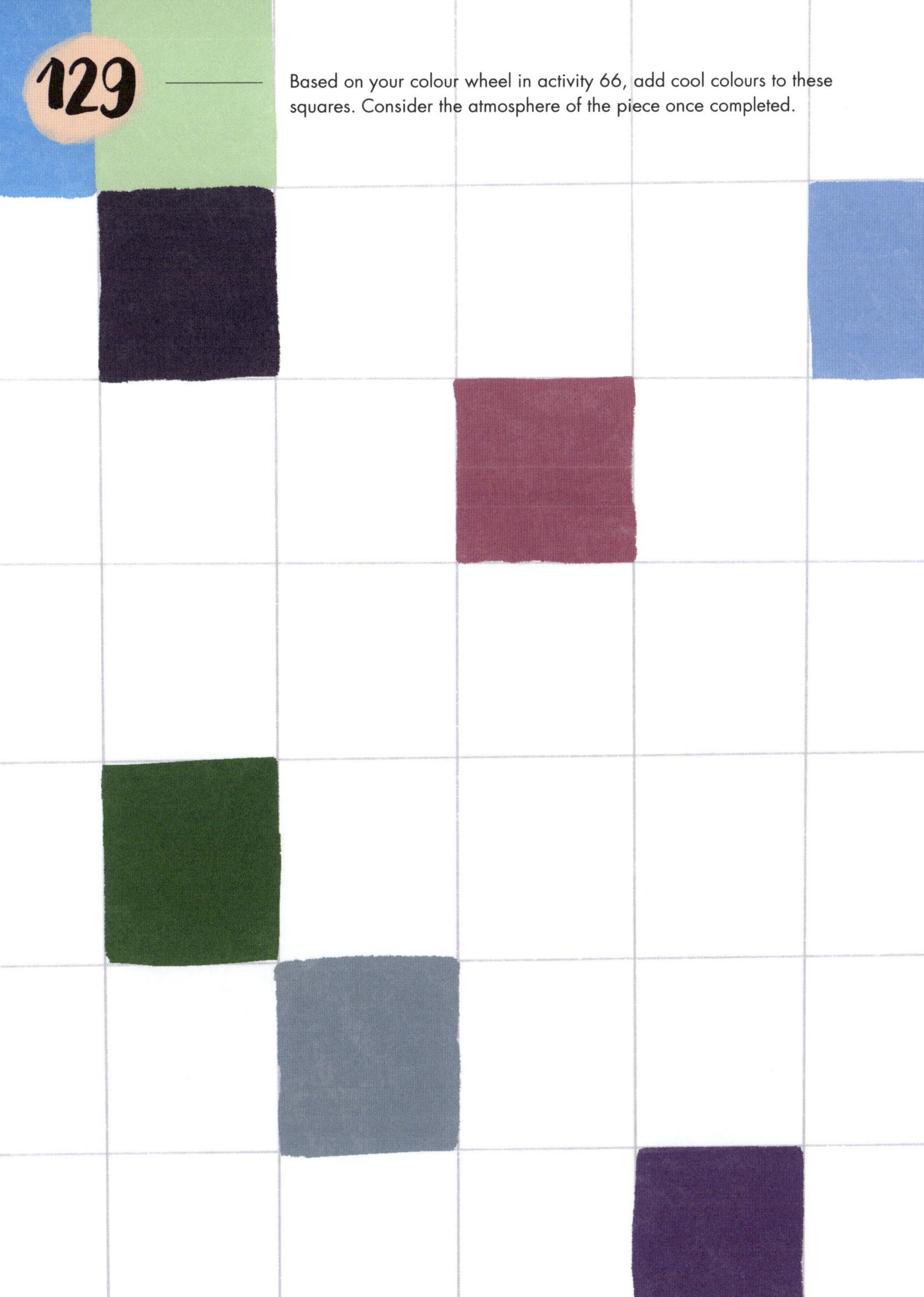

129

Based on your colour wheel in activity 66, add cool colours to these squares. Consider the atmosphere of the piece once completed.

130

Look through a window and draw the shapes and colours you see, without drawing the window frame – instead leave this as white space.

Tip: You could sketch the window frames lightly in pencil first.

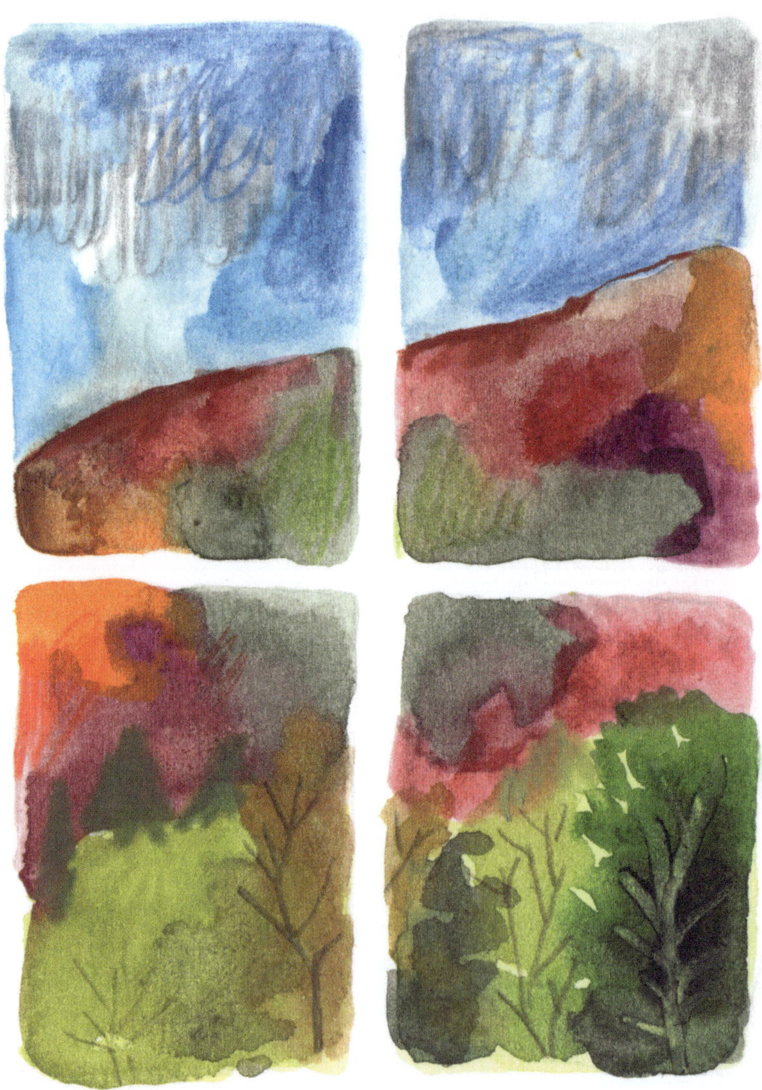

Add some more lines and shapes to this design and then introduce colour and pattern – perhaps spots, stripes and waves.

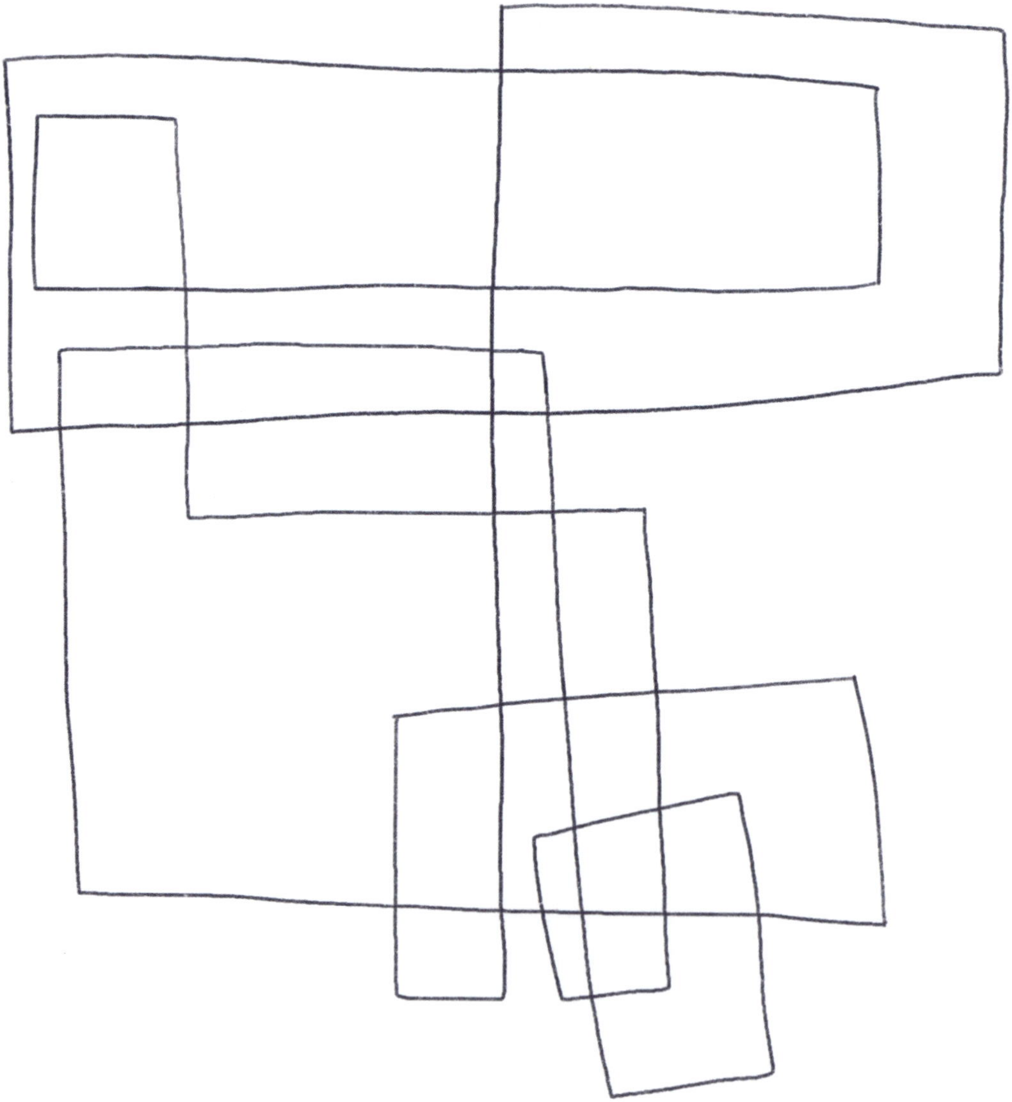

132

We can use colour to add tone to shapes, rather than using black or grey. First, decide which direction the light will be coming from, then use tints and shades of colours to add tone. Or you could experiment with using completely different colours to add shadow. Be playful with your choices.

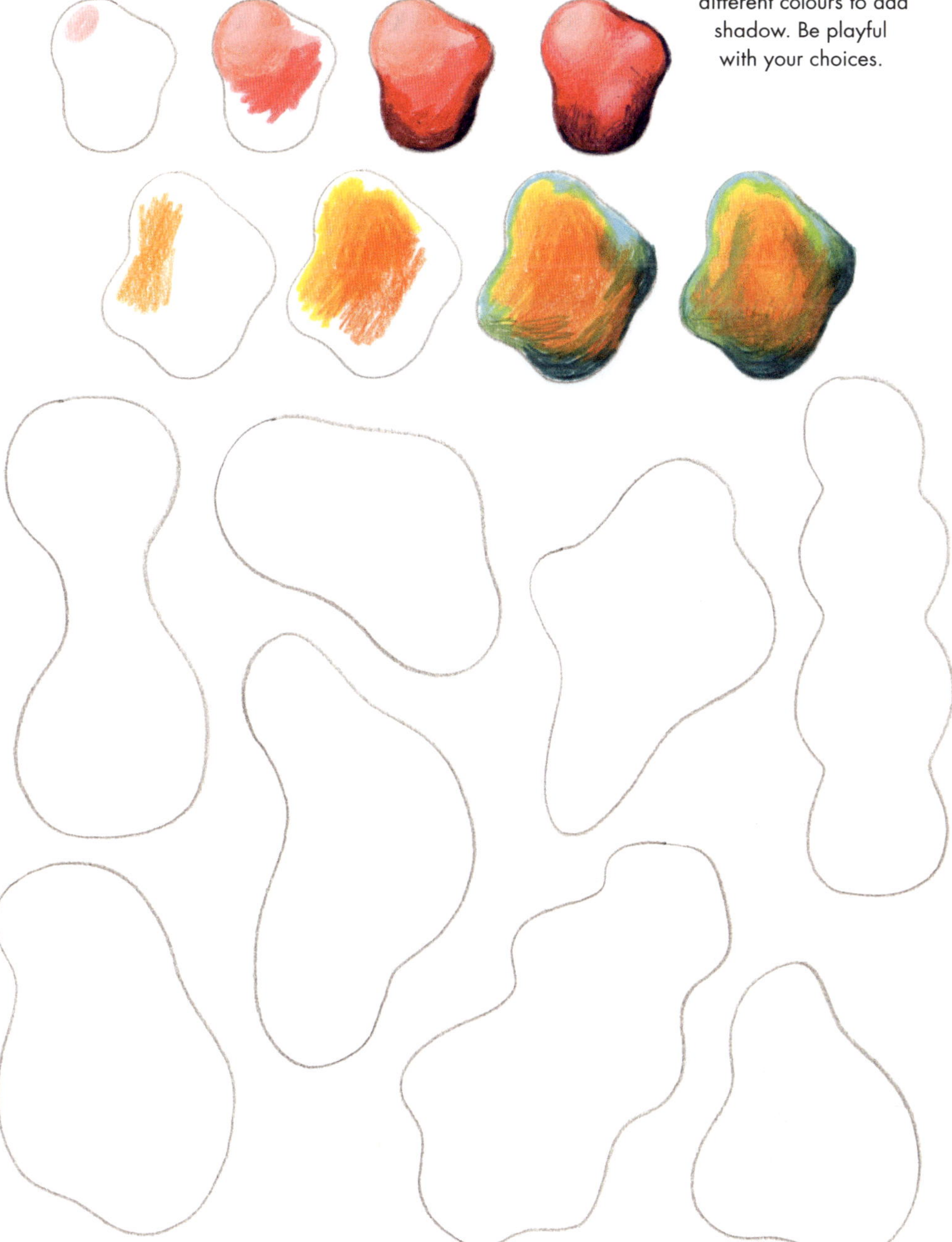

133

Find a greyscale photograph that you like, imagine what it might look like in colour, and draw it here.

134

Yellow can evoke joy and be seen as a happy, friendly colour. What do you think? There's no right or wrong way to feel about colour – it can be subjective. Draw something yellow and consider how it makes you feel.

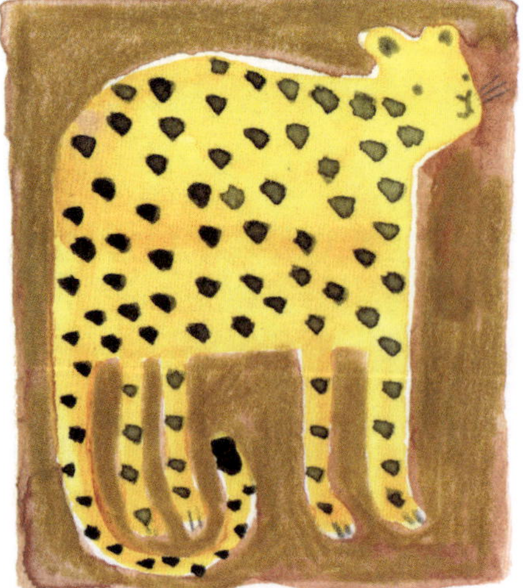

135

It can be tricky to make the leap to using non-realistic colours in your art. Have a play here, colouring each leaf in colours you wouldn't expect to see in nature.

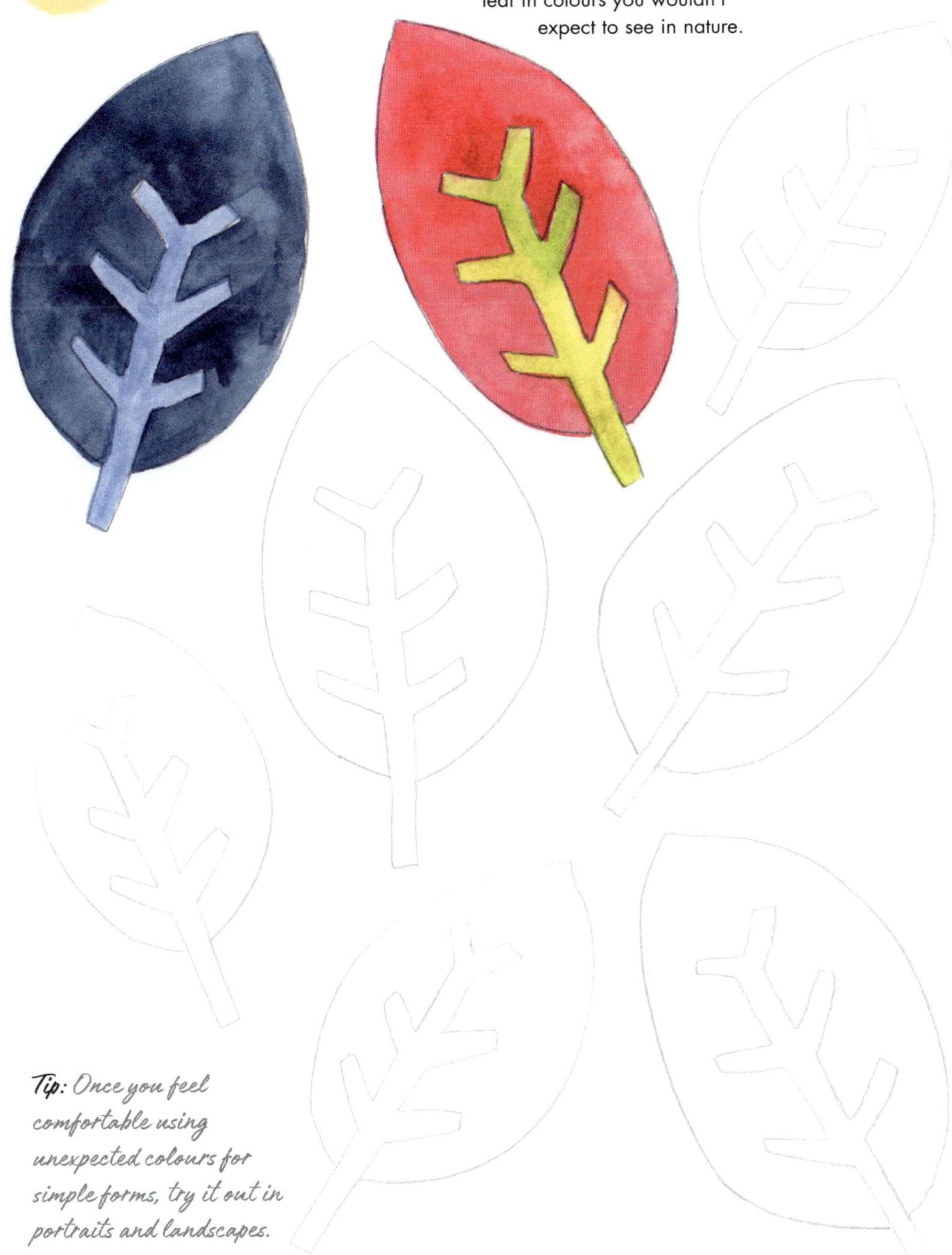

Tip: Once you feel comfortable using unexpected colours for simple forms, try it out in portraits and landscapes.

136

Spend time people-watching in a park or café. Draw lots of people from observation, paying particular attention to their colourful outfits. You could draw the whole scene or individual people.

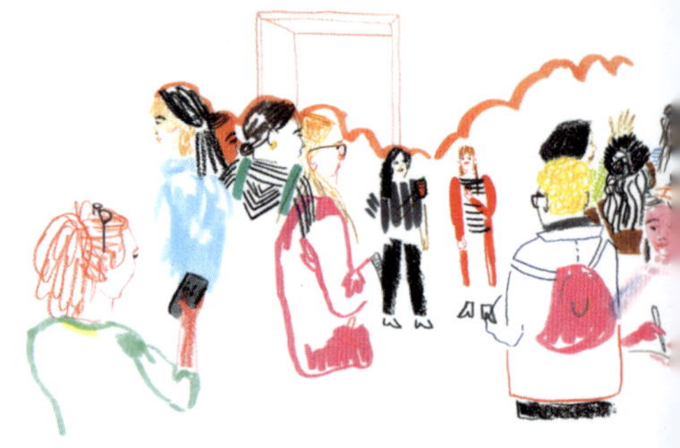

137

It can be useful to break the habit of drawing objects as blocks of a single colour. Choose an object, such as a piece of fruit, and really look at all the colours you can see on its surface. Search for the colours that you wouldn't expect to see at first glance.

Tip: Perhaps start by drawing the outline of the object, then fill in the colours you see, bit by bit.

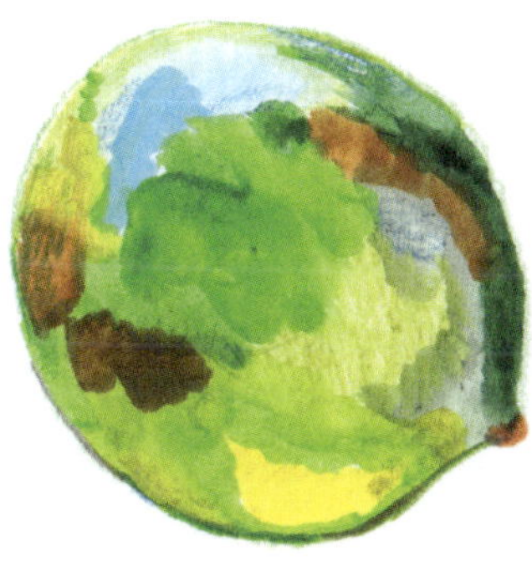

138

Paint a sweep of colour and then add little details to create the silhouette of a horizon.

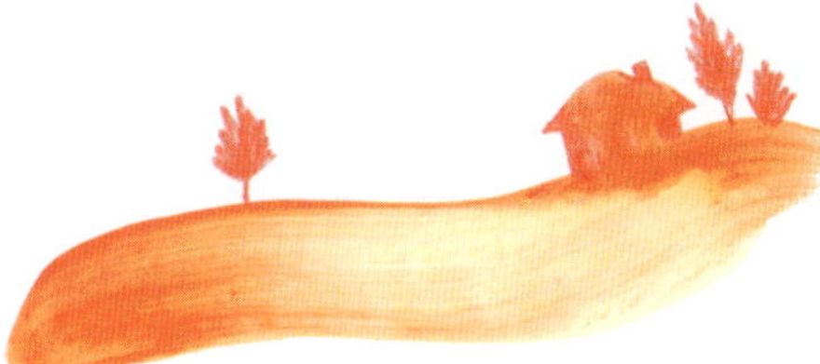

139

Draw something from the natural world, paying particular attention to any vivid colours you can see.

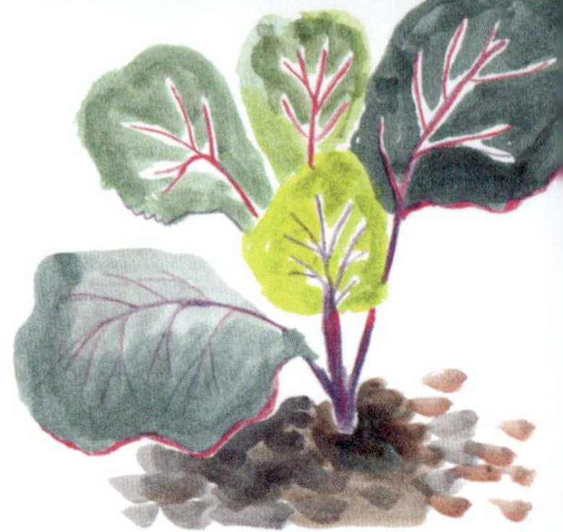

140

When mixing primary colours together, it can be tricky to find a *pure* red, yellow and blue paint, as they often contain a little of other primary colours. However, you can use this to your advantage and explore making even more variations in colour! Choose different hues of primary colours (perhaps a sky blue and a peacock blue, for example) and mix them to make as many secondary colours as you can. Notice the slight variations you create when using different hues.

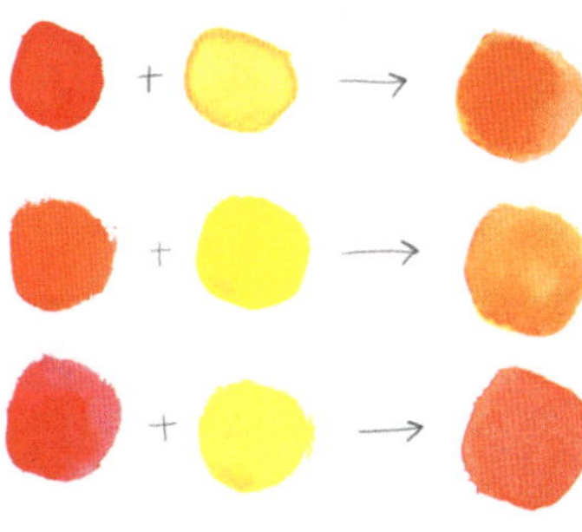

141

We can use colour to show abundance, for example to depict a garden, full of life. Spend up to 20 minutes painting a scene that is bountiful. Explore layering colours on top of each other and embrace the energy of the scene by working quickly.

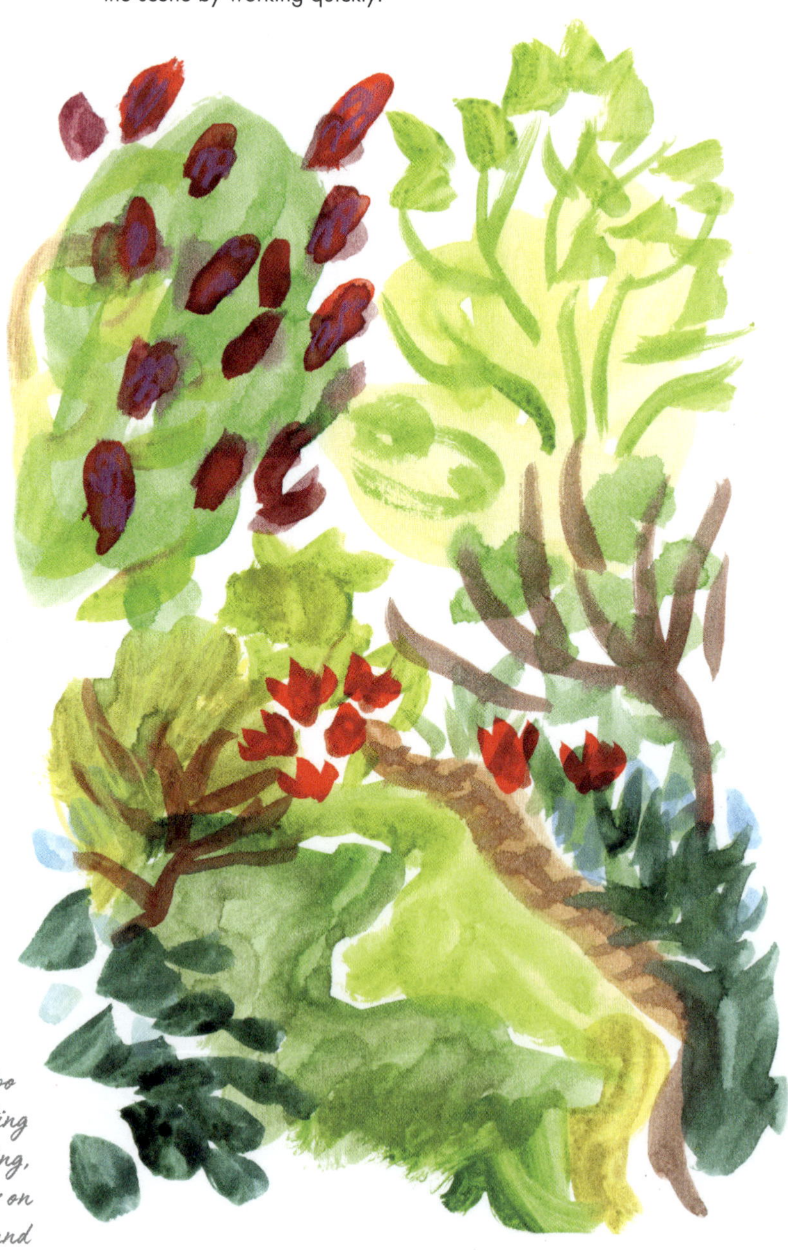

Tip: Don't worry too much about creating an accurate drawing, just get the colour on the page quickly and confidently!

142

By choosing a limited palette of colours – perhaps three or four – you can make an image that naturally feels cohesive. Create a pattern or design using a narrow range of colours.

Design a flag and carefully consider the colours you use – perhaps they have a personal meaning to you.

144

Add a colourful scene to this beach. Include towels, people, parasols and windbreakers.

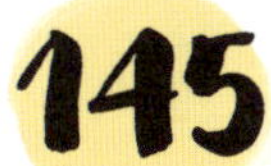

Cut up some paper and create a colourful collage.

***Tip:** Don't think too much about what should go where, just cut shapes and go for it!*

146
Use a triadic colour scheme to colour this pattern.
Refer to activity 94 for tips.

Create a simple, bold collage using this dark background as a starting point. Perhaps be inspired to use bright contrasting colours, or keep the whole design neutral and subdued. You could choose a subject to depict, or create an abstract piece.

Drop some blobs of watered-down paint onto the page and while it's still wet, blow it across the page using a paper straw if you have one, or just your mouth. Have fun and enjoy the unpredictability of the paint!

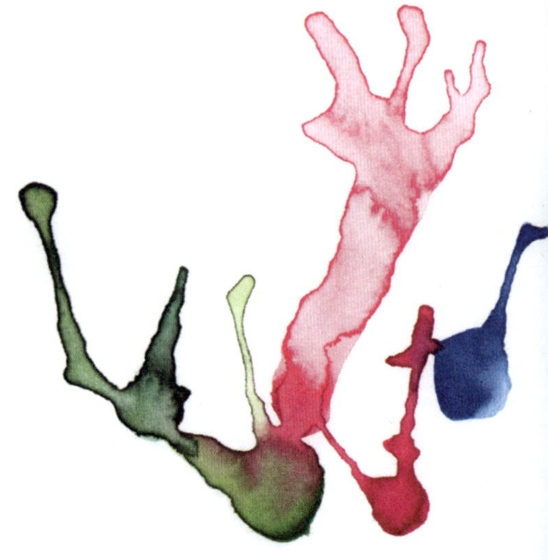

149

Paint or draw a piece of fruit, but use colours that you wouldn't expect, rather than making it look realistic.

Paint or draw a scene (indoors or outdoors) using only pastel colours. How do the colours make you feel, and what mood does this give the scene?

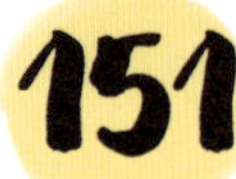

Add more details to the buildings then add colour.

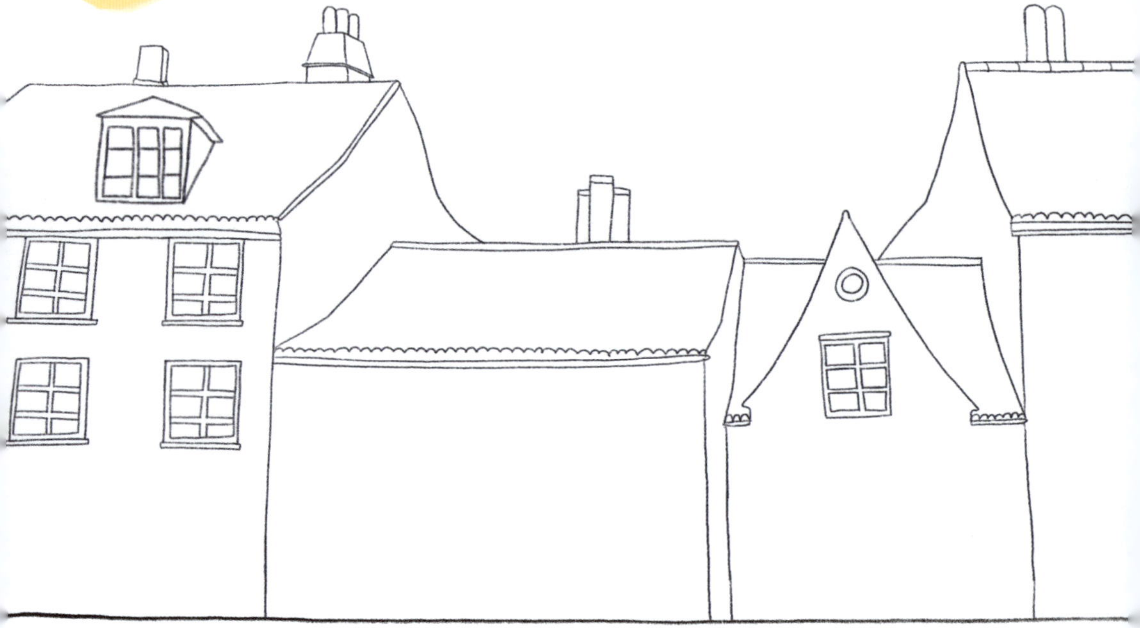

152

Paint a simple landscape using oranges, blues and browns.

153

Explore how different colour backgrounds can change the mood of a portrait. Draw some portraits here and consider how each makes you feel.

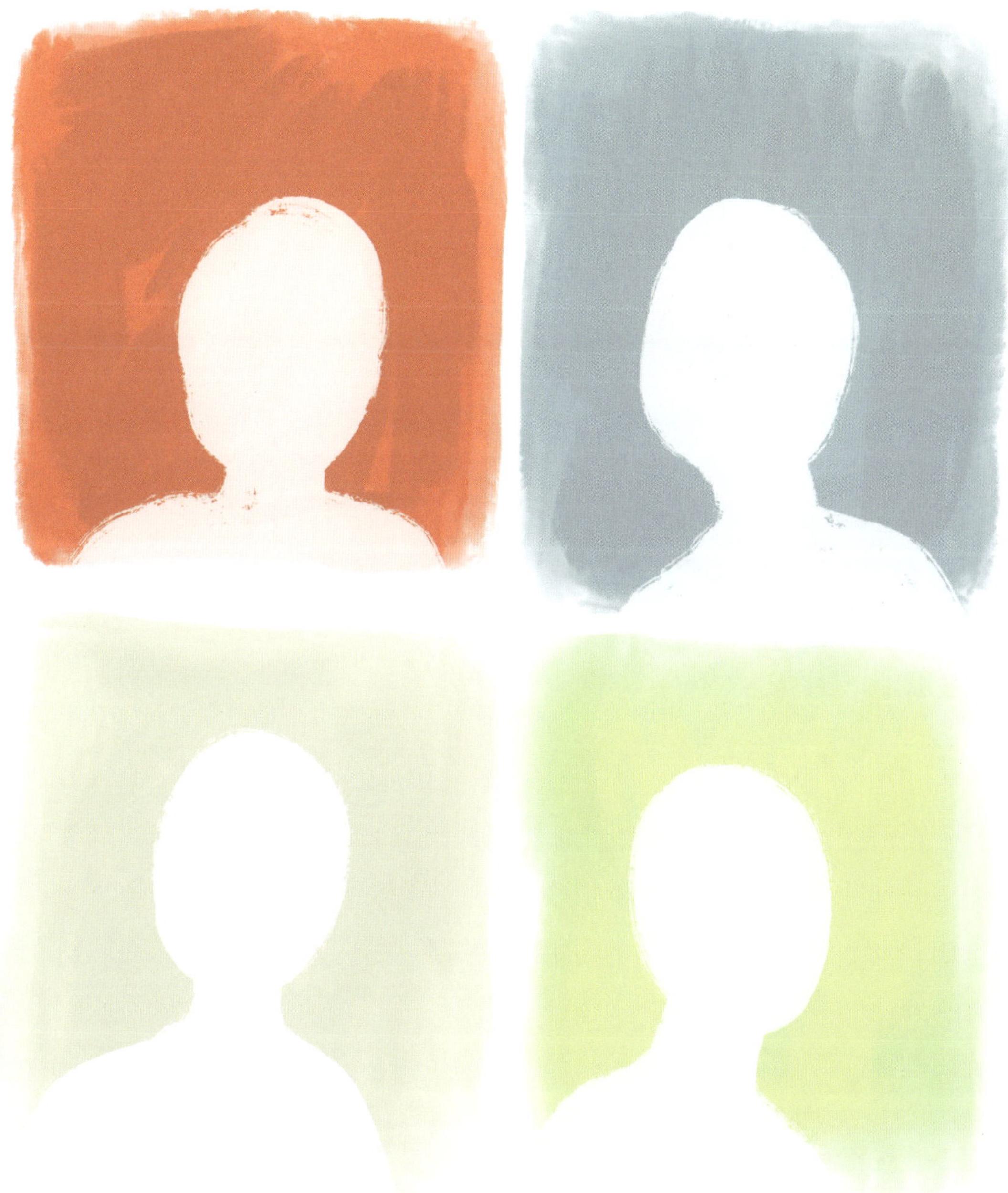

154

Create some mini abstract images using blocks of colour in a range of different art materials.

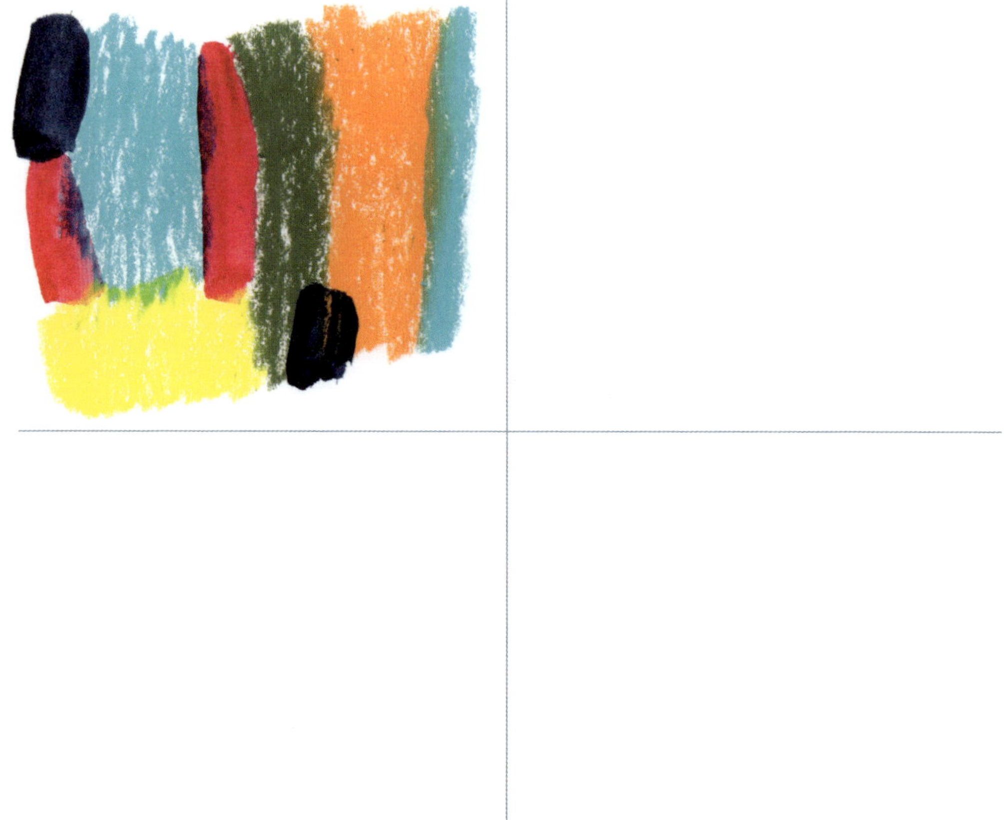

155

Make a colourful piece of art using paper. Choose a subject for your art – perhaps a vase, some fruit or something from your kitchen. Cut shapes based on what you see in front of you.

Tip: You may want to arrange your composition first, before you use glue to fix it down. Or just glue as you go and let your piece evolve naturally.

156

Monochromatic colour schemes are where variations of only one colour are used. This can be a useful way to create a powerful atmosphere in a piece of art. Choose one colour and create a piece of art using only variations of this colour. Consider the mood of the piece once you've finished.

Tip: You could use tints and shades of one colour, or slightly different versions – for example a teal blue and a sky blue.

157

Create a collage using primary colours.

Fill the page with watercolour paint and watch as the colours blend into each other. Once the paint is dry, add a drawing on top using dark colouring pencils.

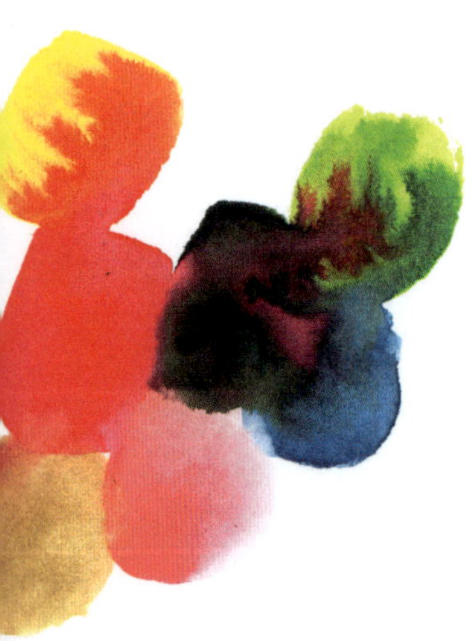

159

Colour can be used in a simple way and still be effective. Have a look at some objects around your home and paint blocks of colour to represent them. Then draw the objects in their simplest forms on top.

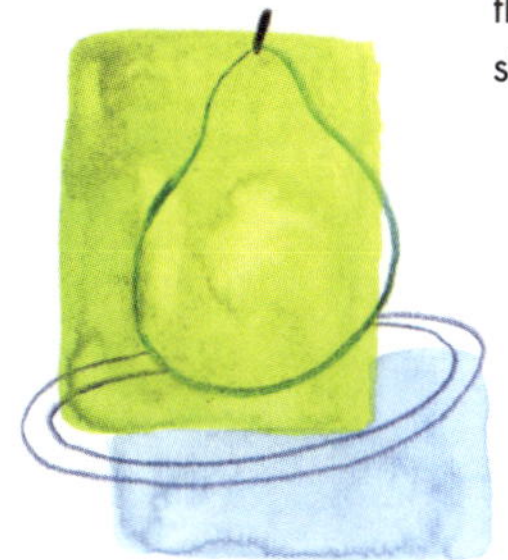

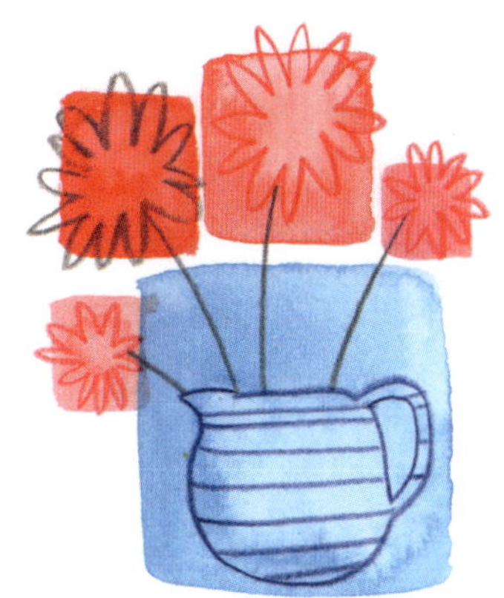

Track your mood throughout the day using colour. When you notice a feeling, draw a segment below and add a colour to represent your mood.

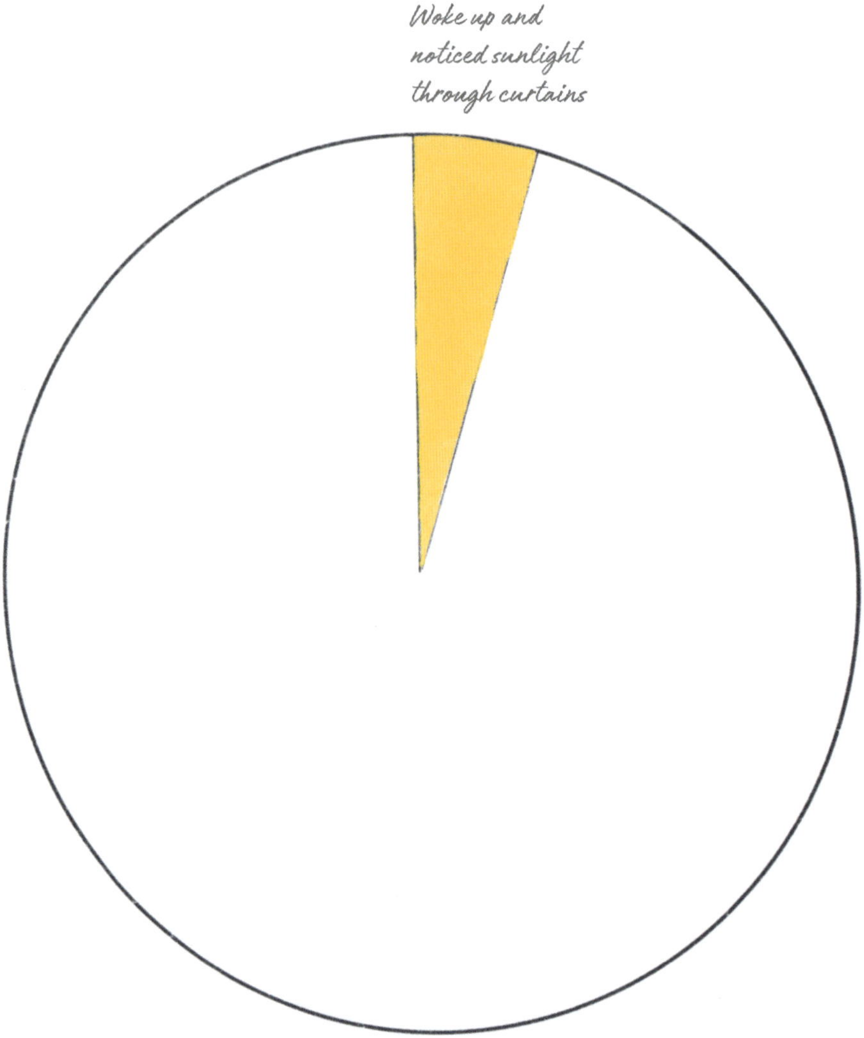

Woke up and noticed sunlight through curtains

161

Create an observational drawing of someone you love using colour.

162

Add bright, colourful leaves to these tree trunks.

Green can suggest nature, life, freshness and new things. How does green make *you* feel? Use those feelings and this shape as a starting point for an image.

164

Create a design for a deck of cards.

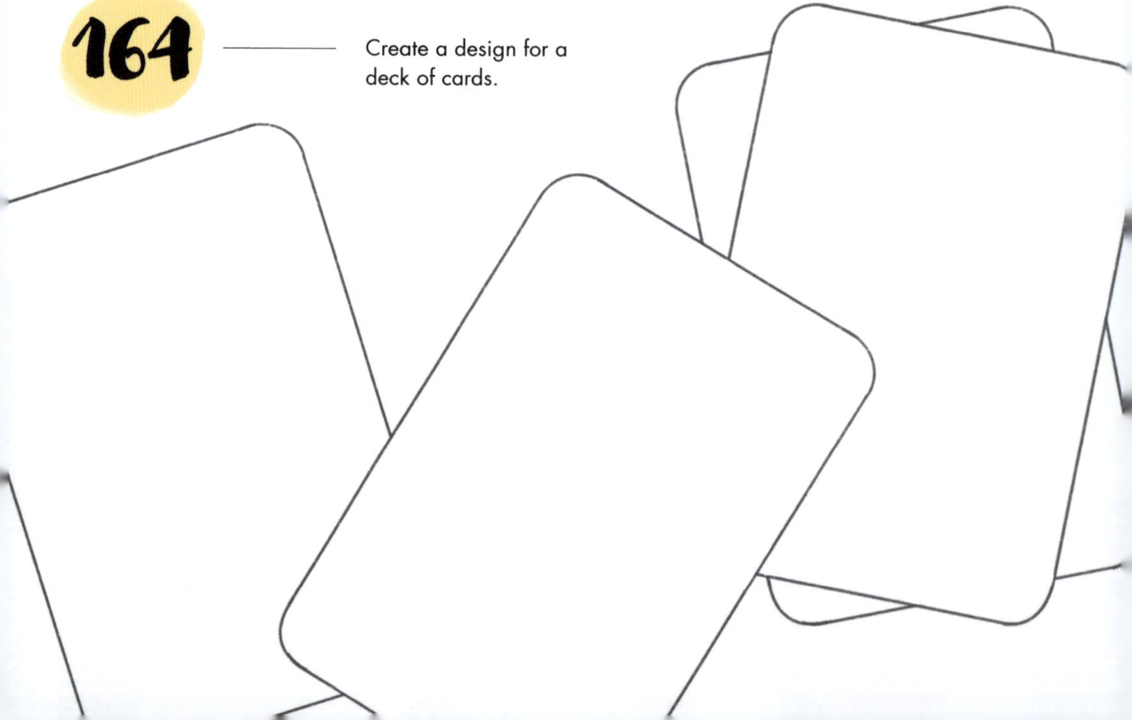

165

Challenge yourself to make an observational sketch in under 25 minutes. Before you begin, paint a brightly coloured background and allow it to dry. This will add even more energy and life to your image.

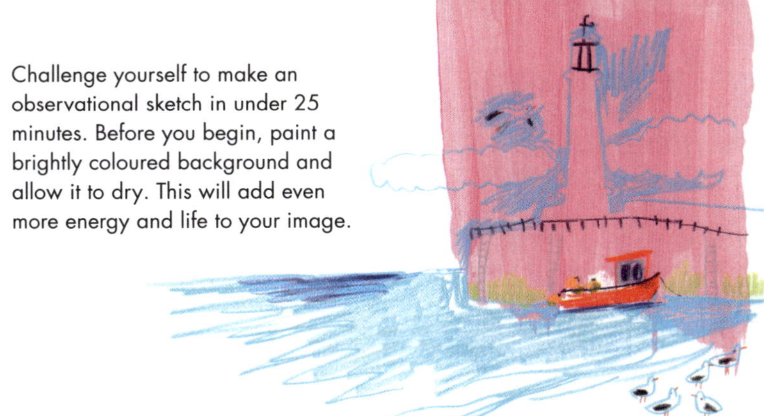

Create a note of all the colours you'd like to use more in your art. Engage with the emotions the colours make you feel and give each colour swatch a name of your own invention.

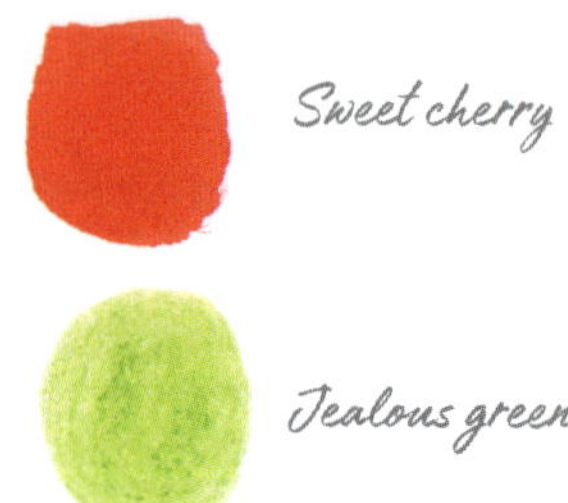

167

Draw as many purple things as you can think of.

168

Sketch a scene, object or person in pencil using only outlines. Then add colour to your drawing using any material you like.

Some individual hues and groups of colours can remind us of particular locations. Think about a place that you love – it could be a room, a town or a holiday location – and create a palette below that conjures up the feelings of that place.

Colour this drawing using only neutrals to create a serene image.

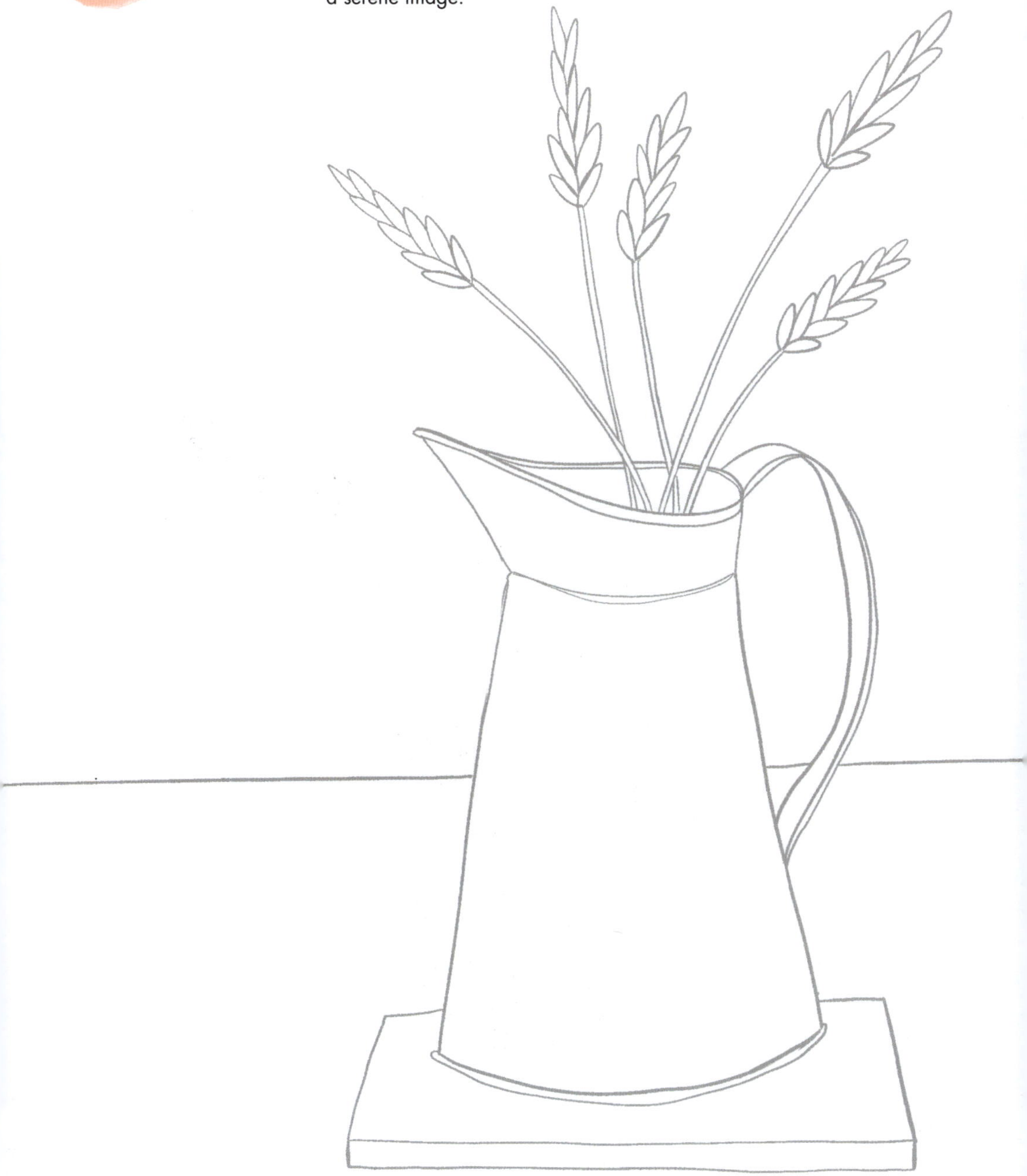

171

Make a piece of art using bright colours against muted or dark background colours. Choose a subject where you can see a strong contrast, and use any material you feel like.

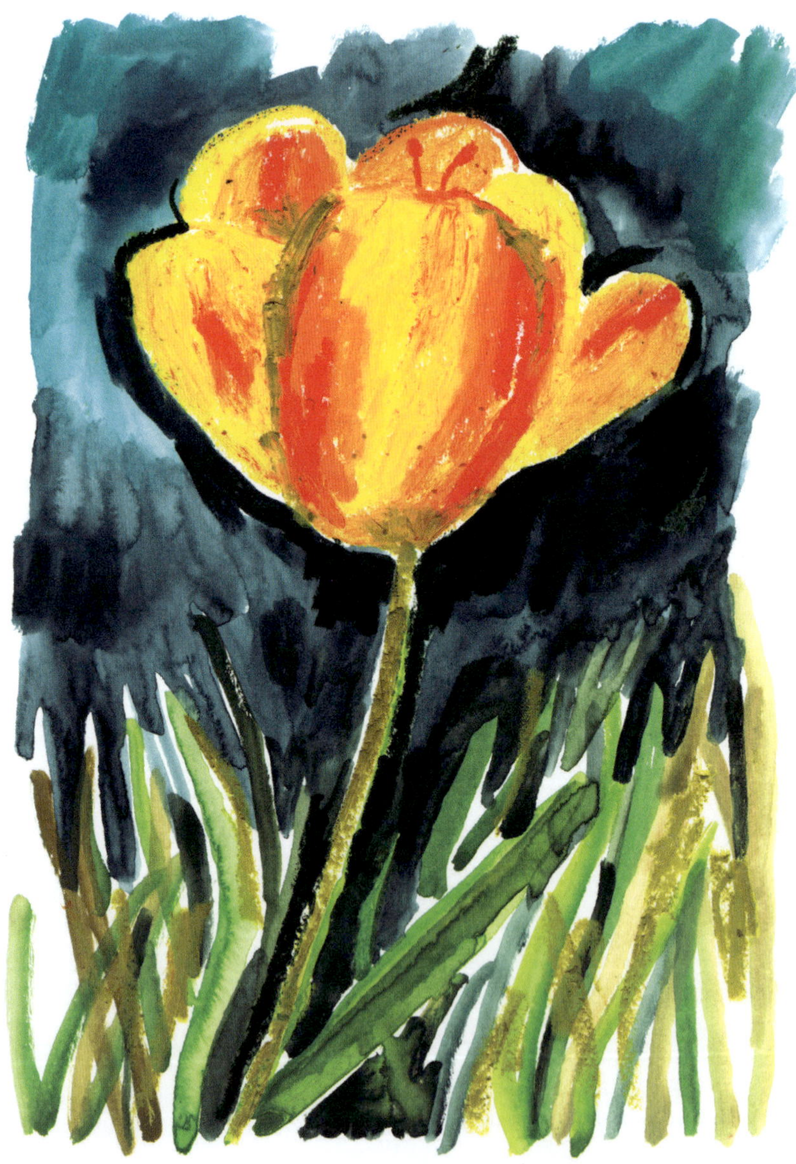

Tip: You may want to draw the light, bright elements first, then add the darker background around them ... but there is no right or wrong way to approach this! Consider what you've learnt about your materials in earlier activities.

172

Continue adding to the design, exploring different art materials.

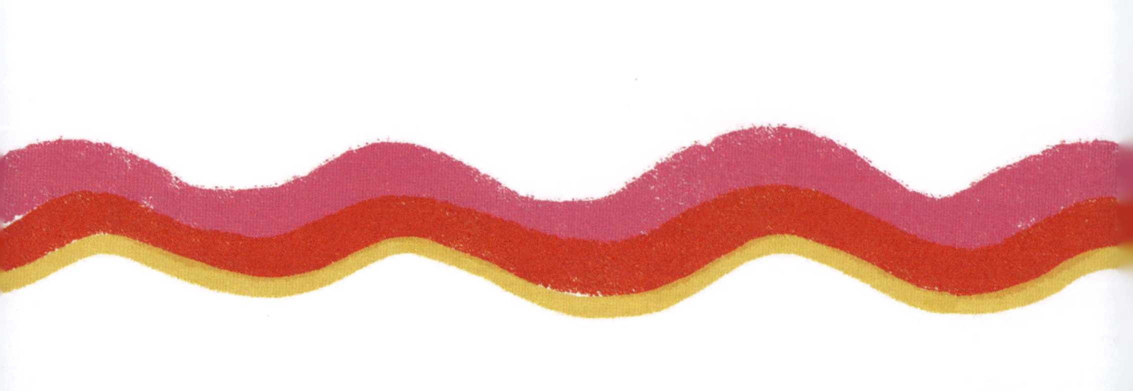

173

Draw some fish in colours that you find harmonious.

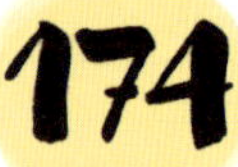

The sea can appear one colour one day, and another the next. Using these backgrounds as starting points, create four depictions of the sea.

175

Paint an object or view using broad, confident brush strokes. Use colour to sculpt your image, rather than an outline. You could layer colours on top of each other to add depth and energy to your image.

Tip: If you are unsure how to begin, paint the background a bright colour – it's far less daunting than a white space!

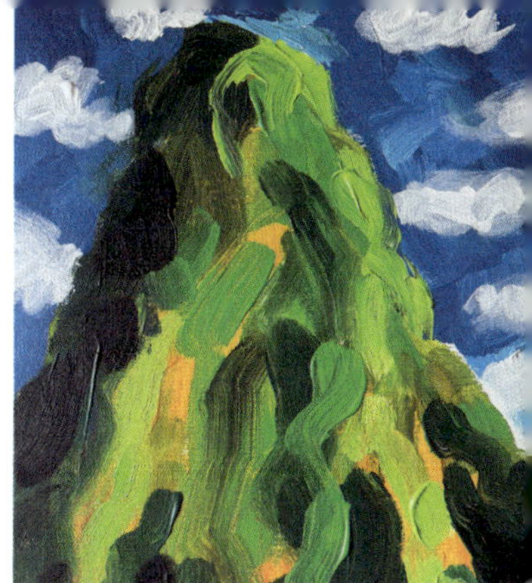

176

Warm colours tend to jump forward in a piece of art, whereas cool colours tend to recede and so can be used to suggest something is in the distance. Draw a landscape and use cool colours like blue to depict elements that are far away, such as mountains or distant buildings.

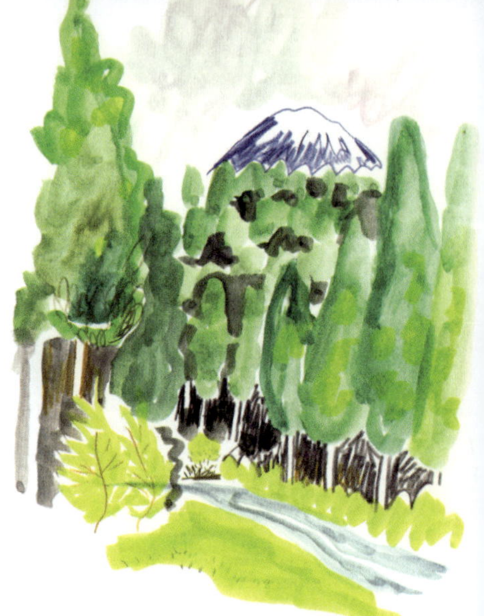

Tip: To add further depth to your image, you could include a warm coloured element in the foreground – a red sign, for example.

177

Add colour to the pattern to create a tartan.

178

Draw a tempest using colours that evoke tumultuous feelings.

179

Add colour.

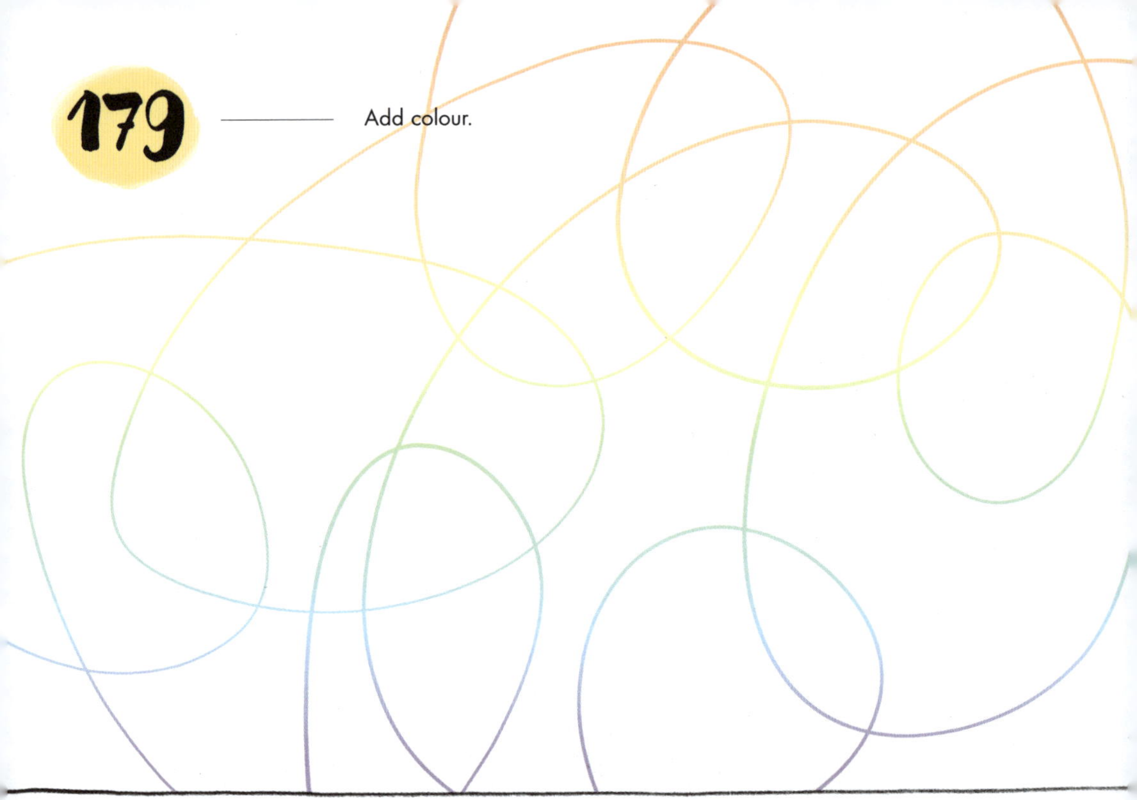

Fill the page with the colour green – how does it make you feel?

You can use a pattern to surround a white image so that the busy 'negative space' makes the clean, white object become the focus. Use a bold pattern to frame a white object.

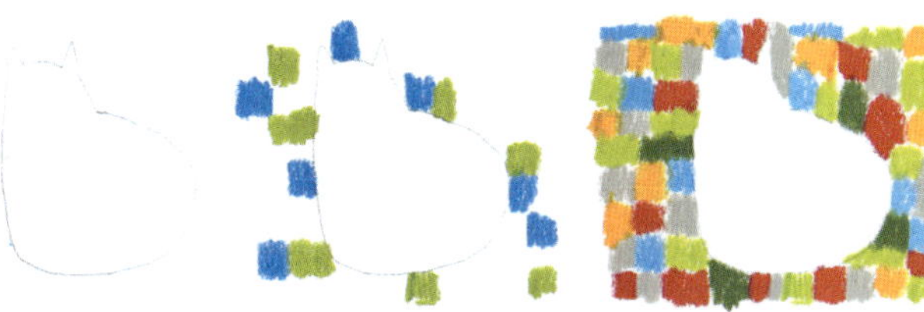

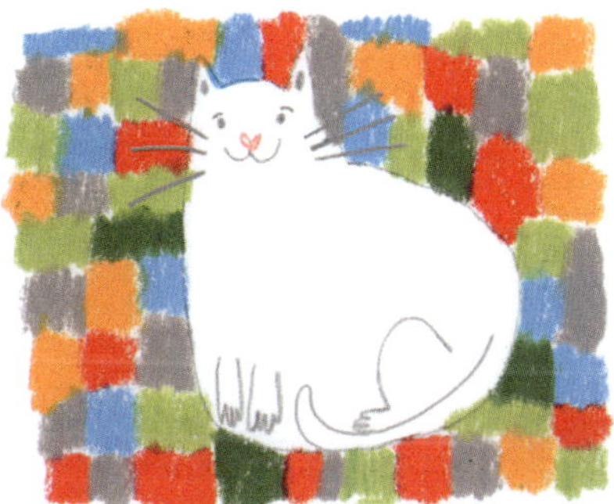

Create a faint outline of your object, then fill the surrounding area with a colourful pattern. Then add details to your object but keep lots of the paper white so that it stands out.

182

Using a limited palette of three to five colours, draw a landscape or object. Use wax pastels if you have some, or coloured pencils.

Tip: *Look carefully at your scene before starting. Which colours could you choose? Perhaps there is a tree trunk that is almost the same tone as some purple leaves, so you choose a purple to represent both. Maybe the palest green leaves you see are a similar tone to the pale sky, so you use a soft green for both.*

Cut lots of shapes out of coloured paper, then create a series of compositions, using the pieces. Work quickly – spend around 10 minutes on each design.

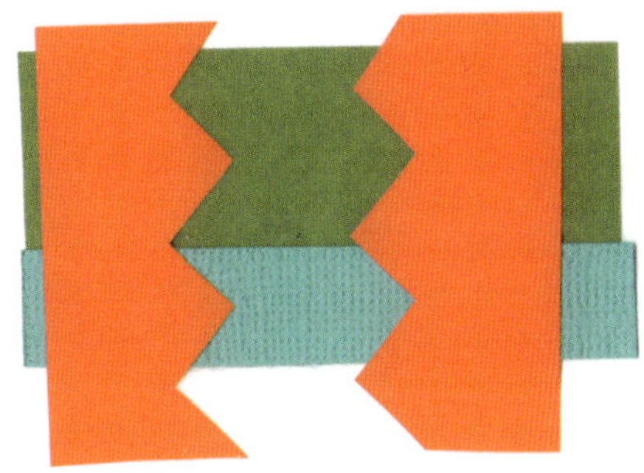

Tip: Working quickly will encourage you to make instinctual decisions – don't worry if your compositions look 'right' or 'wrong' – just enjoy the process of choosing shapes and being playful.

184

Using blues, create graphic representations of tranquillity and water.

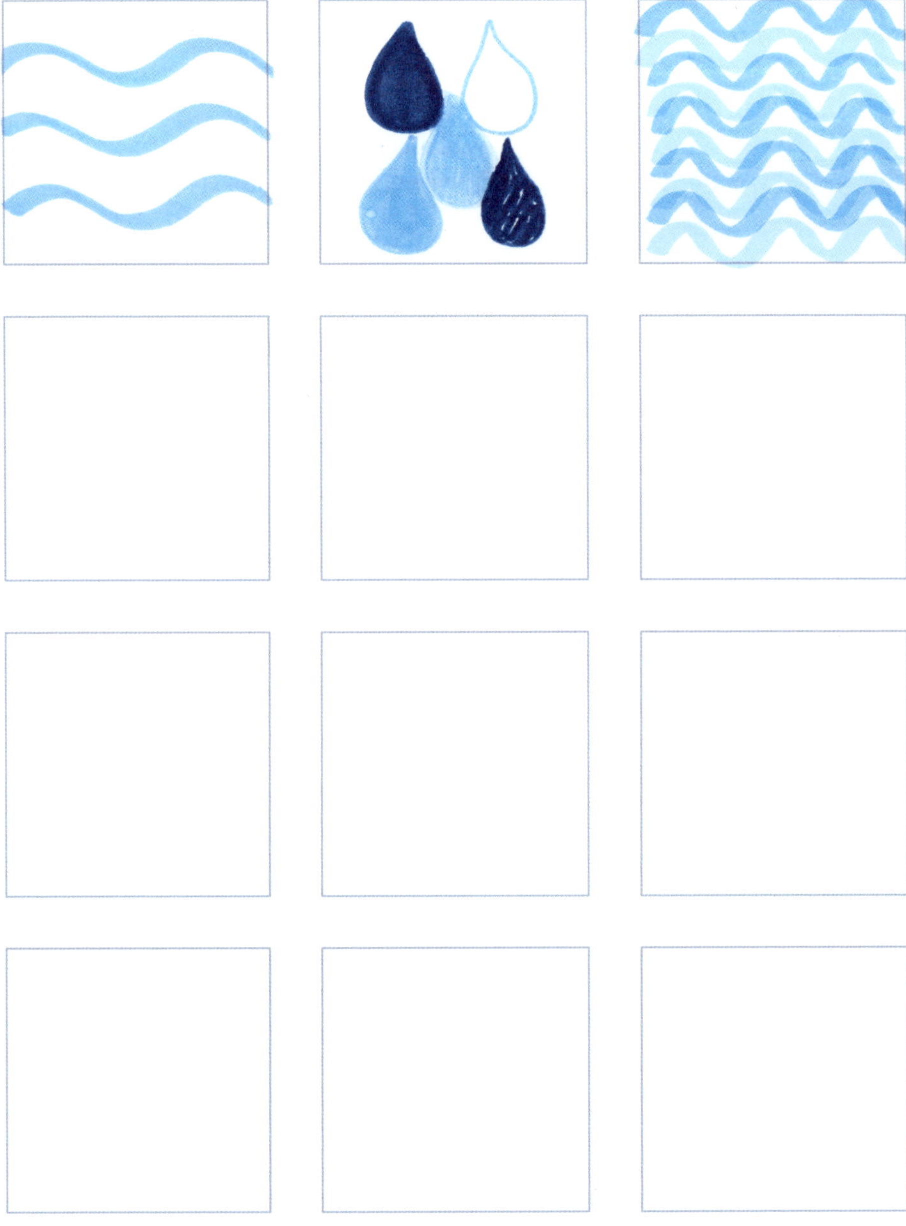

Colour in these pencils.

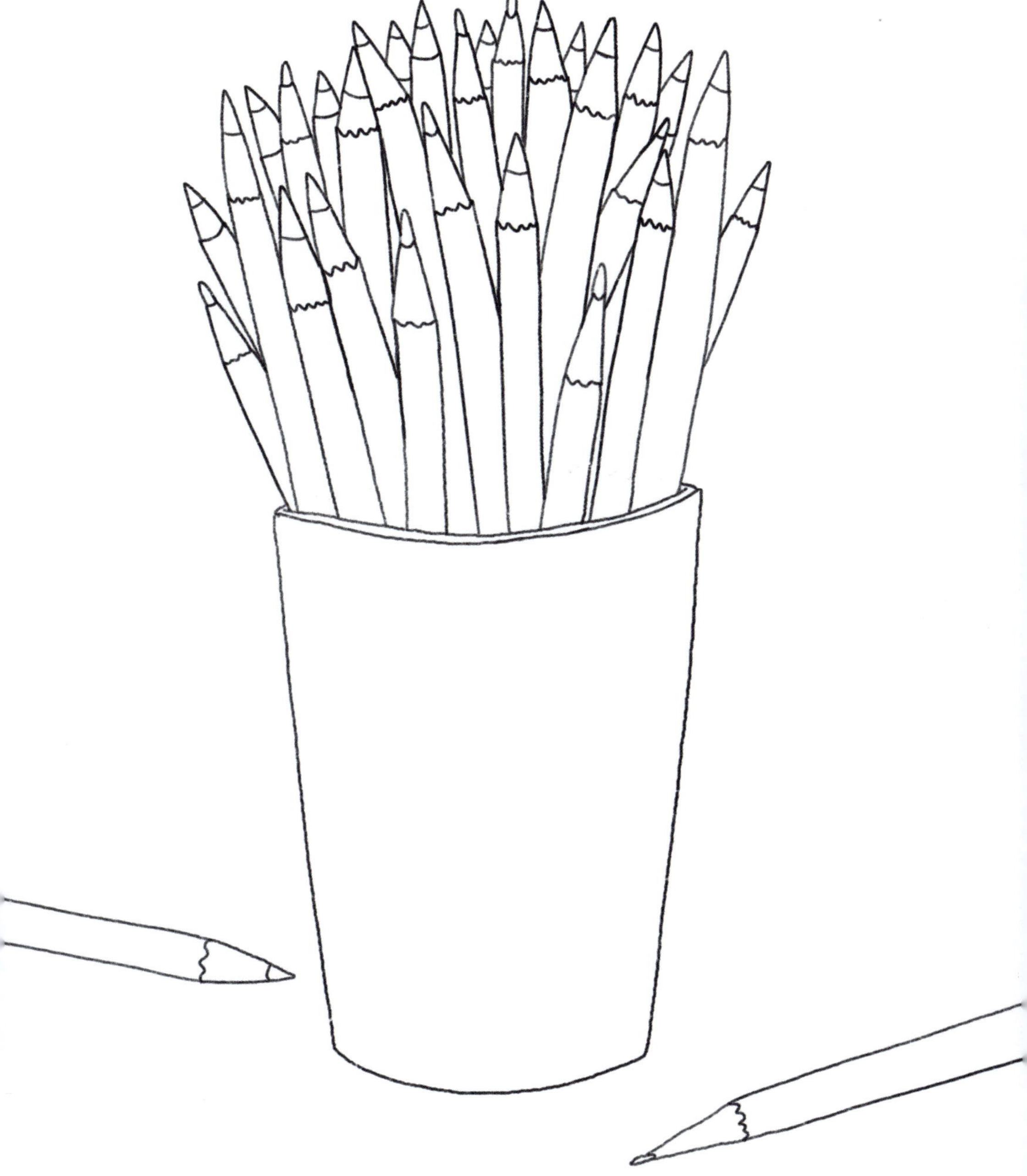

186

Add colour to this design, taking inspiration from the element of either fire or water.

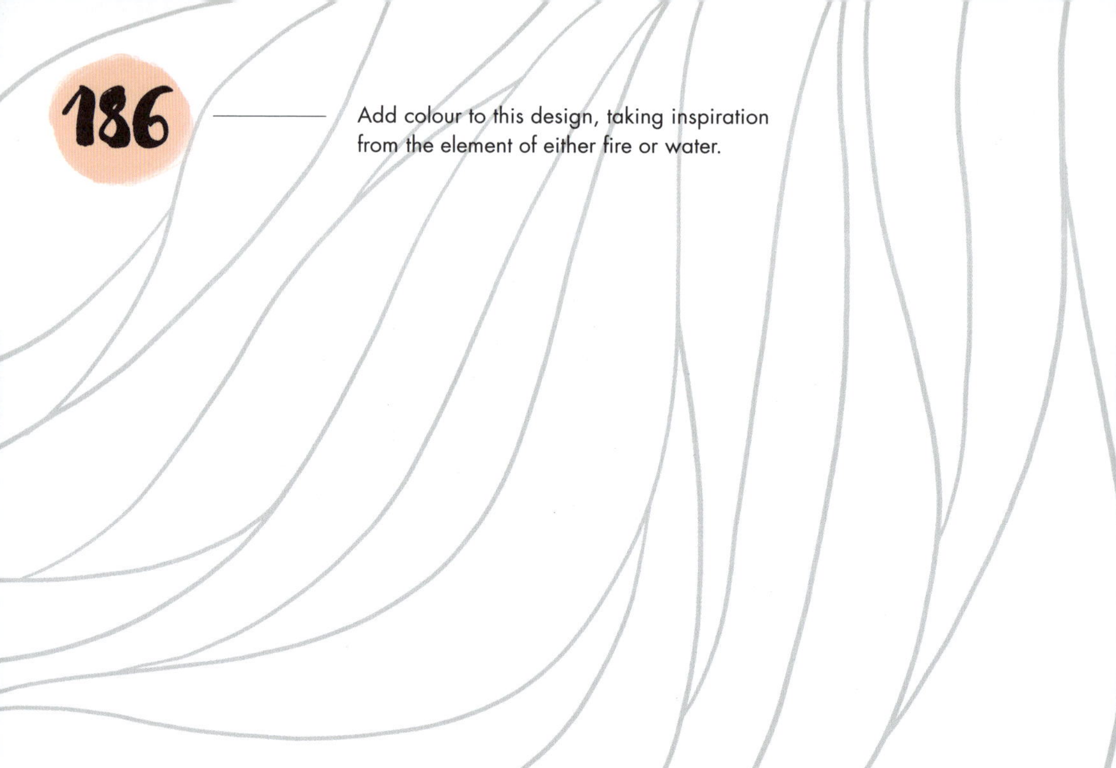

187

Continue adding lines of colour to fill the space.

188

Spend some time observing the shadow on objects and surfaces, noticing all the different colours you see. Look carefully. Draw some simple objects and then paint their shadows as accurately as possible.

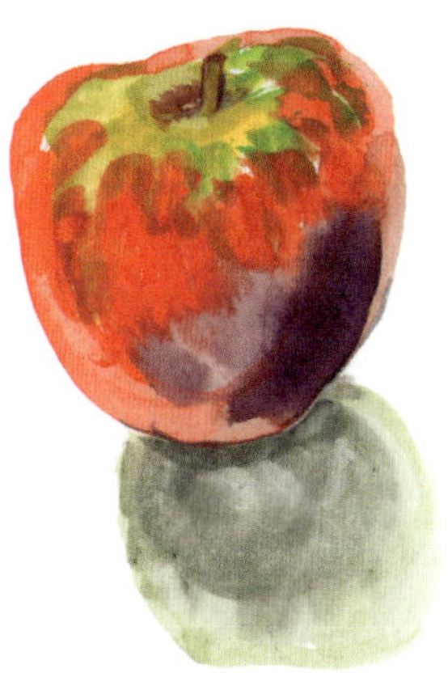

189

Build scenes with colour. Choose three landscapes (from photos, what you see in front of you, or even Google Maps) and paint them using blocks of colour to represent what you see. You don't need the hues to match perfectly – in fact, it can be really fun to overemphasise the colours to make your painting vivid and striking. The boxes are small to encourage you to use fearless marks and not too much detail.

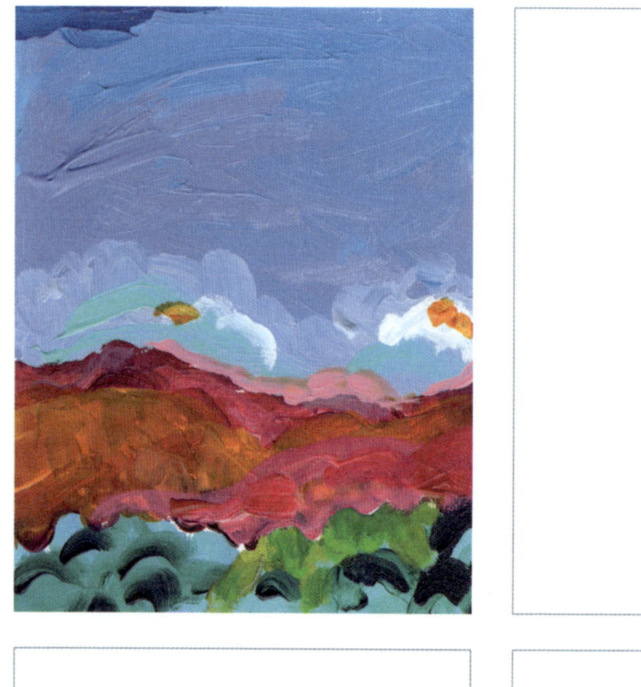

Fill the page with colourful birds.

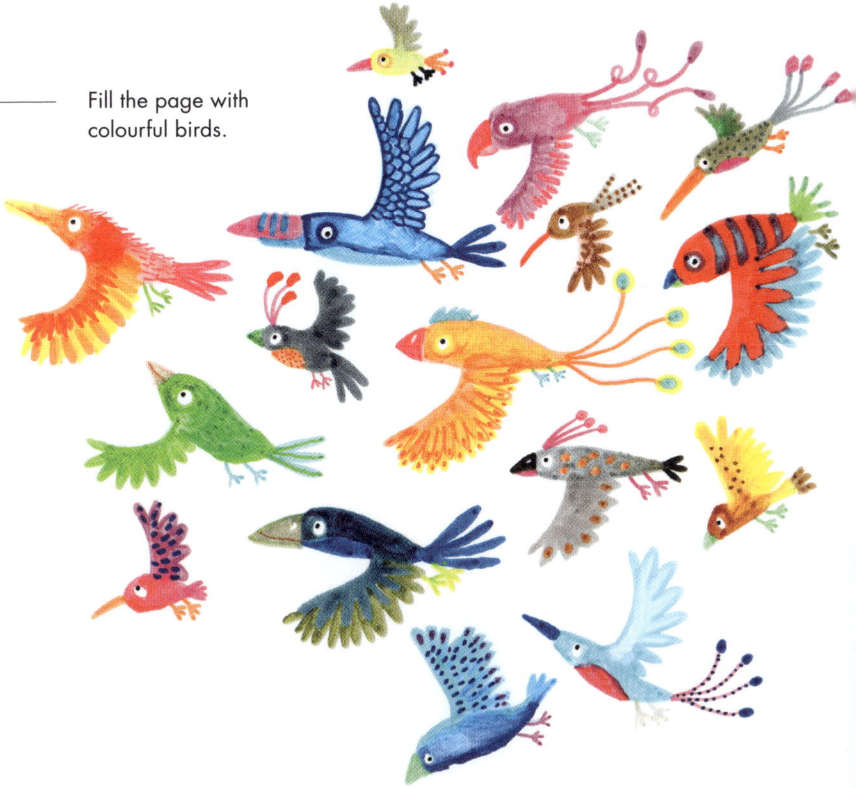

191

Draw a family tree or a tree to depict friendships.
Consider using colour to represent the people.

192

Add watercolour shapes and allow the colours to bleed into each other. Then add bold patterns to the shapes in contrasting colours.

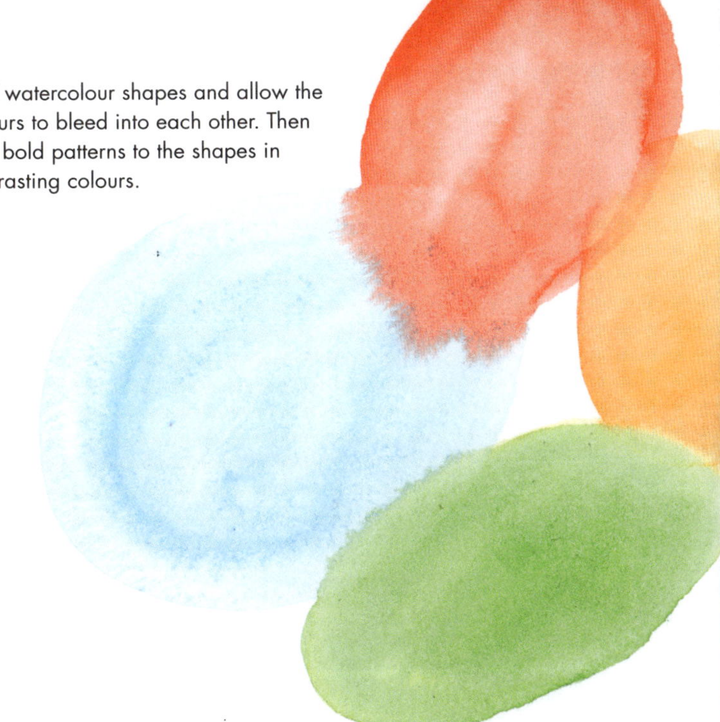

193

Draw the same object twice, when you are experiencing two different emotions. Note down the mood you are feeling, and notice how the colours you naturally gravitate towards vary.

Mood:

Mood:

194

Continue the squiggle using a variety of colours.

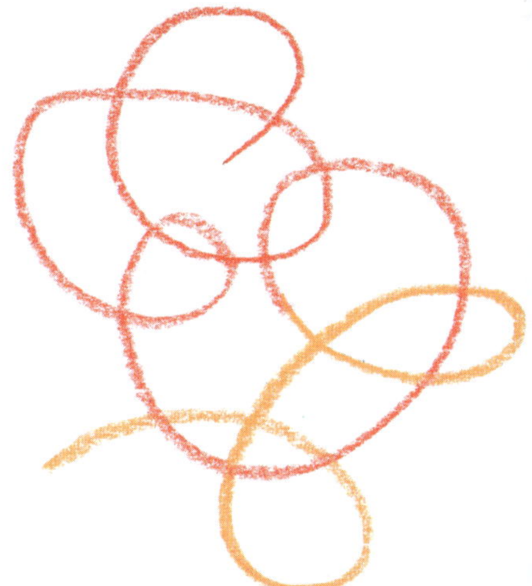

195

Refer to activity 17 to paint a cube using a tint and shade of a colour in order to give it a 3-D effect.

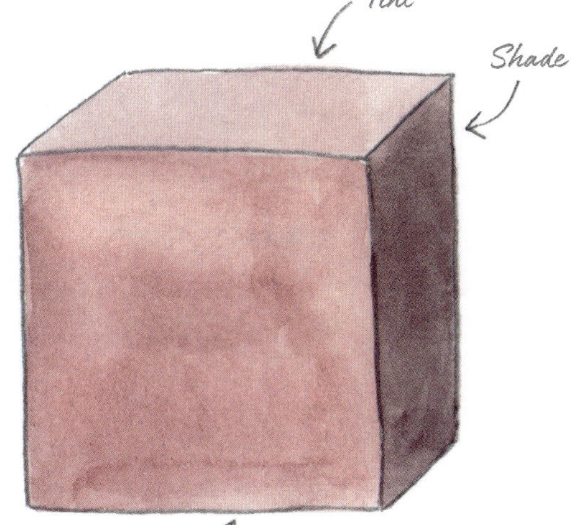

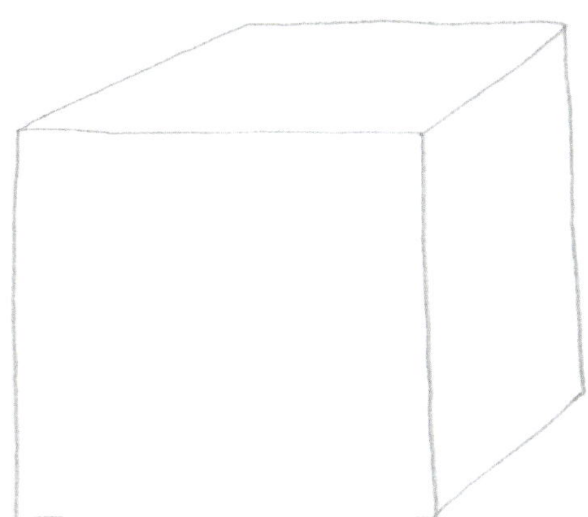

196

Add cheerful flowers to this vase. Create an arrangement that brings you joy.

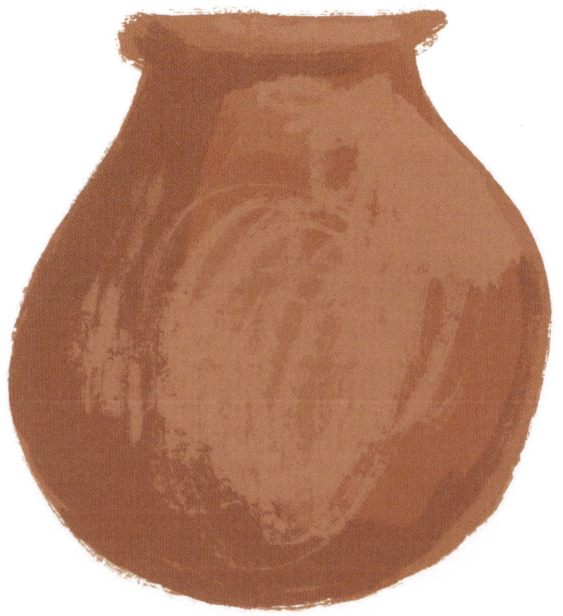

197

Analogous colours produce calm, harmonious palettes. Create some thumbnail sketches in colour for possible paintings using analogous colours. Refer back to your colour wheel and choose three or four colours that are next to each other on the wheel – this will be your palette!

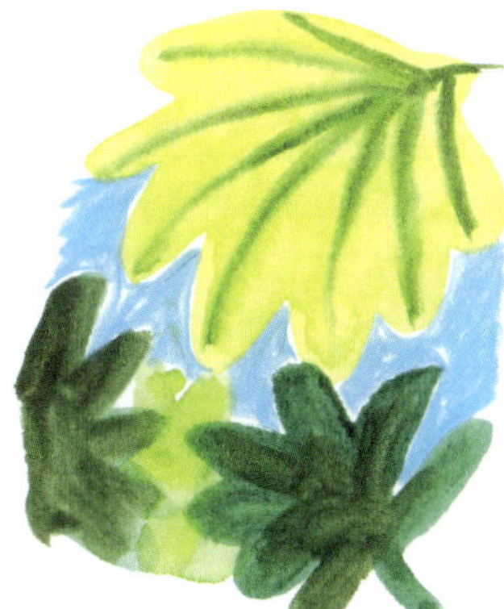

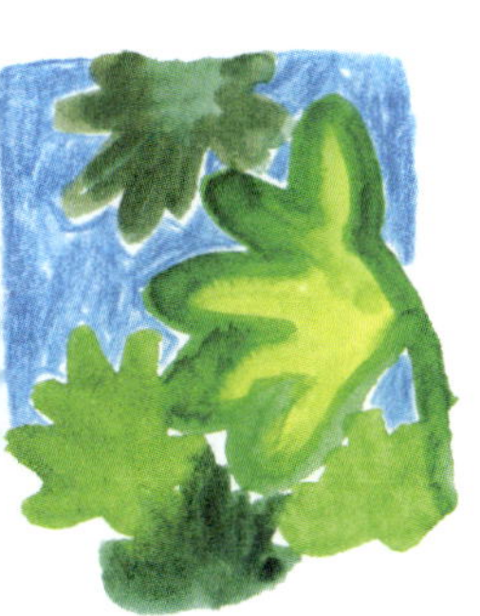

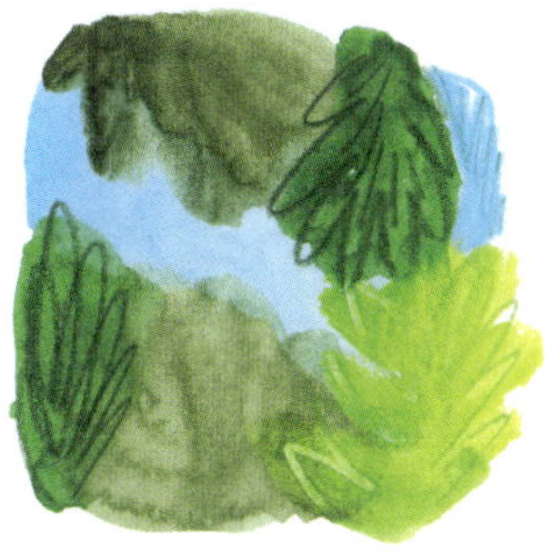

198

You can combine materials within your art, and be led by which colour you'd like to use rather than restricting yourself to one material. Use any art tools you like to create a landscape. Perhaps start by laying out a selection of materials in front of you – paints, pastels, colouring pencils and pens – and choosing from them as you go along.

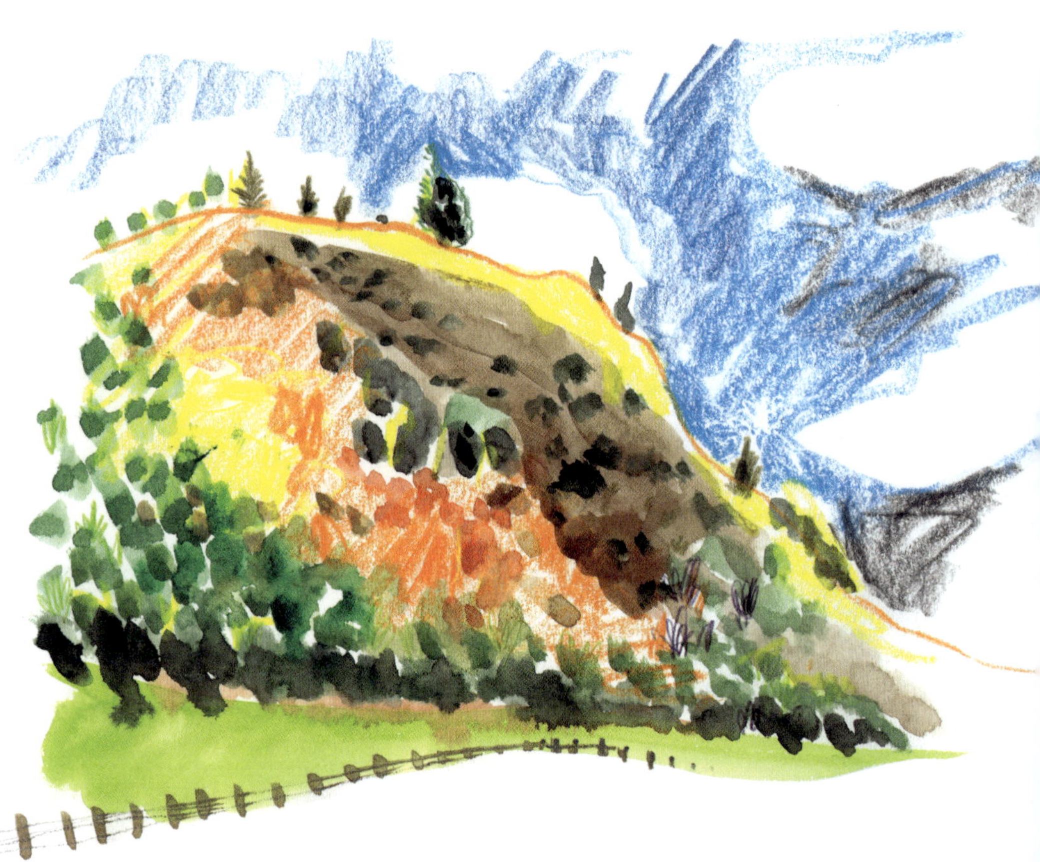

Tip: You can also use the white of the paper as a material – rather than filling the whole page, try leaving some areas of white paper showing through to represent light areas.

199

Use a limited range of colours to create some abstract compositions. Think about what colours could go in each section below to make the piece feel balanced. Then choose your own colours and create your own sections.

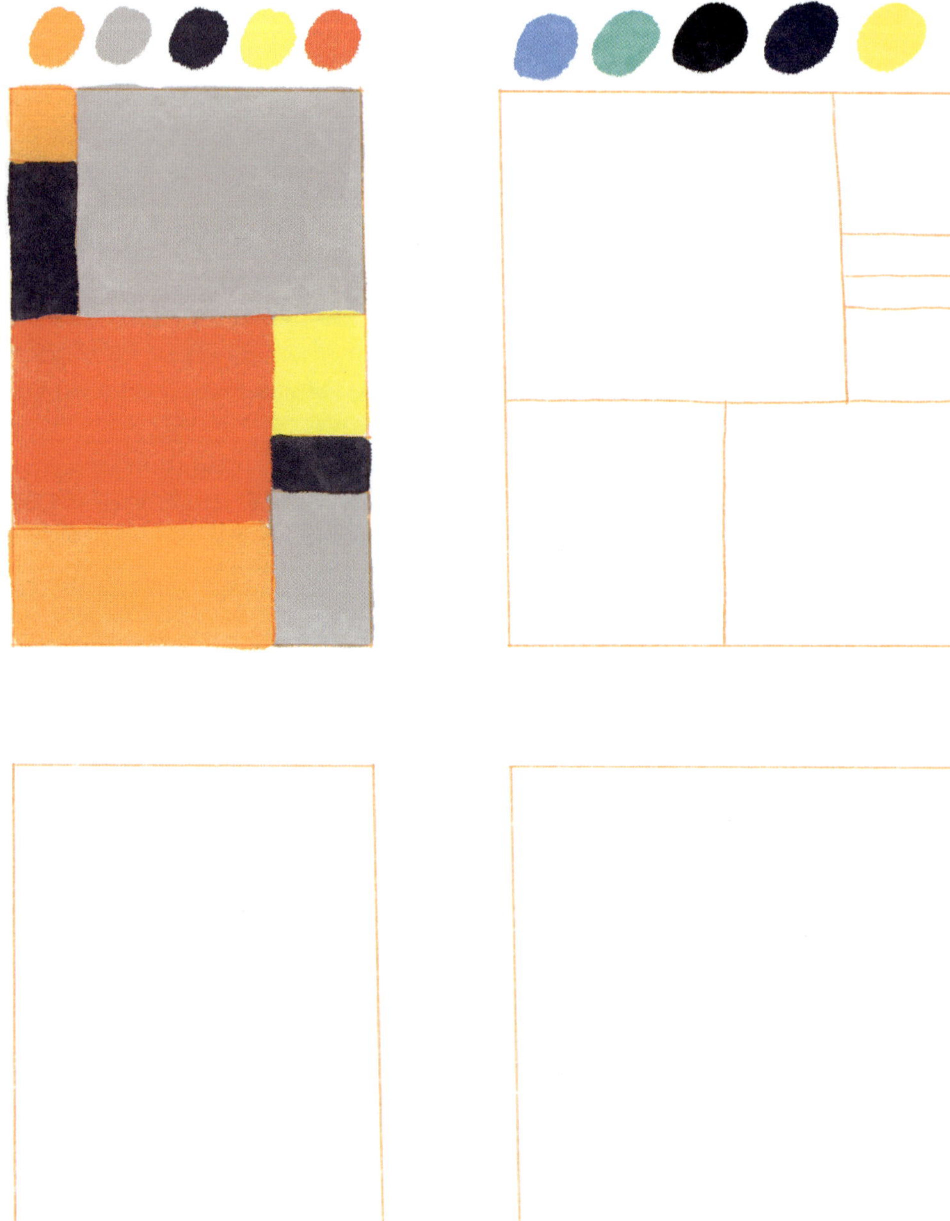

Tip: Small amounts of bright colours can have a big impact among less saturated colours.

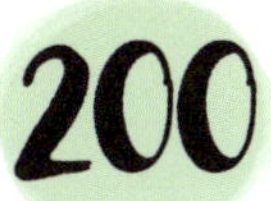

Create colour palettes that represent things you can see around you.

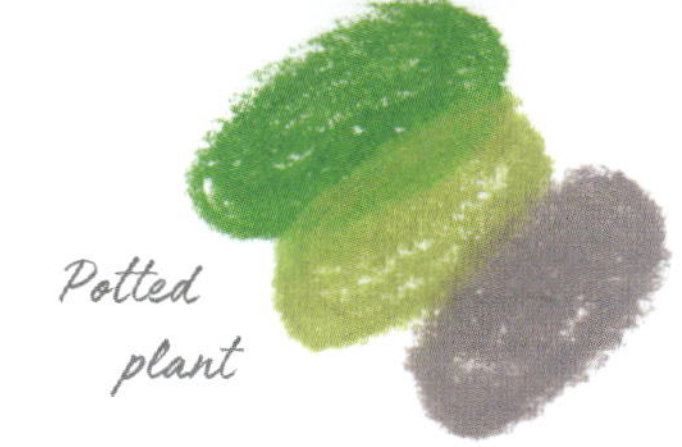

201

Design a pattern using only green triangles.

202

It can be useful to note down colours, even when you are just making a pencil sketch. Draw some people, based on a photo or real life. Jot down anything you observe about the colours – ideas about which colours could go where, or colours you'd like to test out.

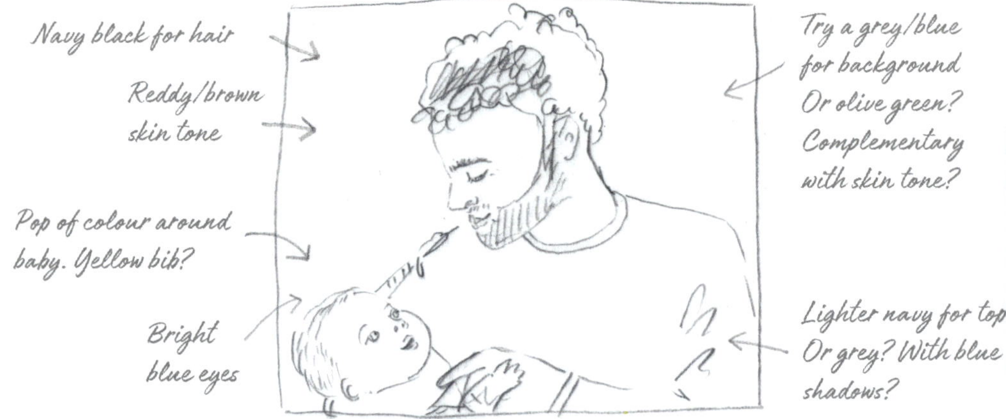

203

Make an image based on this springtime palette. Be inspired by how the colours make you feel.

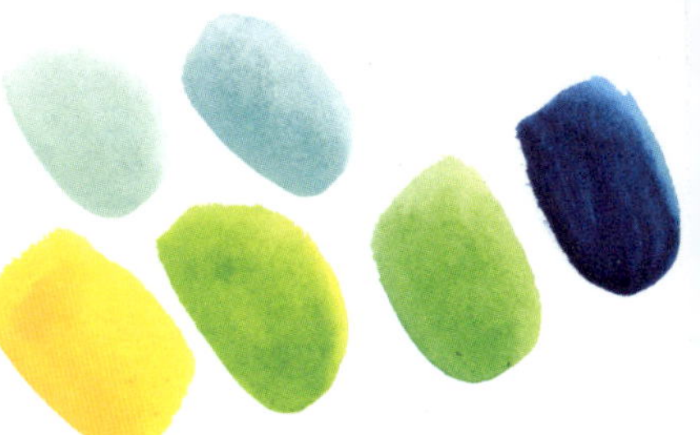

204

Draw a rainbow of food – portray a different food for every colour.

205

Add flowers and plants to the vases. Perhaps some of the leaves could be purple, or red.

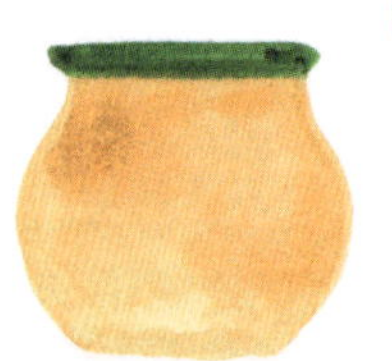
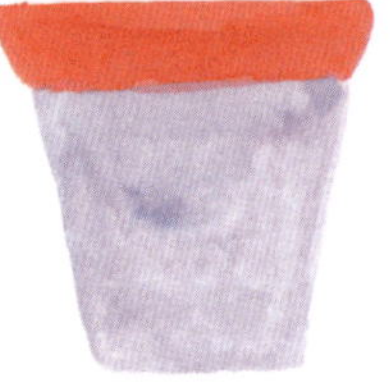
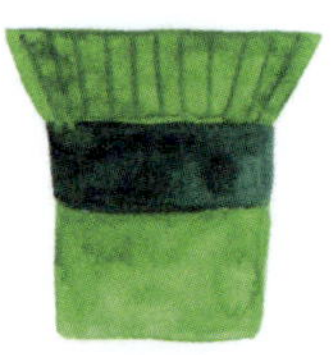
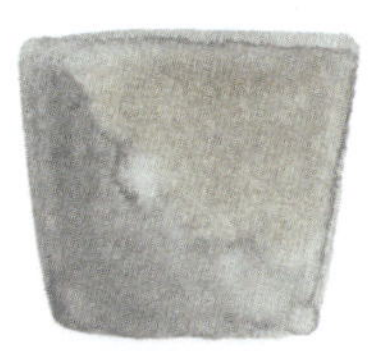
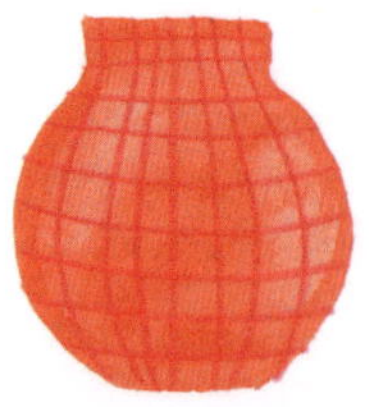

206

Add calm colours to these shapes.

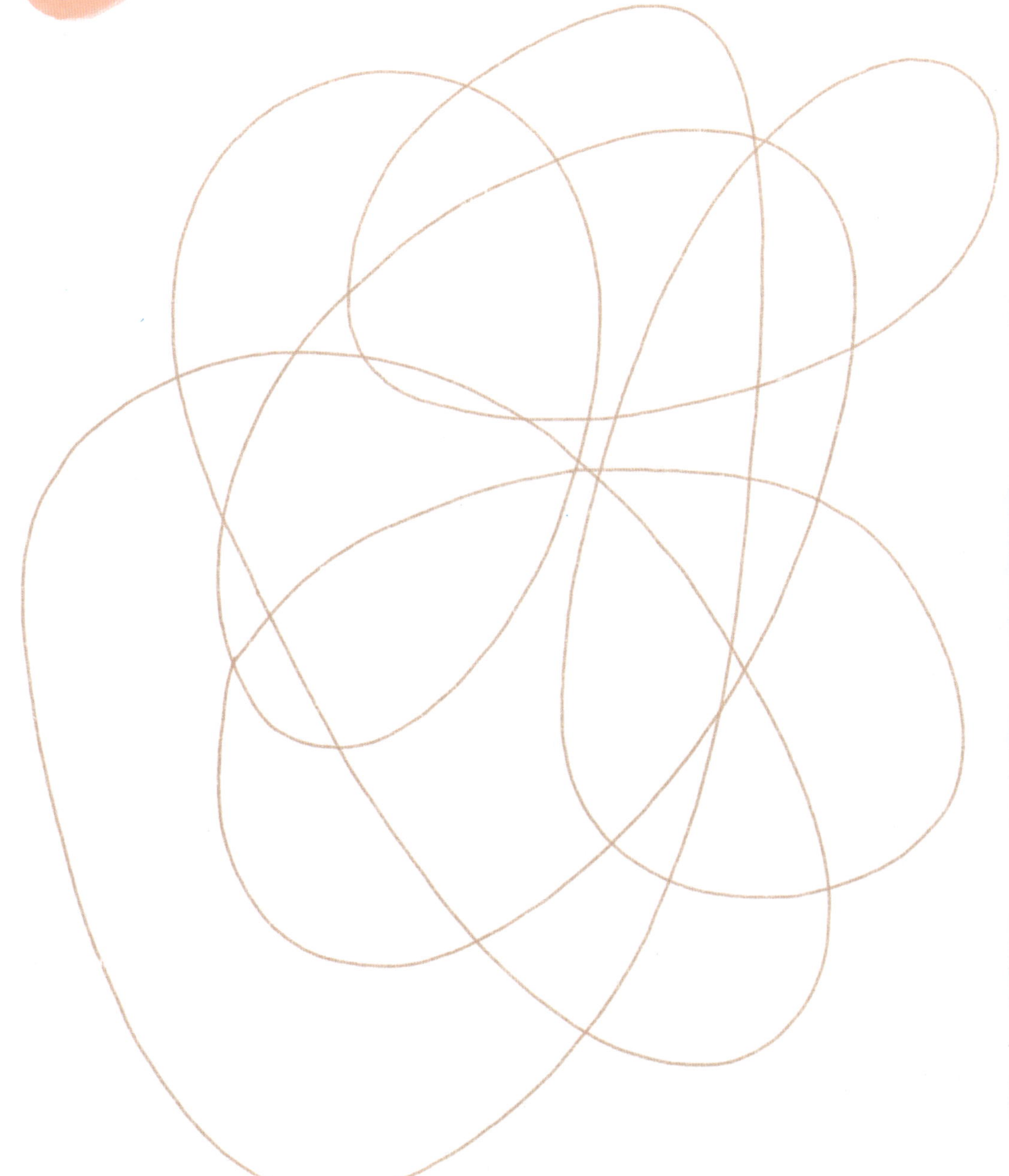

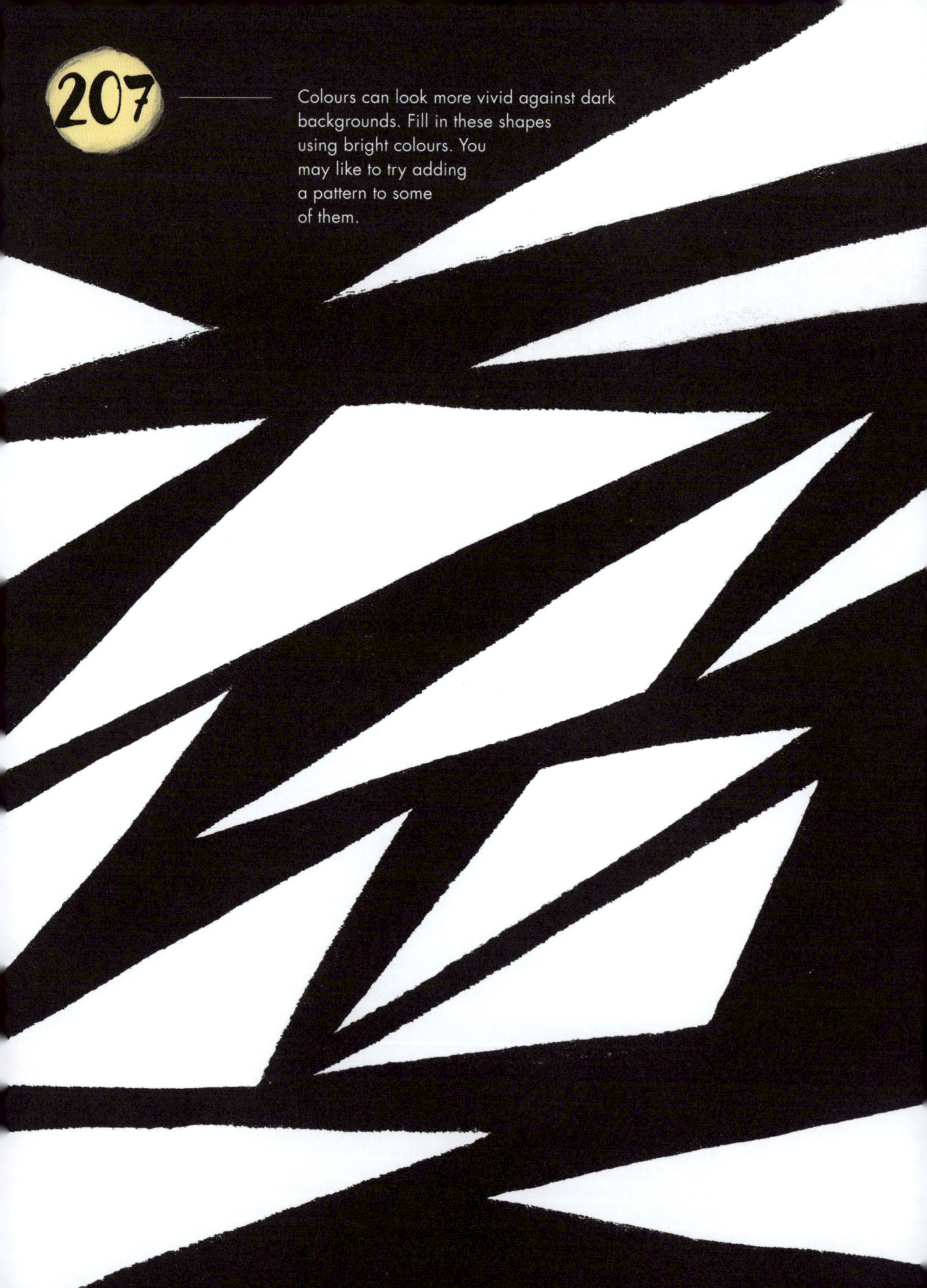

207

Colours can look more vivid against dark backgrounds. Fill in these shapes using bright colours. You may like to try adding a pattern to some of them.

208

The way we use colour can add depth to artwork. Closer objects appear more saturated than those in the distance. Explore this by colouring a forest. As it recedes, colours should become less saturated.

Pink can suggest fun, humour and playfulness. Be inspired by how pink makes *you* feel and turn this shape into an image.

210 —— Draw as many yellow things as you can think of.

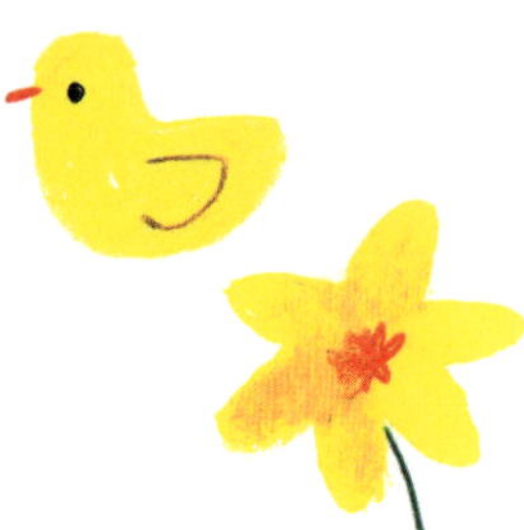

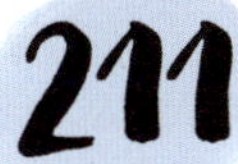

Colour using primary colours, plus black if you'd like to. Notice how bold and striking the image is when you use these hues.

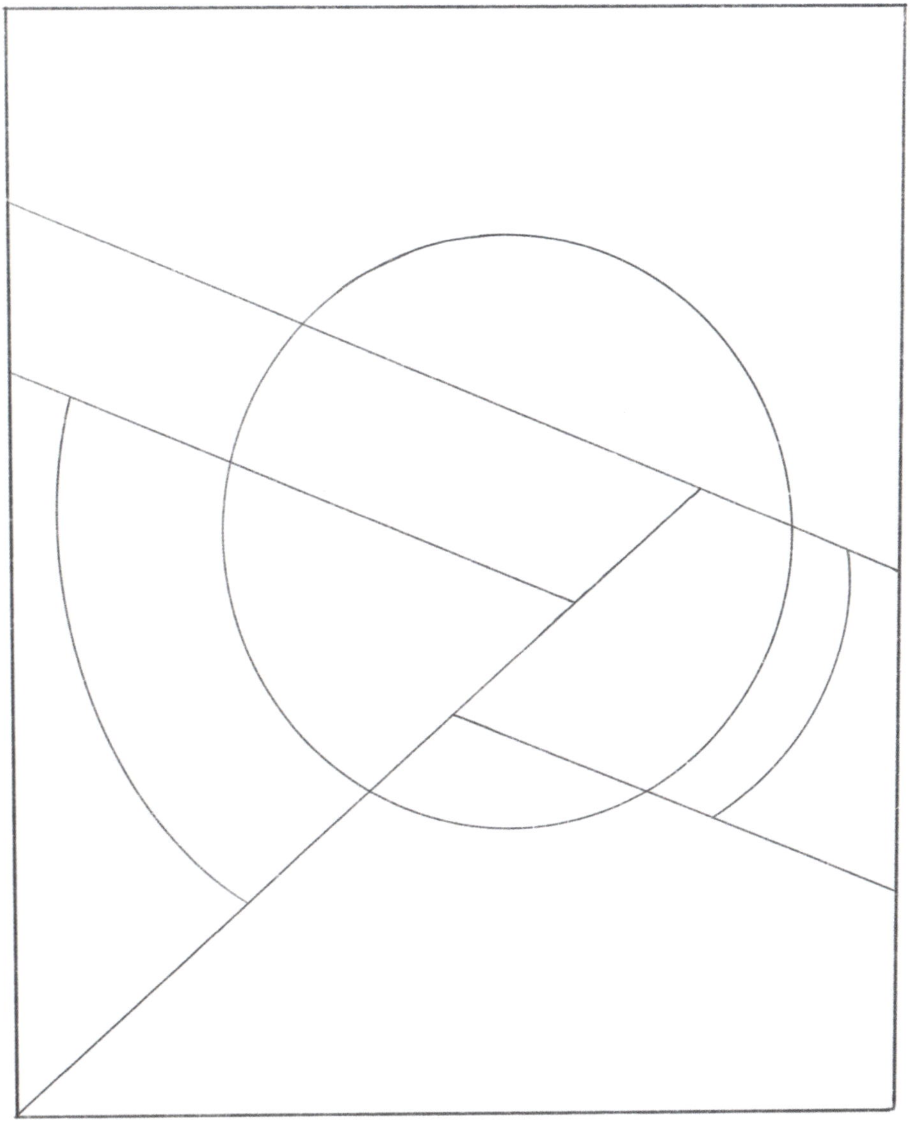

212

It can be useful to use dark colours in your art, and there are lots of ways of creating a black by mixing colours of paint. Using a pure black from a tube can deaden an image, whereas a black or dark colour that is mixed by you can feel more cohesive. This is especially true if your black or dark colour is mixed using colours from the rest of your palette. Explore mixing your own black from a palette of colours, then paint an object using this palette.

Tip: *Mixing green, magenta and yellow will make a black, as will blue, magenta and yellow. Have a go at mixing these and other colours together to make dark colours. Try ultramarine blue and burnt sienna, or perhaps a crimson, blue and a brown.*

213

Use colour to express your feelings today.

214

Create a landscape using blocks of colour. You could use torn paper.

215

Add a stormy sky.

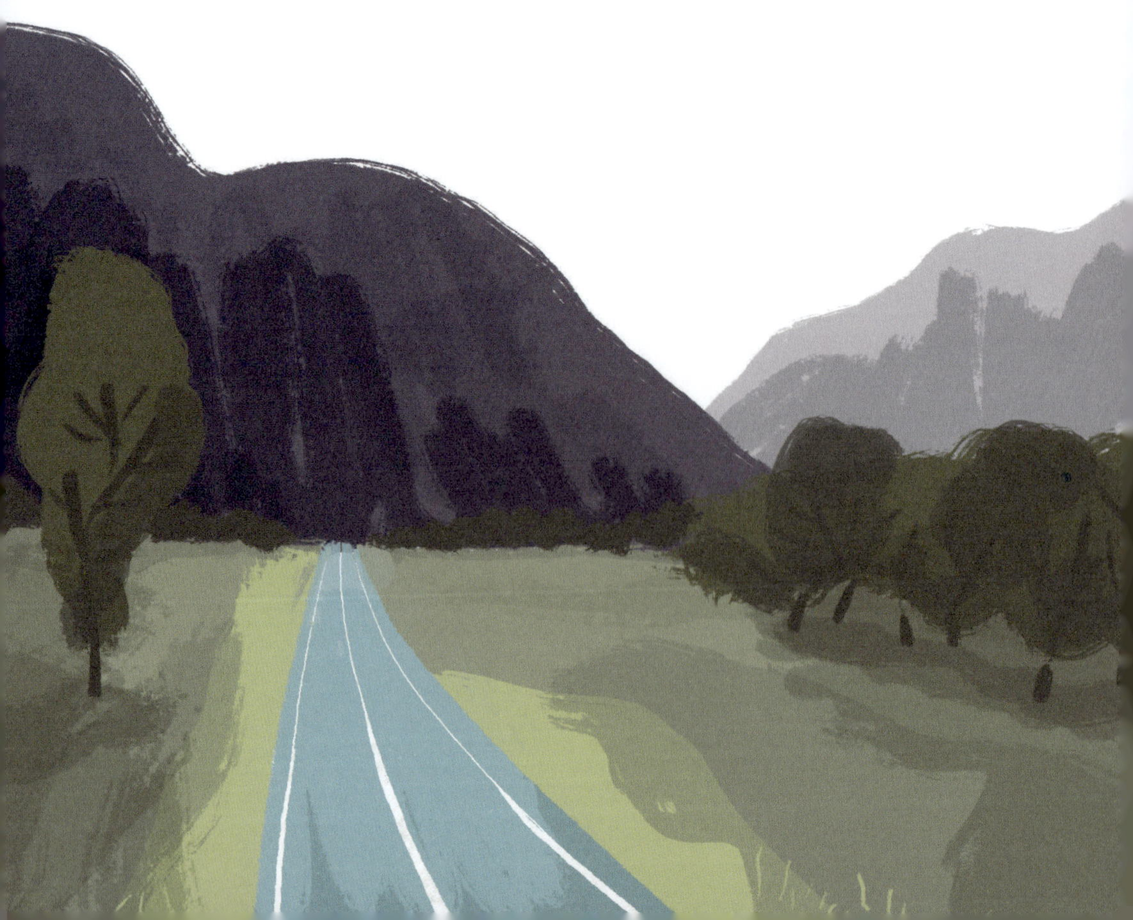

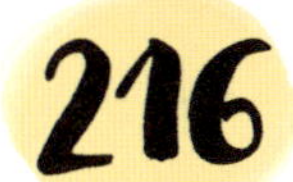

Choose five colours and create abstract thumbnail compositions.

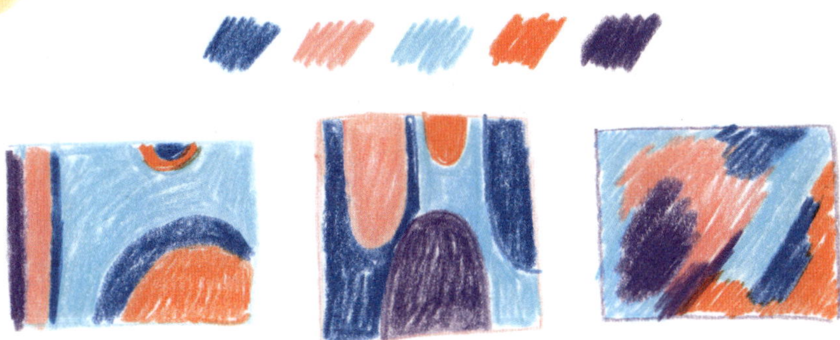

217

Based on your colour wheel in activity 66, add warm colours to these squares. How do these colours affect the atmosphere of the piece?

218

Continue this colourful beach scene.

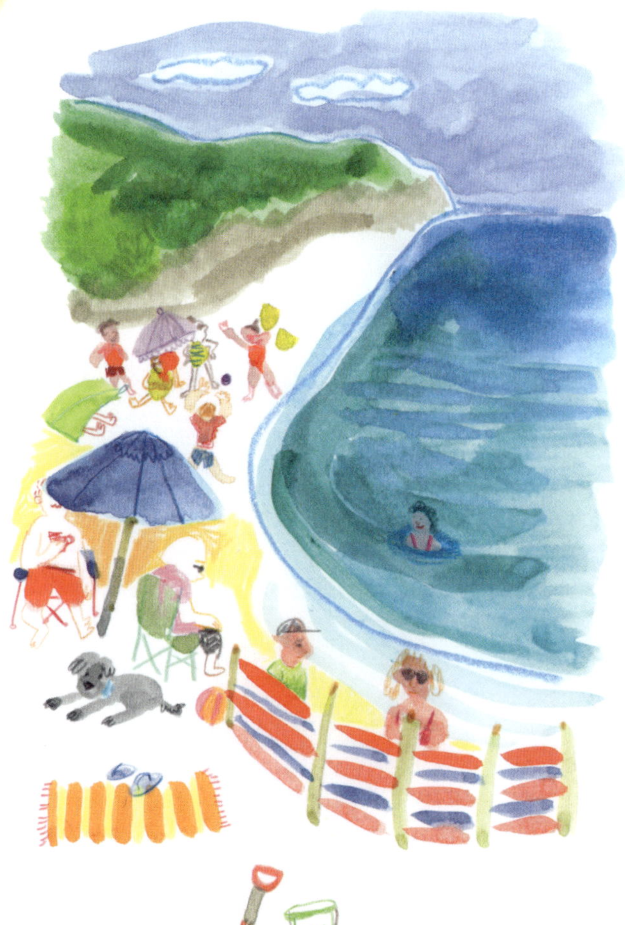

219

Draw the view out of a window today.

220

Add colour.

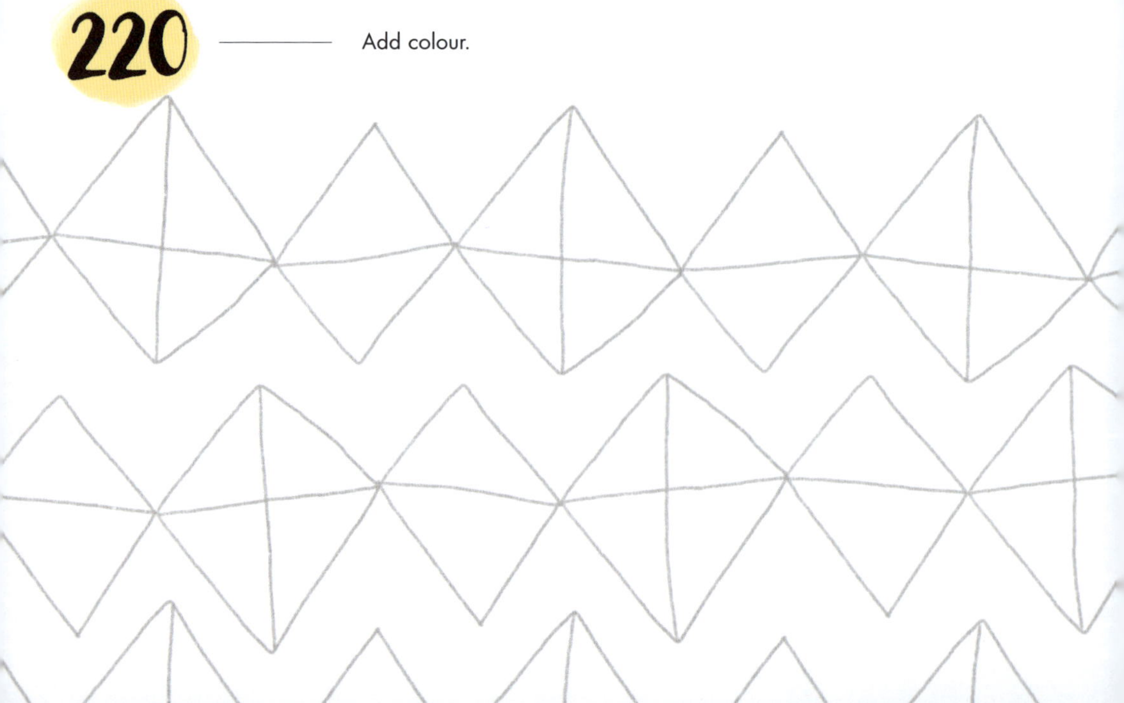

221

Use complementary colours to create an eye-catching graphic image. Your subject could be an everyday household object. Half of the image should show one combination of colours, and the other half should show the same image, but with the colours inverted.

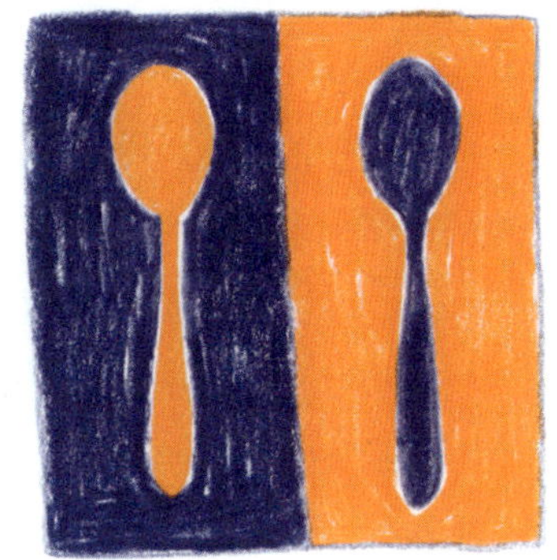

222

When used in an image, primary colours will automatically jump out, so you can use them intentionally in your art. If the main subject of your painting is a primary colour (whether that's something abstract or an object) the eye will be drawn to it. Create a drawing where the focal point is in a primary colour. For example, you could draw a red apple in a bowl of oranges and grapes, or a person wearing a bright yellow top.

223

Turn these splodges into objects, characters or mini scenes. Let your imagination run wild!

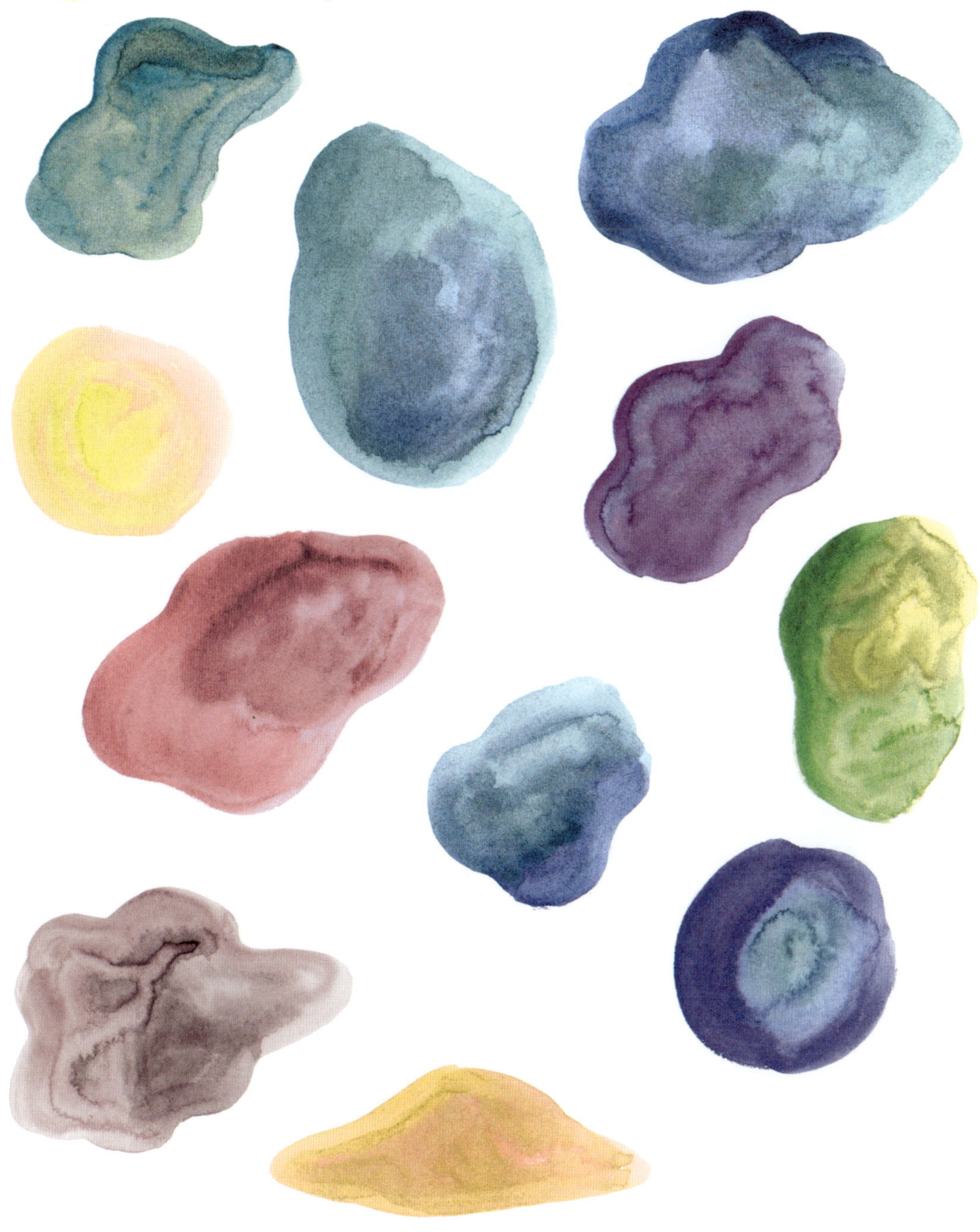

224

Draw a scene using only blues and greens. You could use a variety of materials. What atmosphere does your artwork evoke?

225

Find a photograph you like, stick it down and then add colours around it to represent your feelings when looking at the image.

226

Fill the page with balloons.

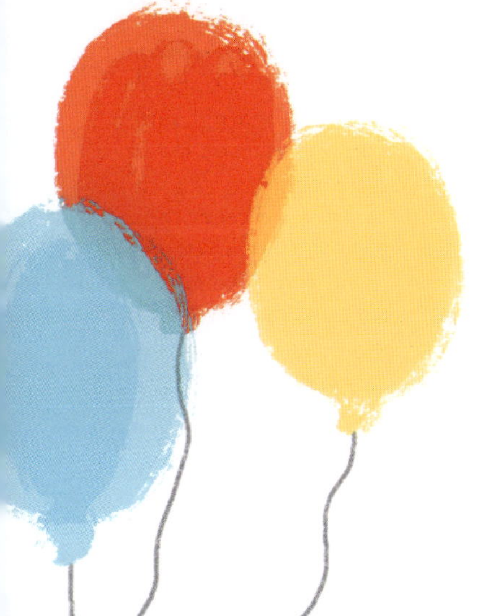

227

Refer to your clean and dirty colours in activity 75. Choose some items from around your home and set up a still life, being sure to include objects that have dirty colours (muted, murky) as well as clean colours (bright, pure).

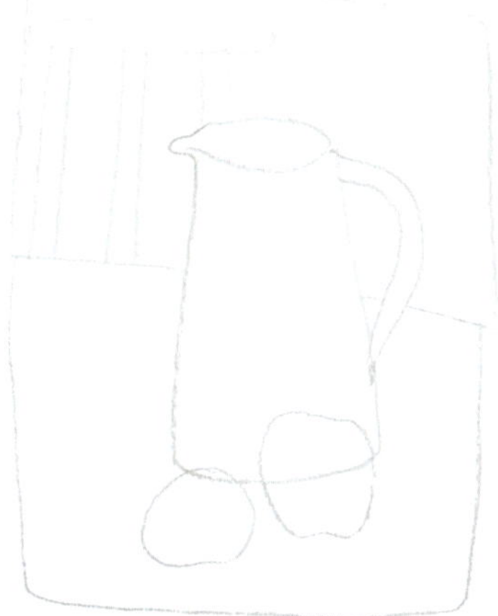

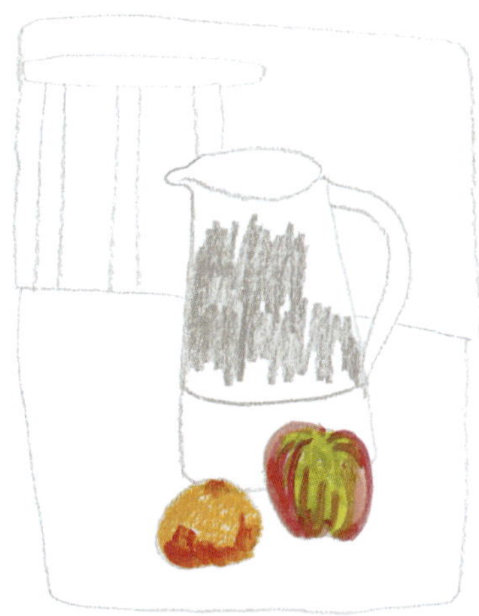

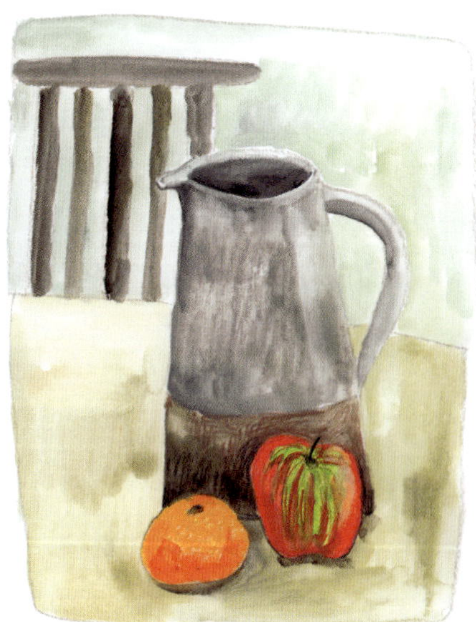

Begin by making a simple sketch of the scene. Map out the prominent elements and consider the composition – where could you place the objects on the page?

Choose your palette and materials and add blocks of colour to your sketch. Work into these, adding tone, detail and texture. Perhaps consider adding more detail to the areas you want to highlight, and keep background elements looser.

Notice how using the clean and dirty colours together can create a harmonious image. The more muted areas of the image offer a place for the eye to rest, and the clean colours become the focus.

228

Draw your hand and then add colour. Pay particular attention to the exact colours you see in your skin tone. Hands can be tricky to draw. Take your time and don't worry if it doesn't look quite right – this exercise is about studying the colours rather than capturing accurate proportions.

Tip: *You may like to create some swatches of the colours you see in your skin tone before starting.*

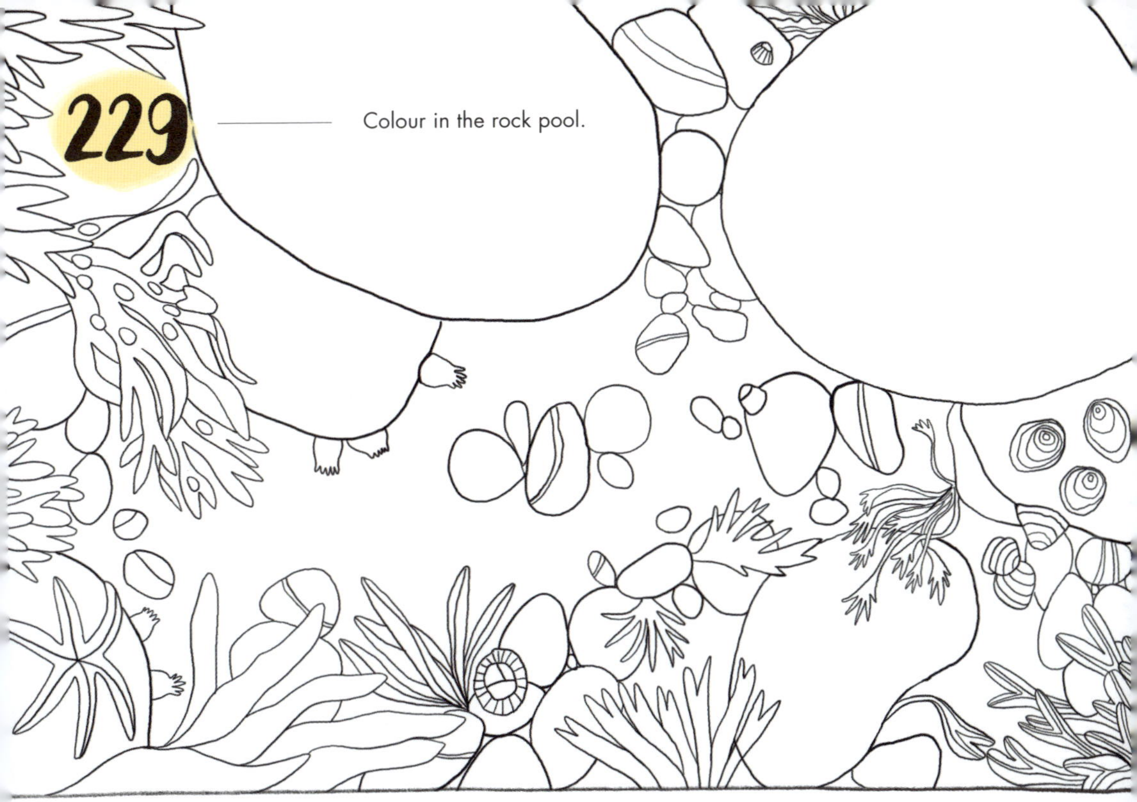

229 Colour in the rock pool.

230 Blues can be used to create a peaceful mood as they can evoke water, the sea and a day clear of clouds. You may feel like blues evoke different emotions. Use blues to fill the circle and consider what the colours make you feel.

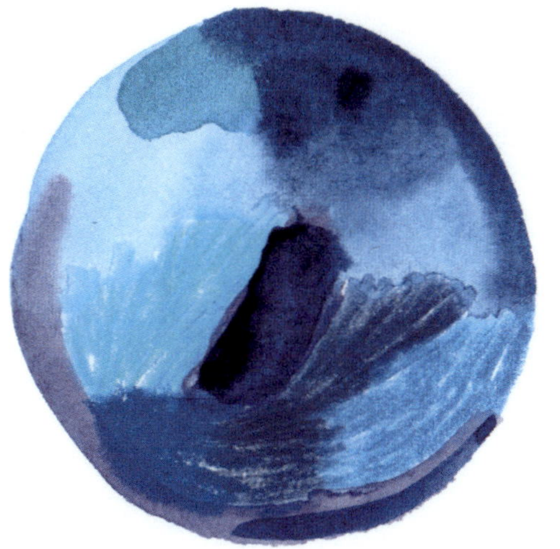

231

Set up some items for a mini still life and make colour studies of what you see. These can be a quick, handy way to test various colour combinations, and also to try some bold ideas that you wouldn't initially think to use. It can be useful to create a palette of colour options first, and then paint lots of quick versions of the same scene. Try lots of different versions, keeping the images very simple and rough, without detail.

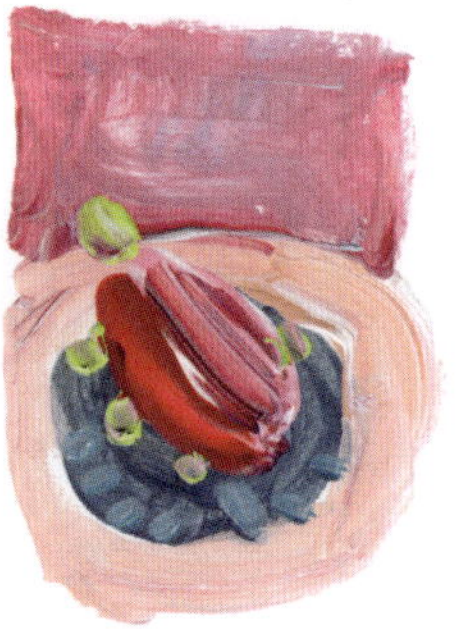
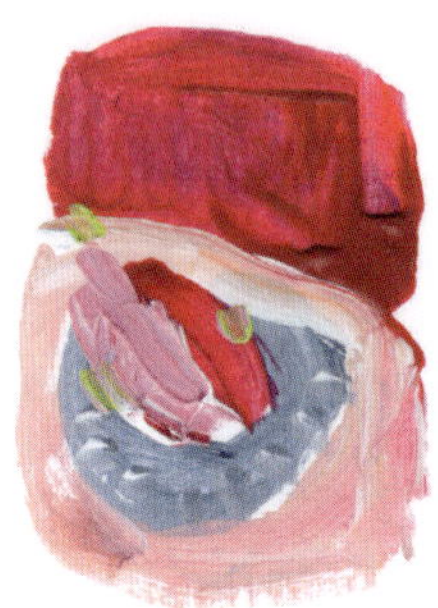
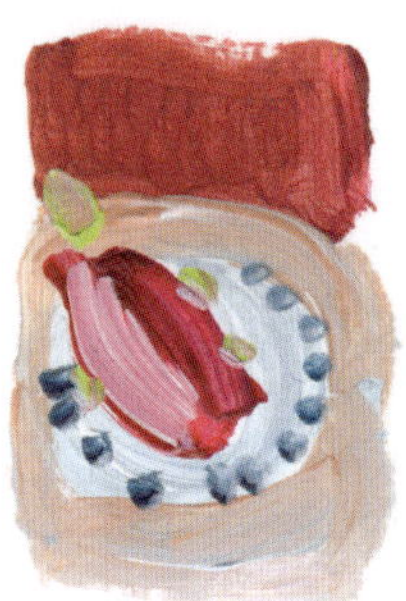

Tip: Perhaps do a few with unusual colour choices – what have you got to lose?!

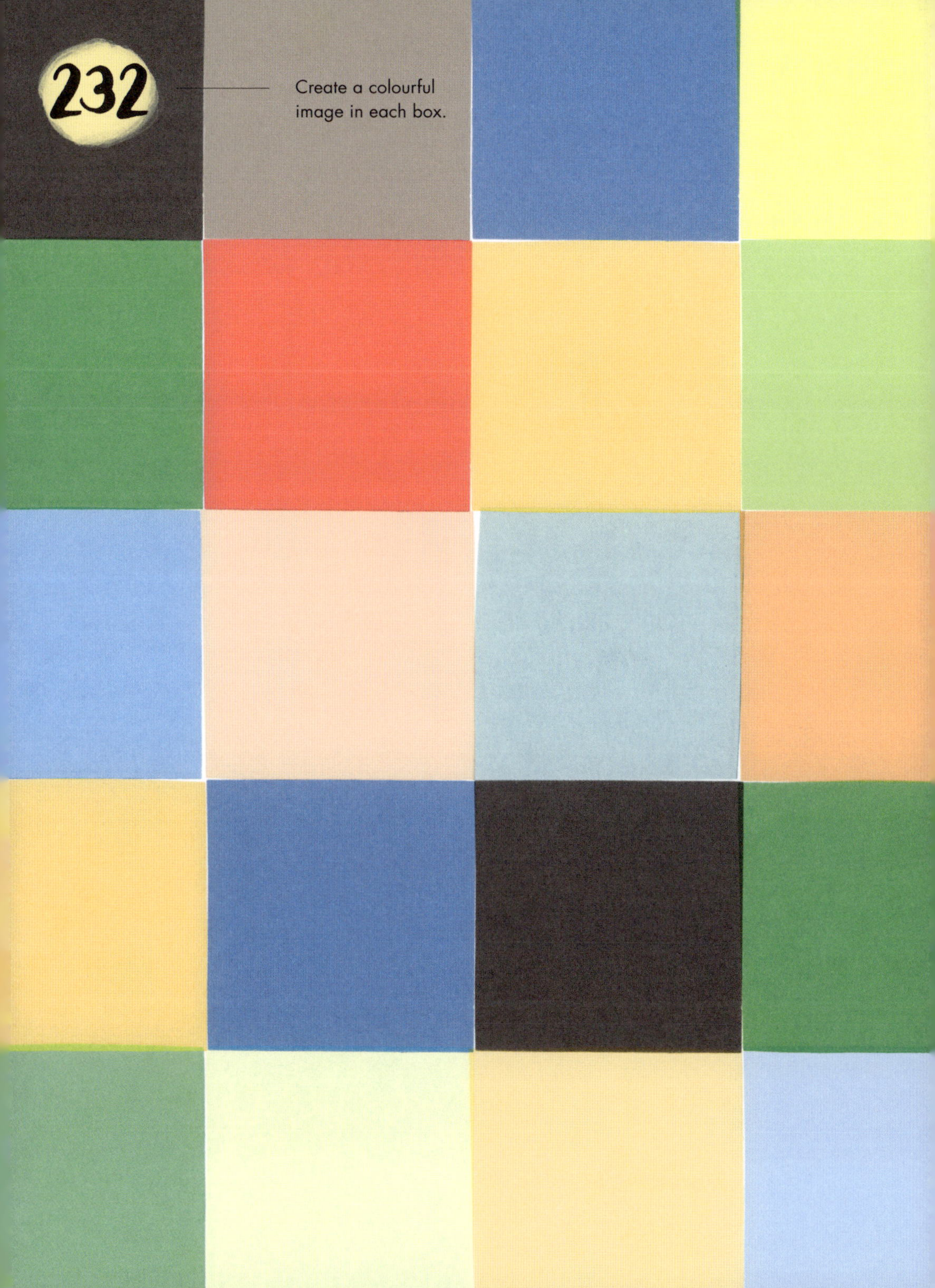
232
Create a colourful image in each box.

233

Doodle using coloured pastels. Try holding two at the same time and moving them across the page together.

234 Blend colouring pencils to add colour to these hearts.

235

There are so many tones in our skin. Create swatches or mini drawings of all the colours you can see in your skin and the skin of your friends and family.

236

Turn these marks into a scene.

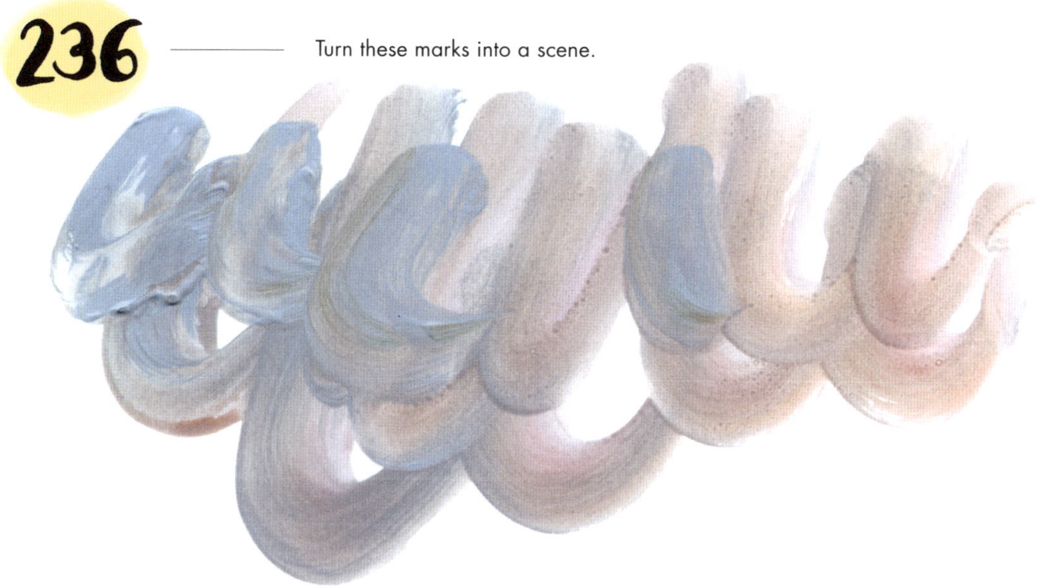

237

What colours and imagery suggest strength and bravery? Make an image here based on those emotions.

238

Draw a portrait of someone using only cool colours. How does the image make you feel? What mood does it evoke?

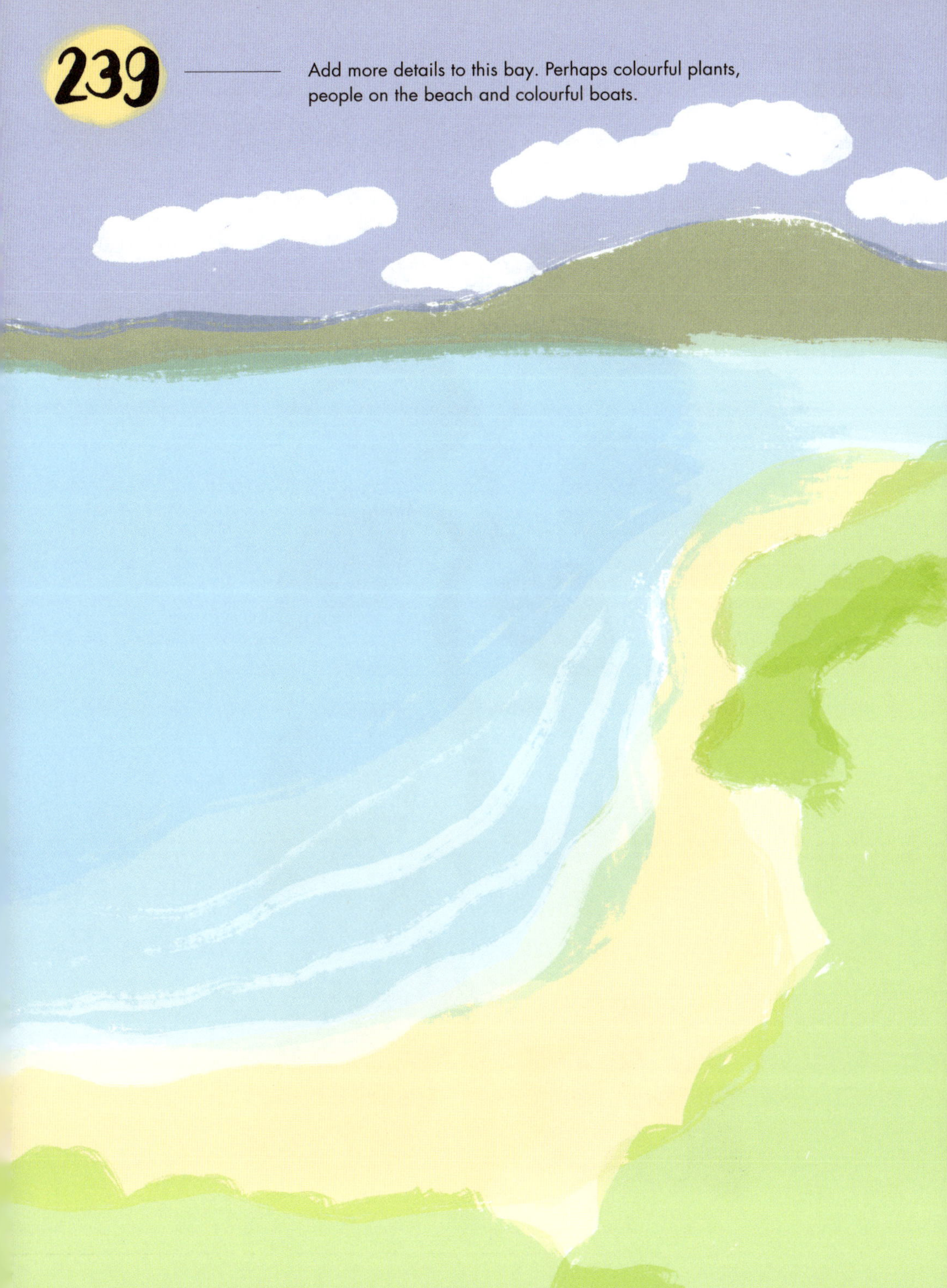
239
Add more details to this bay. Perhaps colourful plants, people on the beach and colourful boats.

240

You can use dark shades to create bold, contrasting images, especially against white. Draw or paint an image using only dark shades. Don't worry about what should look dark and what should look light, just have fun with the dark tones to create a graphic drawing.

Tip: You could mix your dark shades before starting, or use them straight from the palette. It doesn't matter which colours you use, focus on enjoying shape and contrast instead.

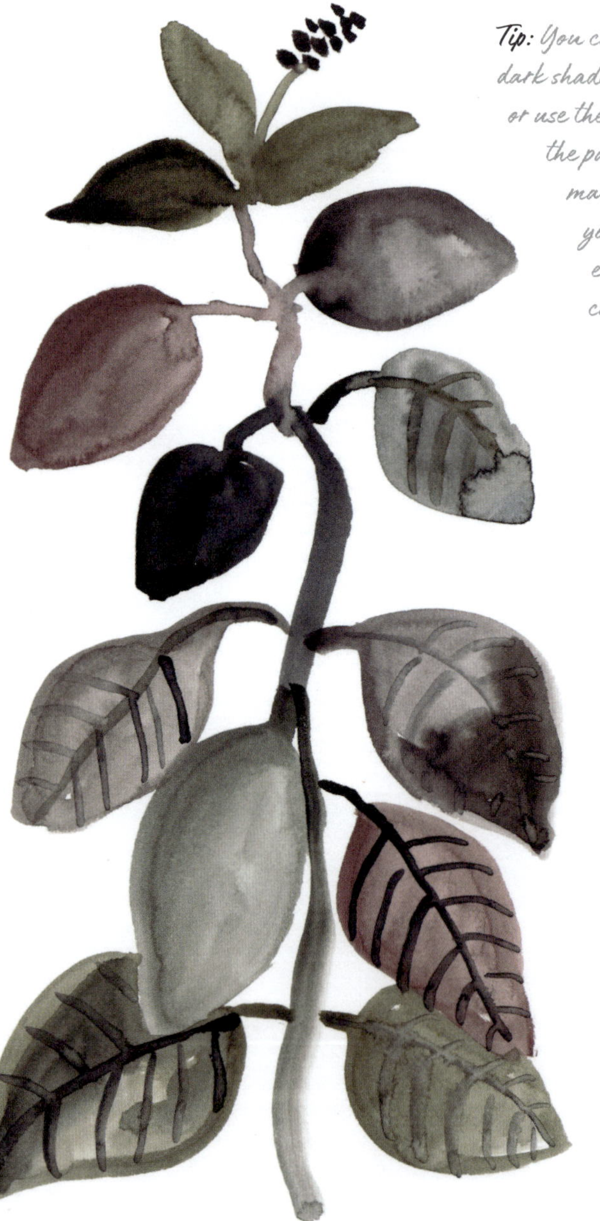

241

Fill the page with diamonds.

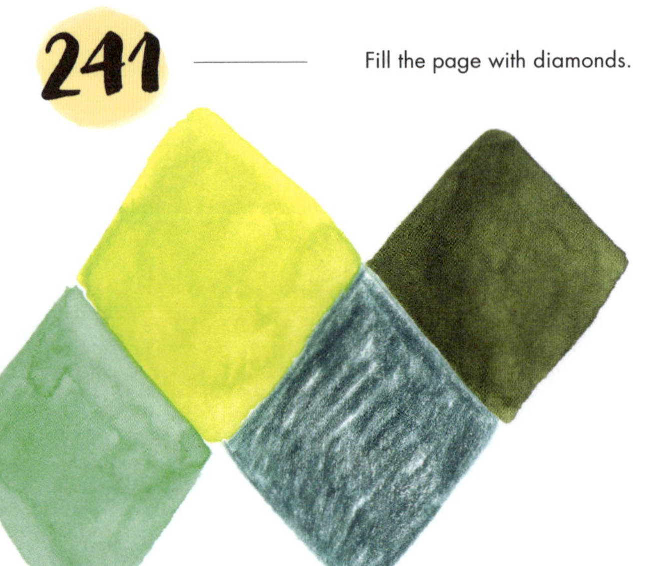

242

Look at an artist's work that you like – in a book or gallery. Notice which colours you are drawn to, and draw your own version of little areas that you particularly like in the artworks.

243

Draw ripples on a swimming pool. What colours do you notice?

244 — What colours and shapes evoke joy for you? Make an image here in response to those emotions.

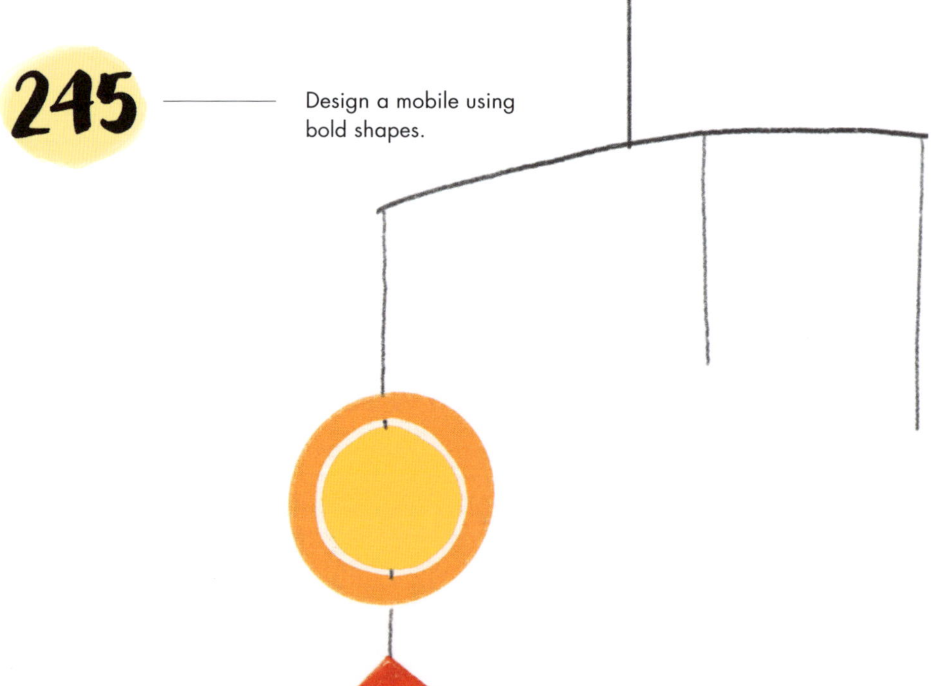

245 — Design a mobile using bold shapes.

246

Mix or blend colours together to match these colours as closely as possible.

Tip: Look at the colour and think about what colours might have been used to make it. Perhaps the green looks slightly yellowy so there may be a lot of yellow and just a tiny amount of blue. This can take time! It's no problem at all if you aren't able to get close to matching the colours – it's a skill that takes practise and a lot of trial and error too! Don't be afraid to try many combinations.

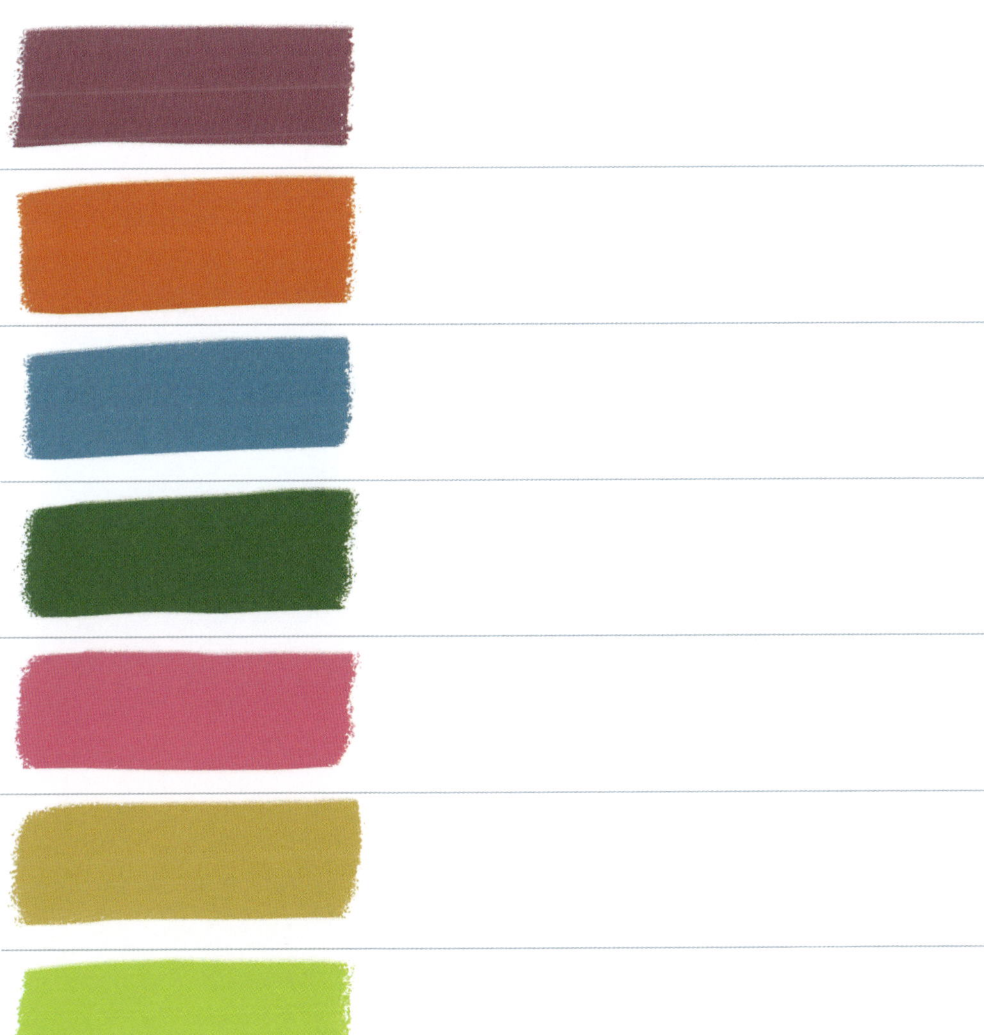

247
Create a pastel flower pattern.

248

Paint an everyday scene with bold colours. Use any that inspire you. Start with big coloured shapes and then add detail, keeping the image loose and free to give it lots of energy.

249

Draw a colourful animal from observation. Perhaps look at images in a book or online.

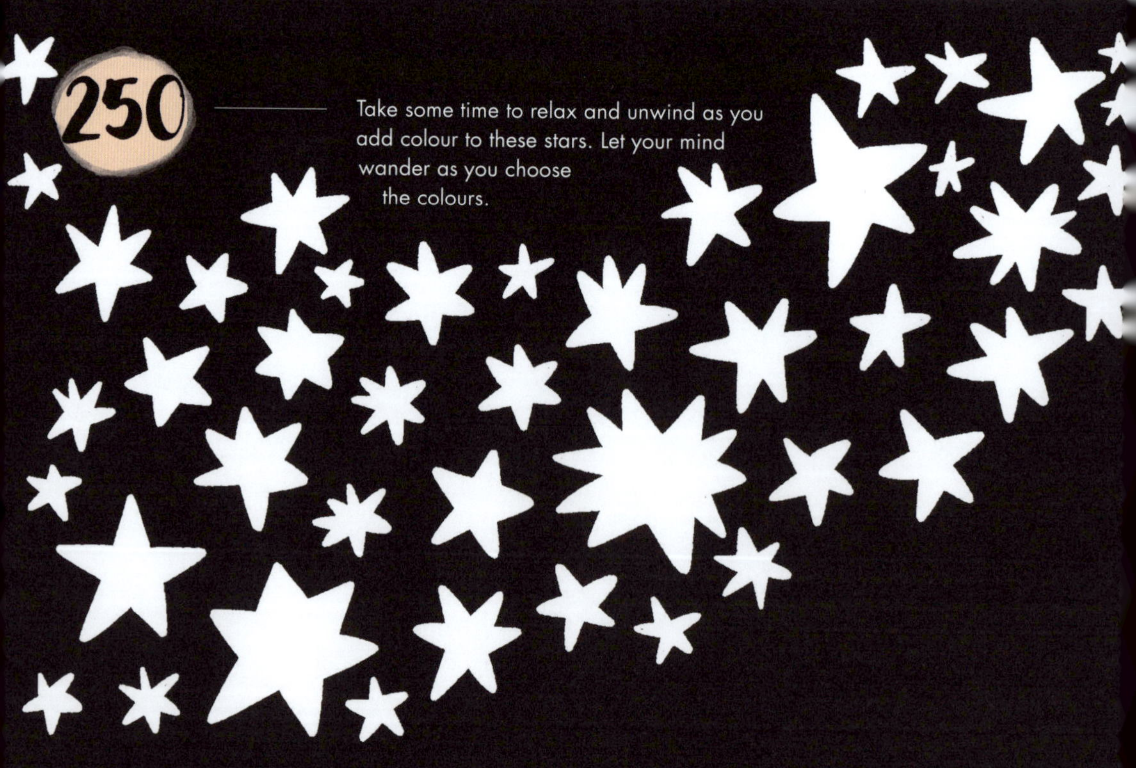

251

Create an image using only secondary and primary colours. You can use as few or as many as you like.

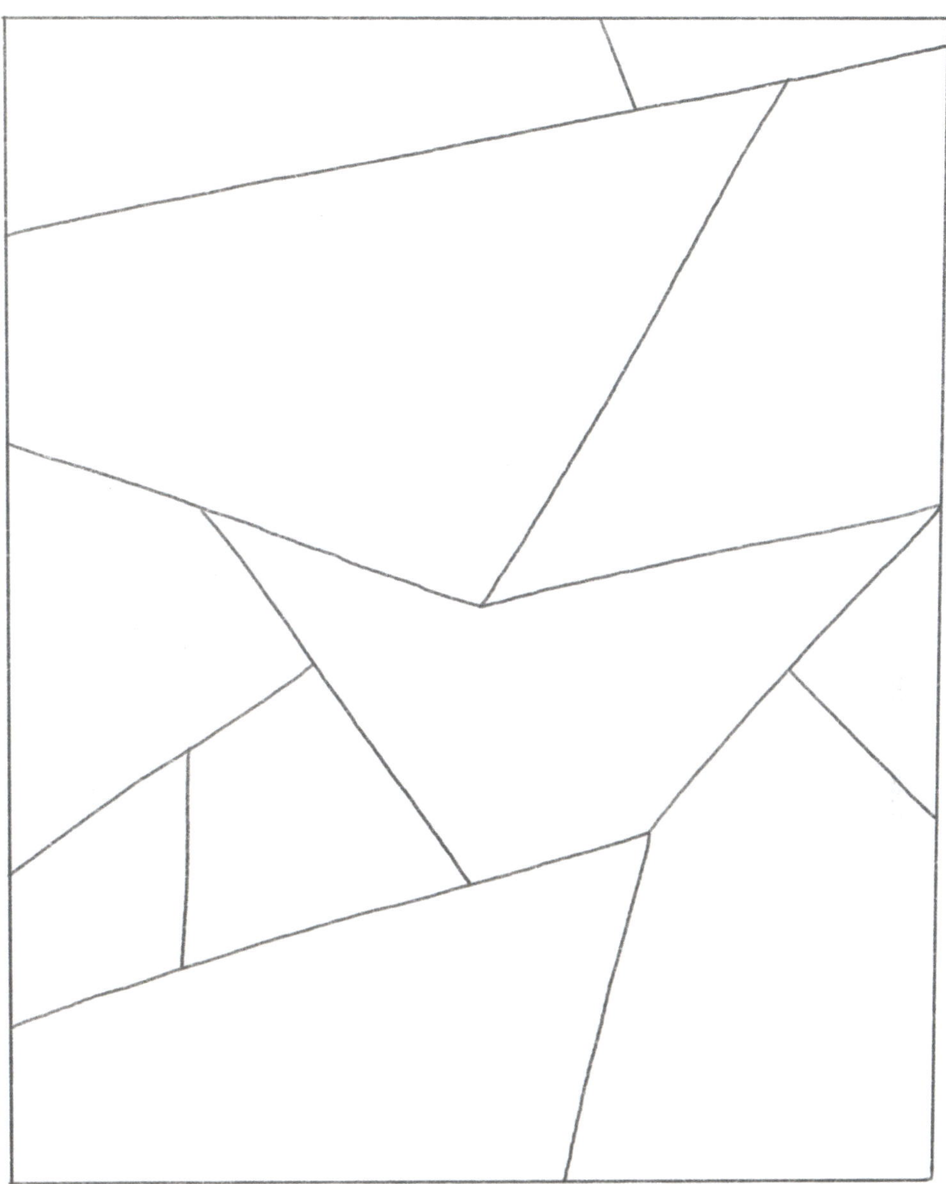

Tip: Primary colours are red, blue and yellow. Secondary colours are made by mixing the primary colours – violet, orange and green.

252 Turn these simple blocks of colour into objects.

253

Draw a shell. Look carefully at the colours you see, especially the areas of light and dark.

254

Including a small amount of a clean, bright colour against neutrals can make it appear eye-catching and jewel-like. Draw some abstract designs where there is just a pop of bright colour among muted tones.

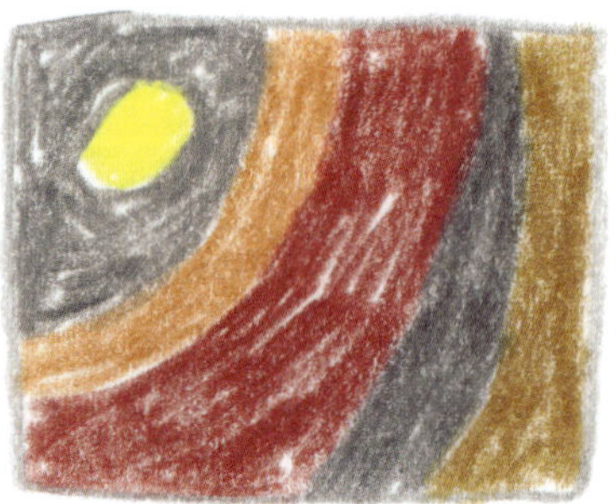

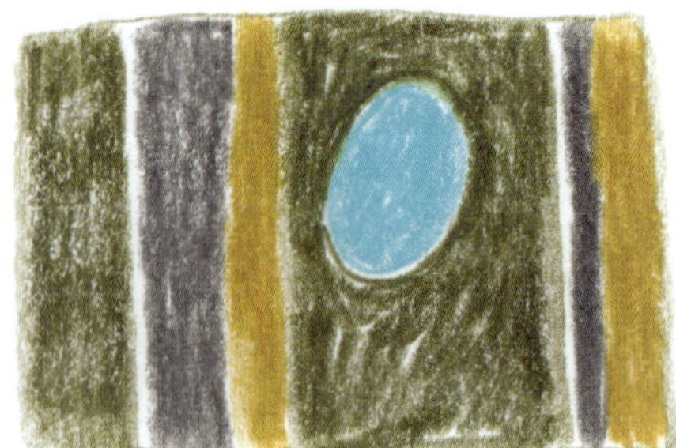

255 Fill the page with colourful squiggles.

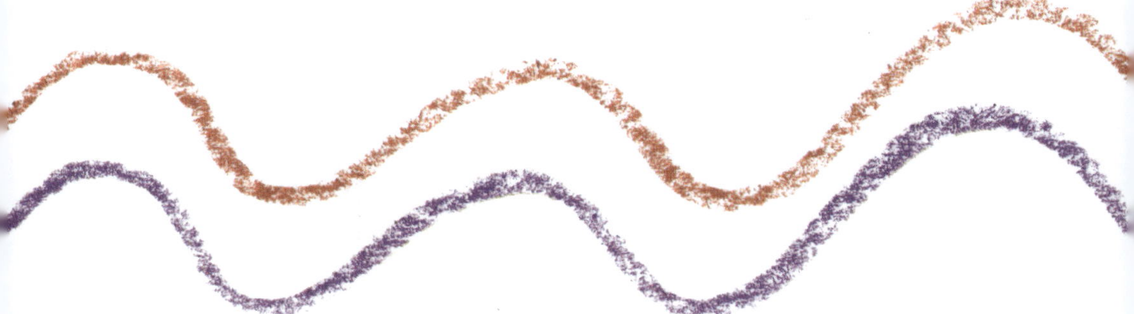

256

Take some time to make a sustained, detailed colour study. Choose your subject and look carefully at what colours you can see before starting. In a green plant, for example, you will be able to see many hues of green and perhaps yellows, purples, browns and others. Gather the appropriate materials and add specific colours deliberately, rather than rushing.

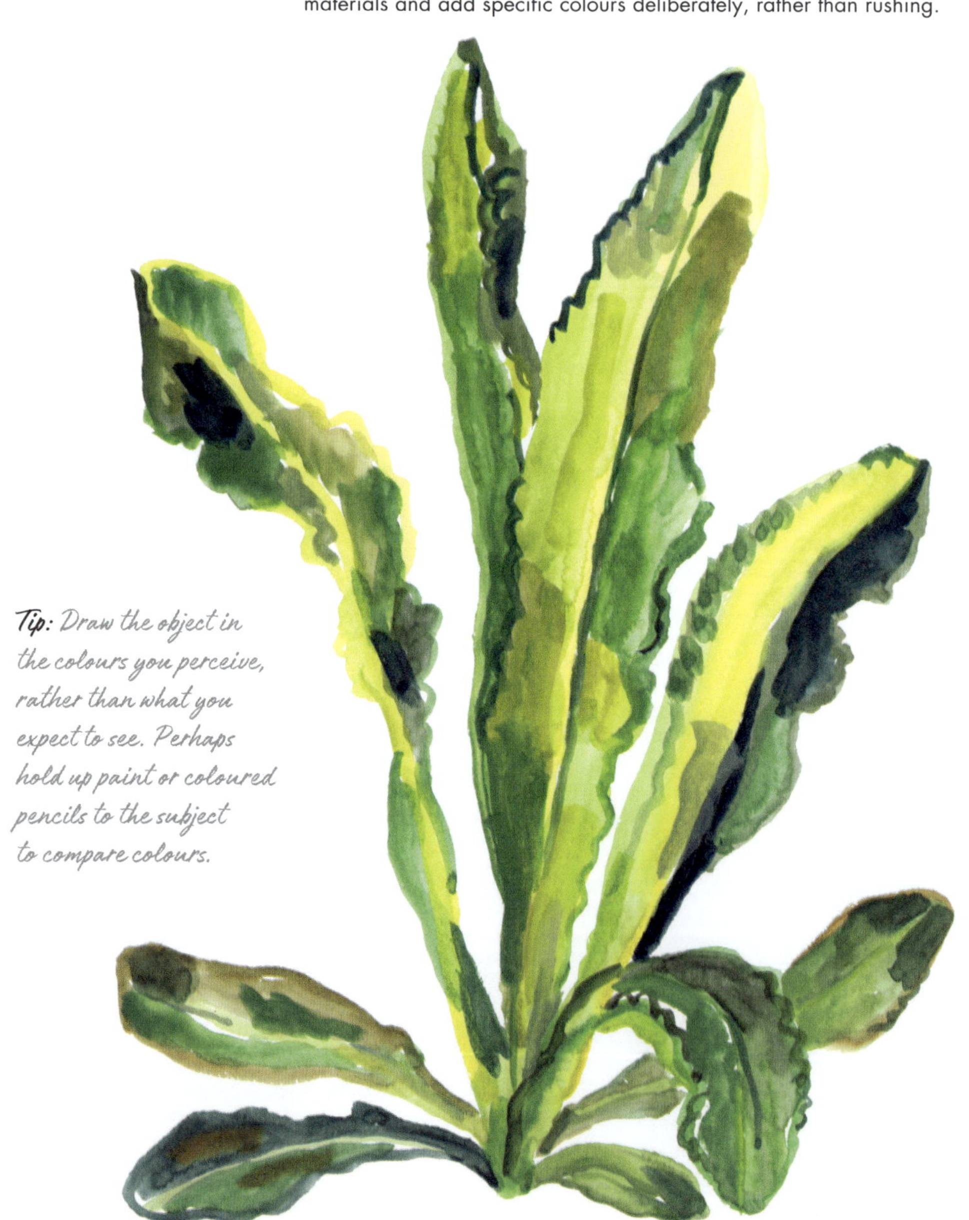

***Tip:** Draw the object in the colours you perceive, rather than what you expect to see. Perhaps hold up paint or coloured pencils to the subject to compare colours.*

257

Groups of gourds and pumpkins create a pleasing autumnal palette, perhaps because the colour palette is often analogous (these colours are found alongside each other on the colour wheel). Paint some vibrant gourds.

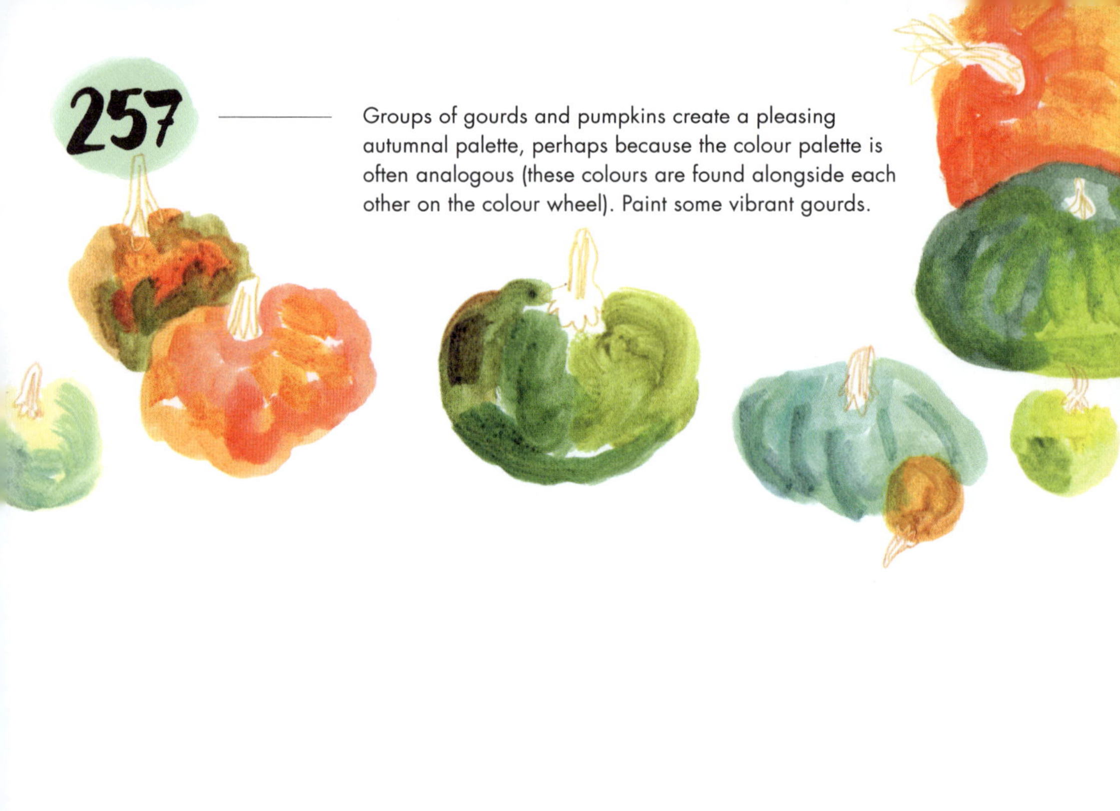

258

Match these flavours to colours. Fill in each shape using one colour you'd use to describe the flavour that comes to mind.

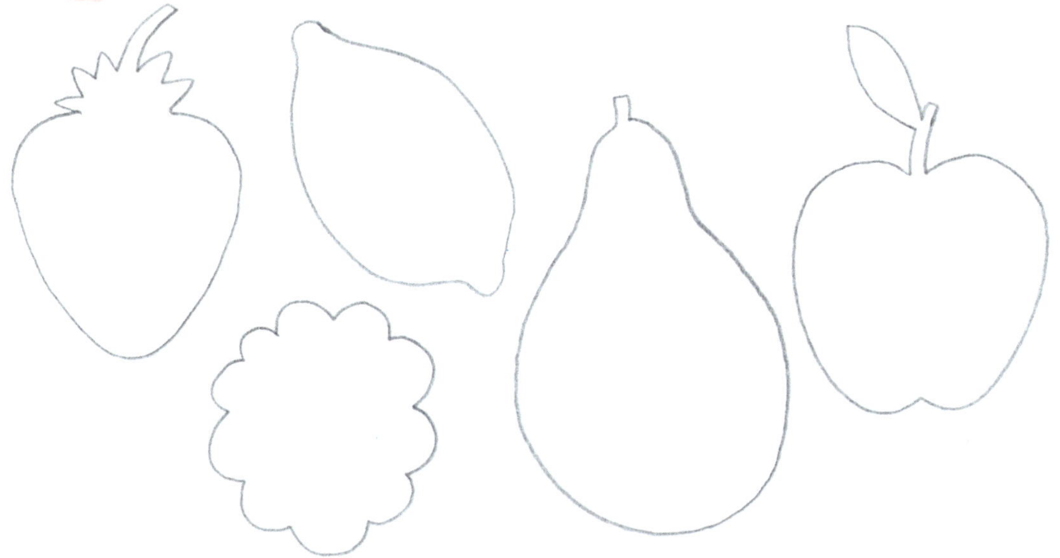

259

Put on some lively music and draw!

260

How does the colour violet make you feel? Create a pattern using violet. Perhaps use it alongside small amounts of yellow to explore the effect of working with these complementary colours.

261

Fill the design with patterns and colour.

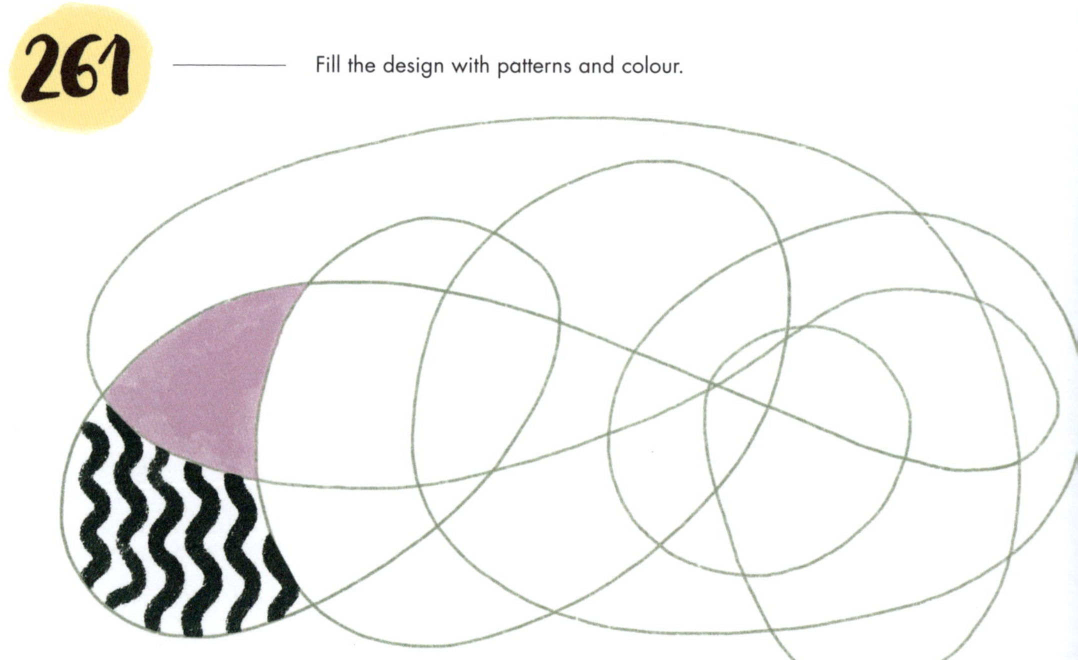

262

Paint a sky on a day where you can see many different colours.

263

Warm, dark colours like burgundy, deep oranges and reds can make an image feel intimate. Use these colours to depict a cosy space.

264

Spend just five or 10 minutes capturing a colourful still life. Choose some items from your home to draw, then select the coloured materials you'd like to use. Work quickly with lots of energy to add line and blocks of colour to the page.

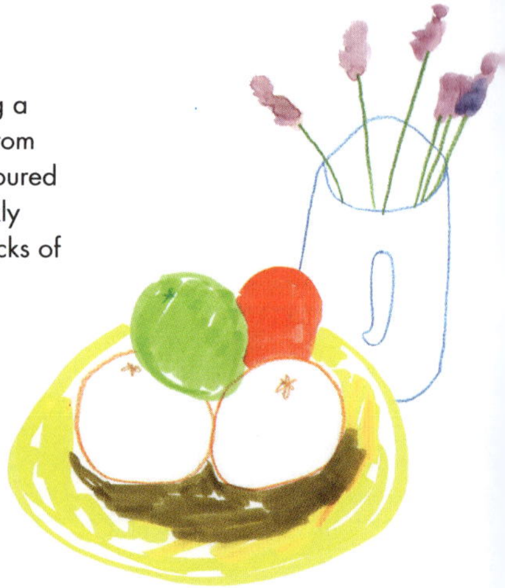

265

Add colour to this design.

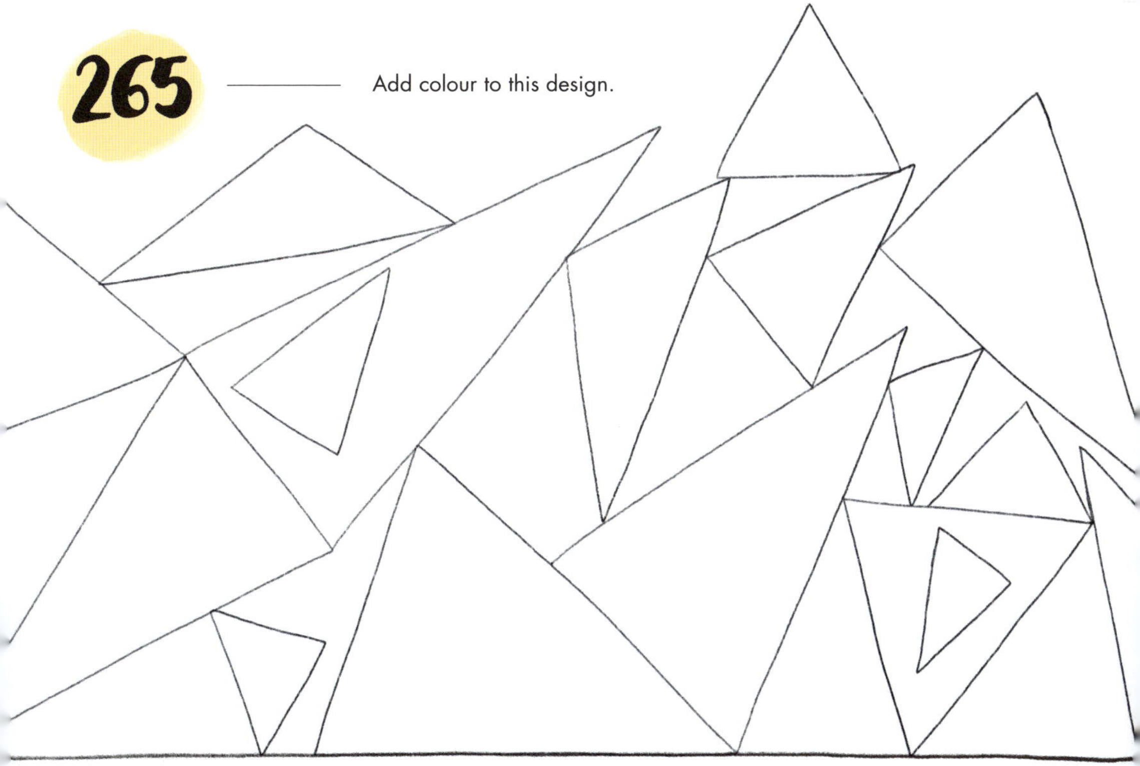

266

We can use cool and warm colours deliberately in art. Colour these three subjects and backgrounds using warm and cold colours, and notice how you can achieve different effects and atmosphere.

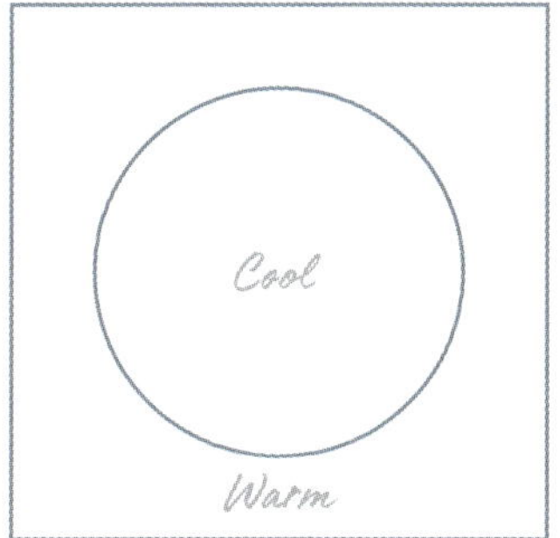

Cool colours will recede. How does a cool subject affect the mood of the image?

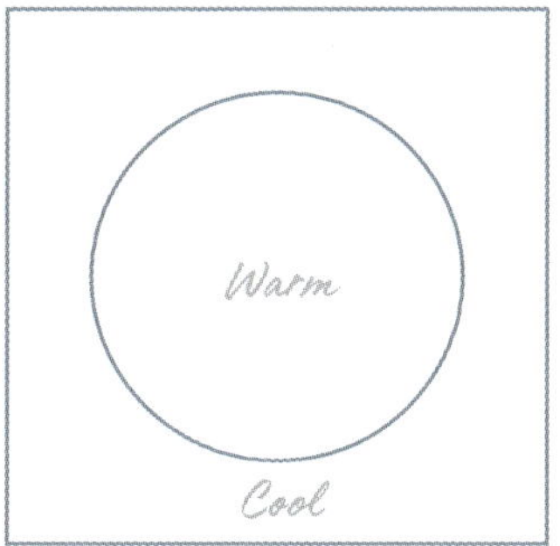

Warm colours will advance. How does a warm subject affect the mood?

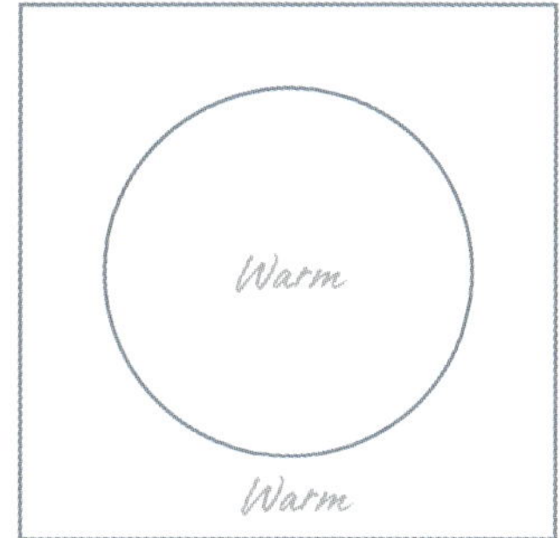

A warm colour may seem cooler when placed on an even warmer background.

267

Make a painting of your eye, focusing on all the different colours you can see in your eye and in the skin around it.

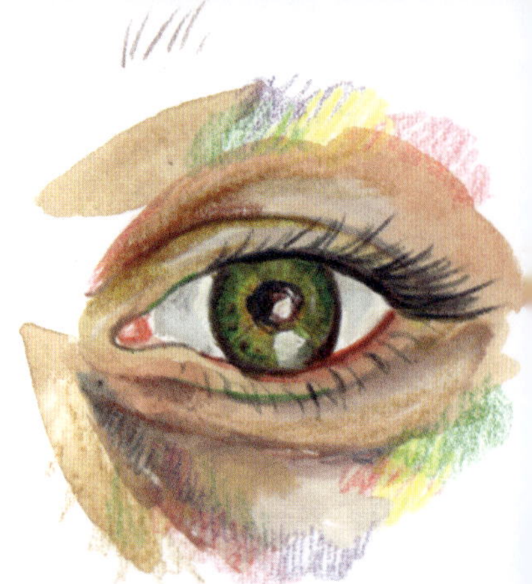

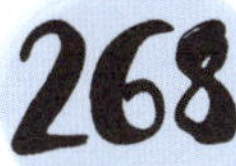

268

Continue adding rings of colours to fill the page, but choose a colour that is analogous to the colour before it.

Tip: Analogous colours are those that appear next to each other in the colour wheel. So, for example, after the purple ring you could add a different purple, or a blue or red ring.

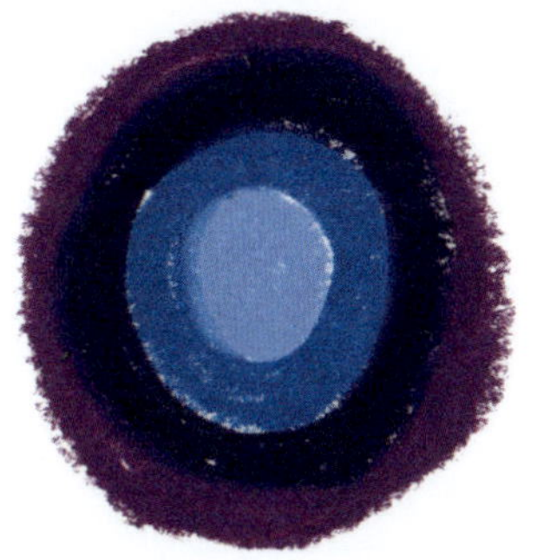

269

Design colourful pots and vases. Perhaps some are abstract and some have patterns.

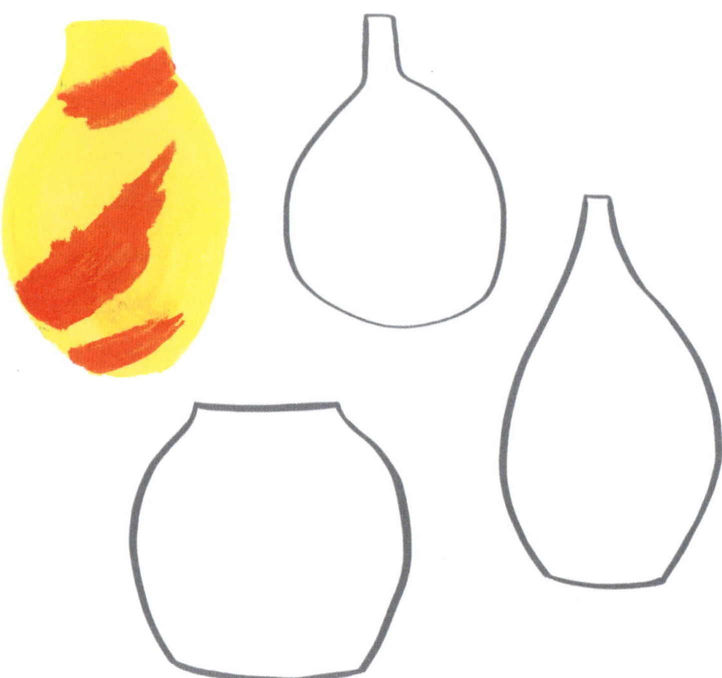

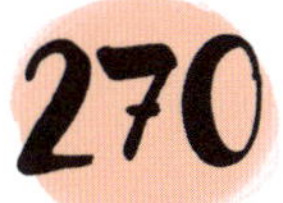

Consider which colours evoke feelings of happiness.
Create an image using only happy colours.

271

You can create powerful drawings with simple use of colour. Choose a subject, then draw it using a restricted palette of three to five colours. Rather than creating blocks of colour, focus on just rendering the outlines of the object.

Tip: You don't need to draw all the lines that you see, just choose a few to keep the drawing delicate. Stop the composition as soon as it feels balanced.

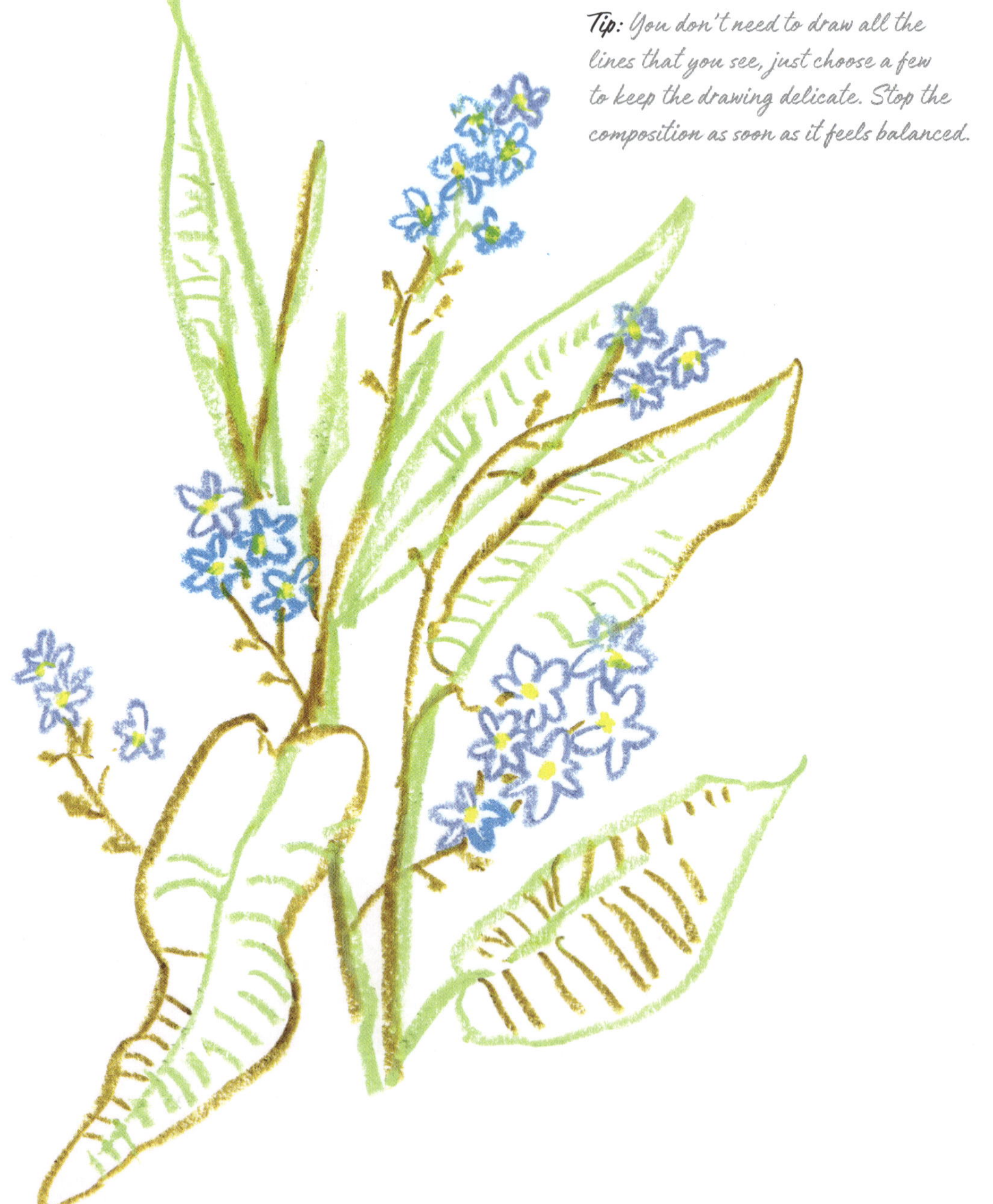

272

Add leaves using different colours. Notice that because the shape is recognisable, the colour doesn't have to be accurate to show what it is.

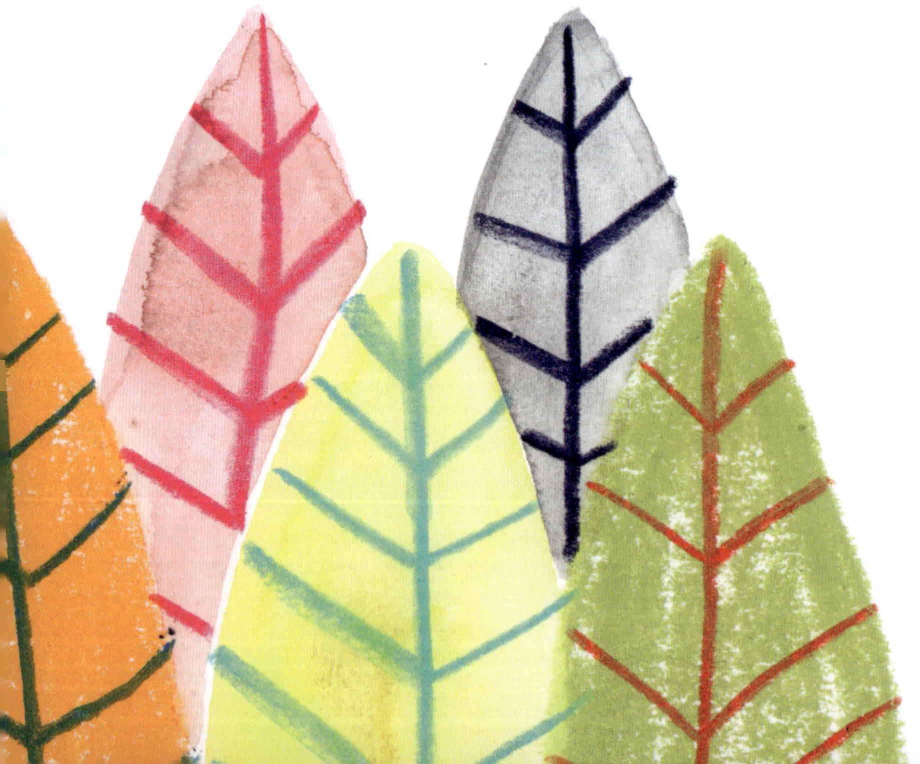

273

Colour the polka dots.

274

Different background tones can make a subject appear brighter or duller. A dark tone can make a colour really pop. Choose a bright object and draw it here on a dark-toned background.

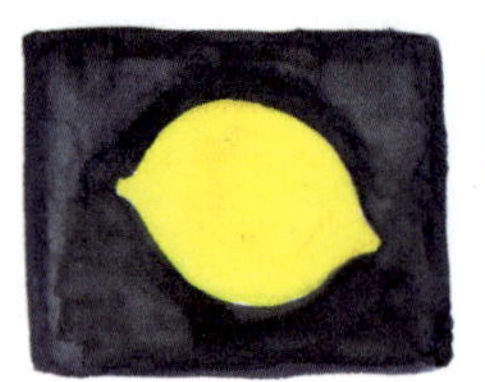

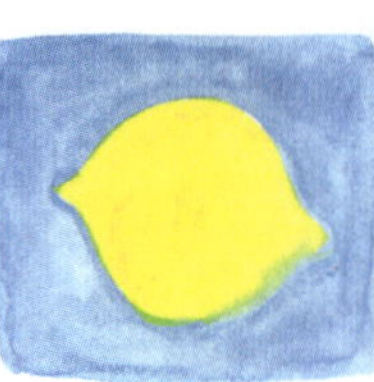

275

Draw a portrait of a friend or pet using vibrant colours.

276
Explore how straight, coloured lines can have a powerful visual impact. Add straight lines to this grid. Try different colours.

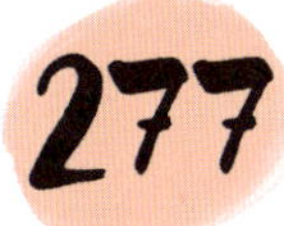

You don't need to always be in a good mood to create art! Create a piece of art when you aren't quite feeling yourself. Notice which colours you reach for, and how you feel after you've been creative.

278

Add colour to this garden. There could be leaves and flowers on the tree and in the pots. Perhaps wildlife, a pathway, some grass and shrubs?

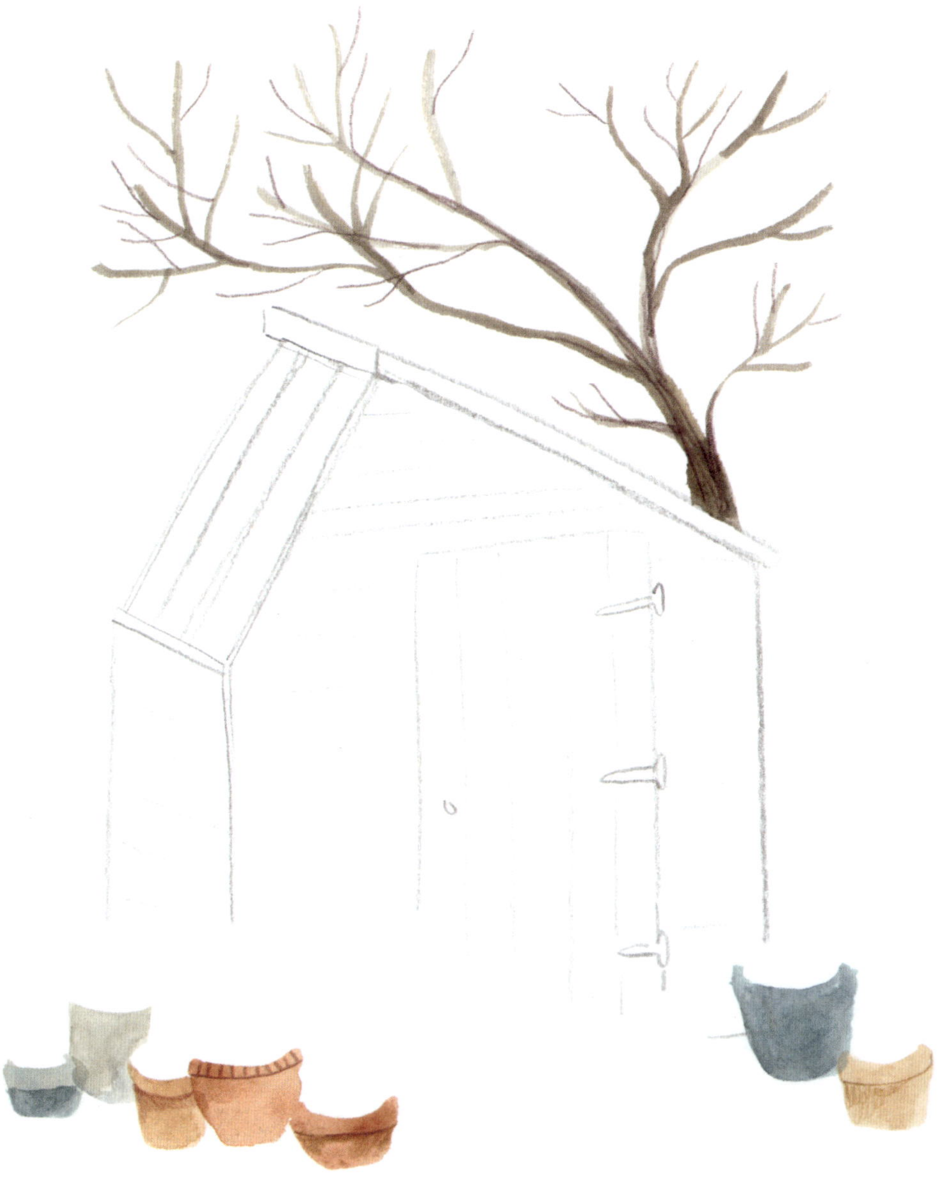

279 — Create a piece of art using primary colours.

While letting your mind wander, add colourful shapes.

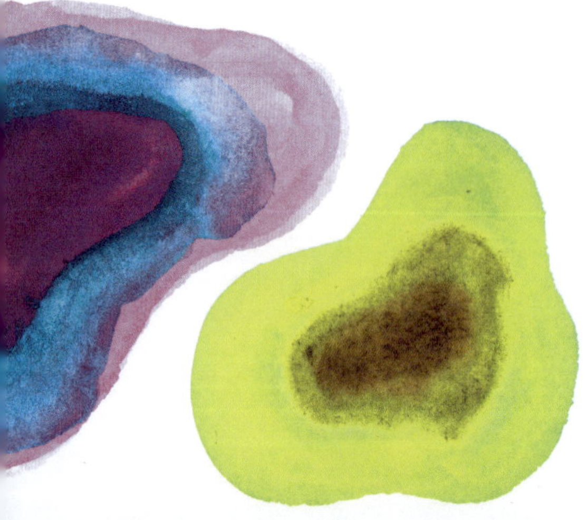

281

If you look carefully at colours that appear black, they are often not *pure* black, but dark shades of colours – very dark blues, violets and greens, for example. Fill the page with lots of dark shades that aren't pure black.

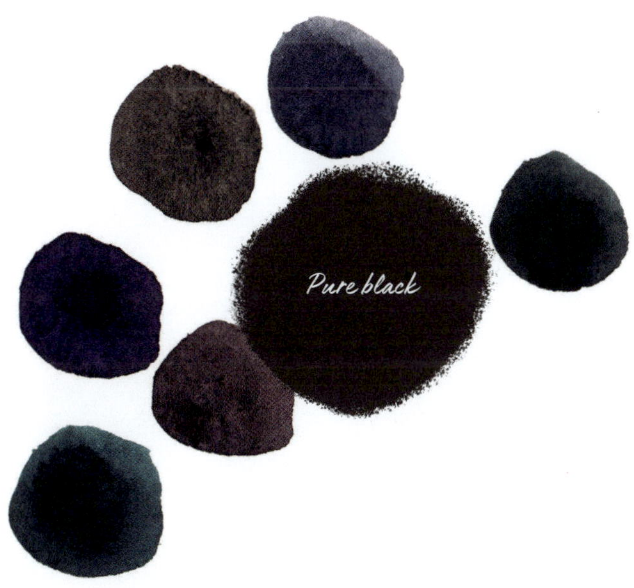

Tip: *Using pure black can sometimes drain the energy and life out of your art, so you could opt for dark shades instead. Refer back to this page when considering which near-black shades to use in your art.*

282 Design a mural for where you live.

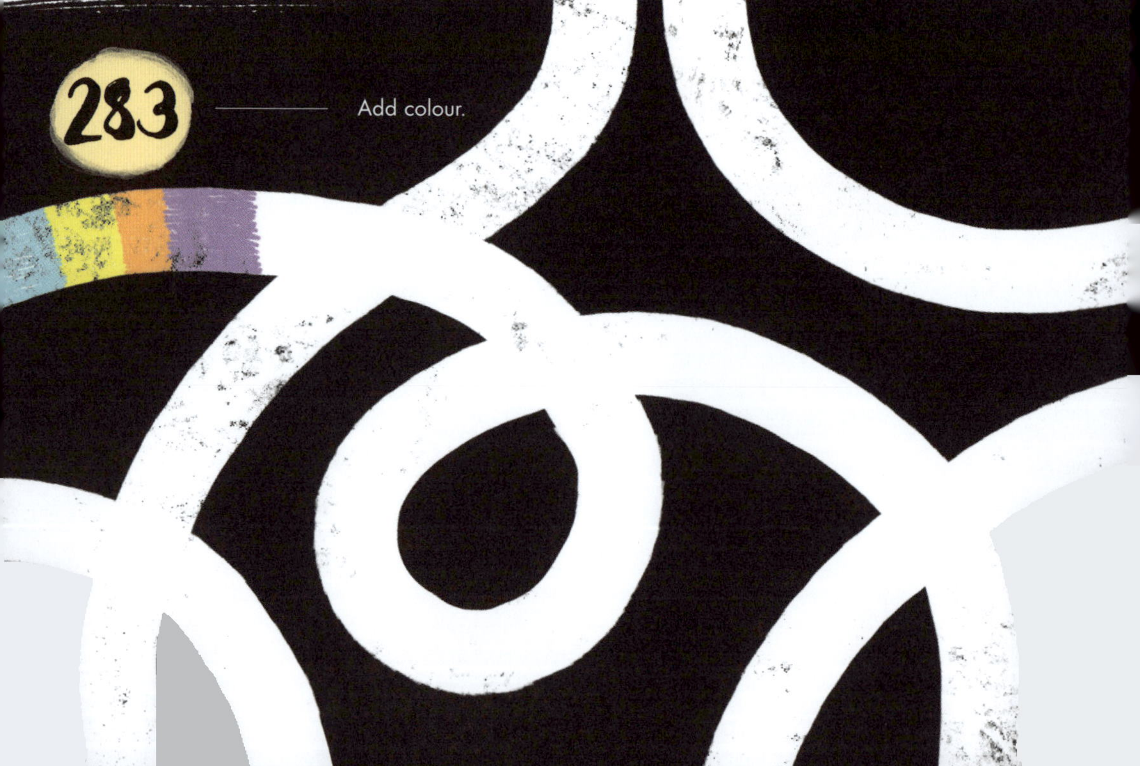

284

Draw two red things you can find in your home.

285

Create an image using collage and any other material you like. Explore texture – perhaps with the paper you use, how you cut or tear the paper, and the marks you make with additional materials.

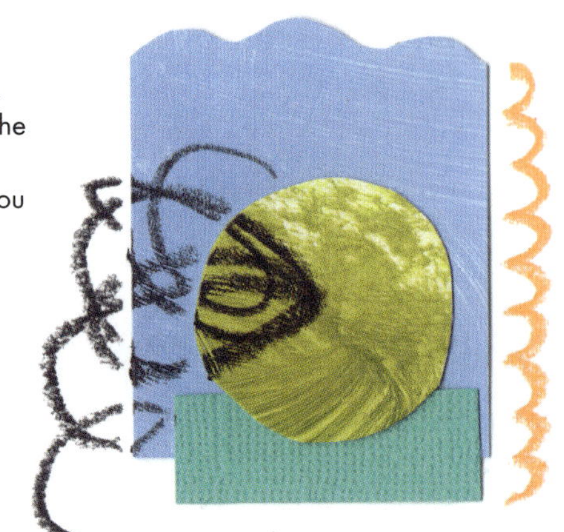

Tip: *You could make lots of these on a separate piece of thin card and turn your images into greetings cards!*

Using jagged shapes can bring an energetic, assertive quality to artwork. Add colours to this design to enhance the feeling of force, movement and dynamism.

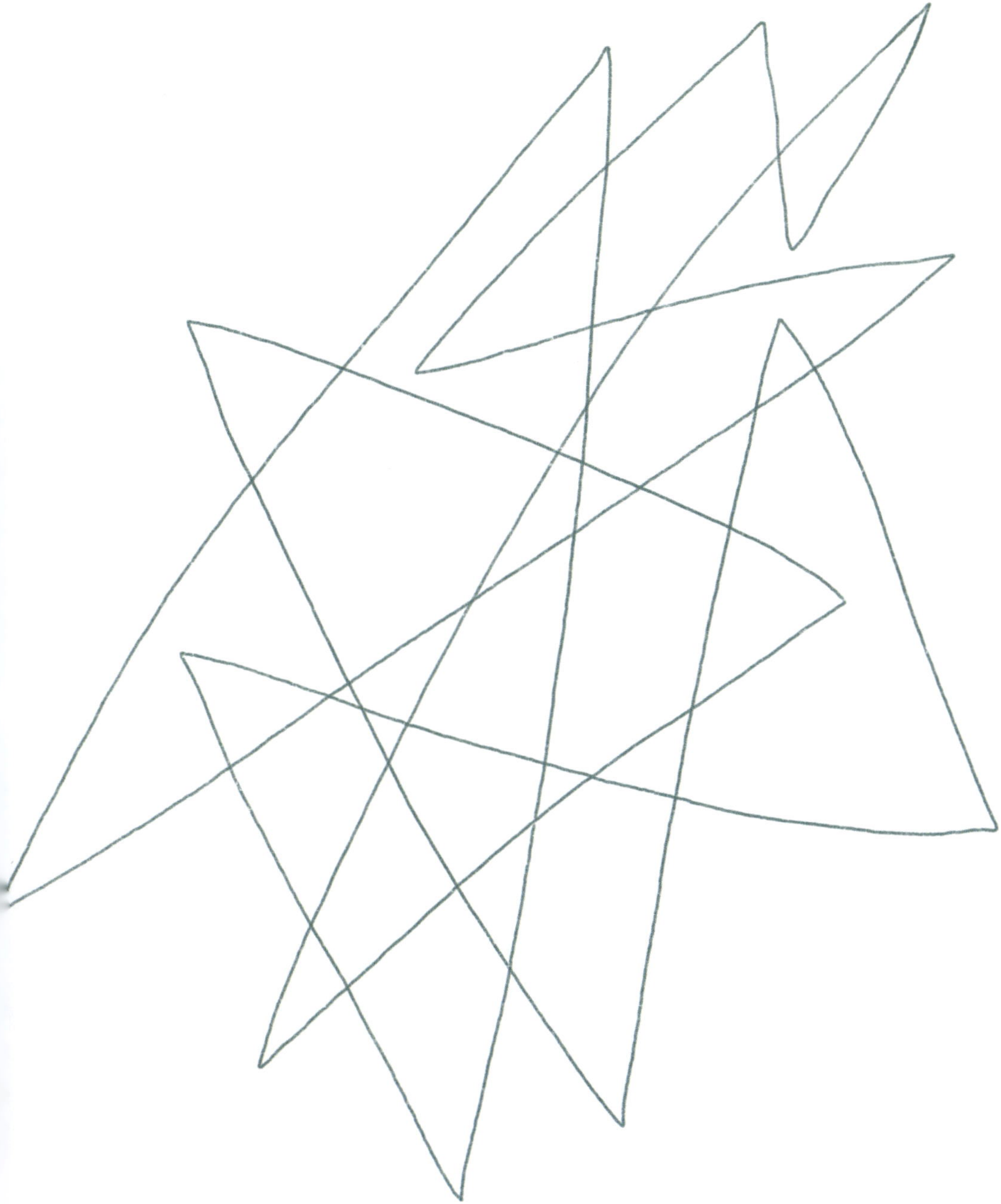

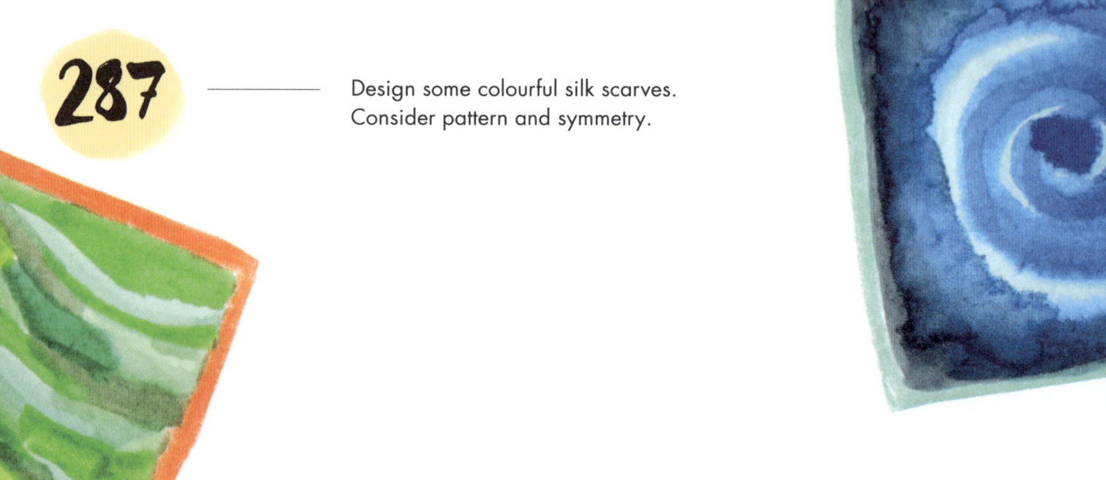

Design some colourful silk scarves.
Consider pattern and symmetry.

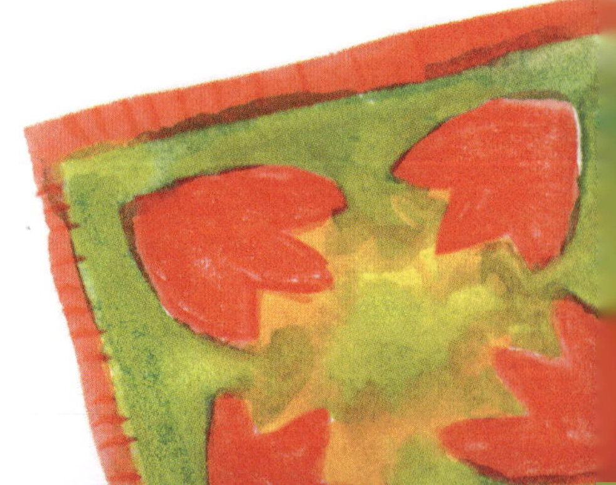

288 What colours would you choose to represent feeling optimistic? Design a pattern here using those colours.

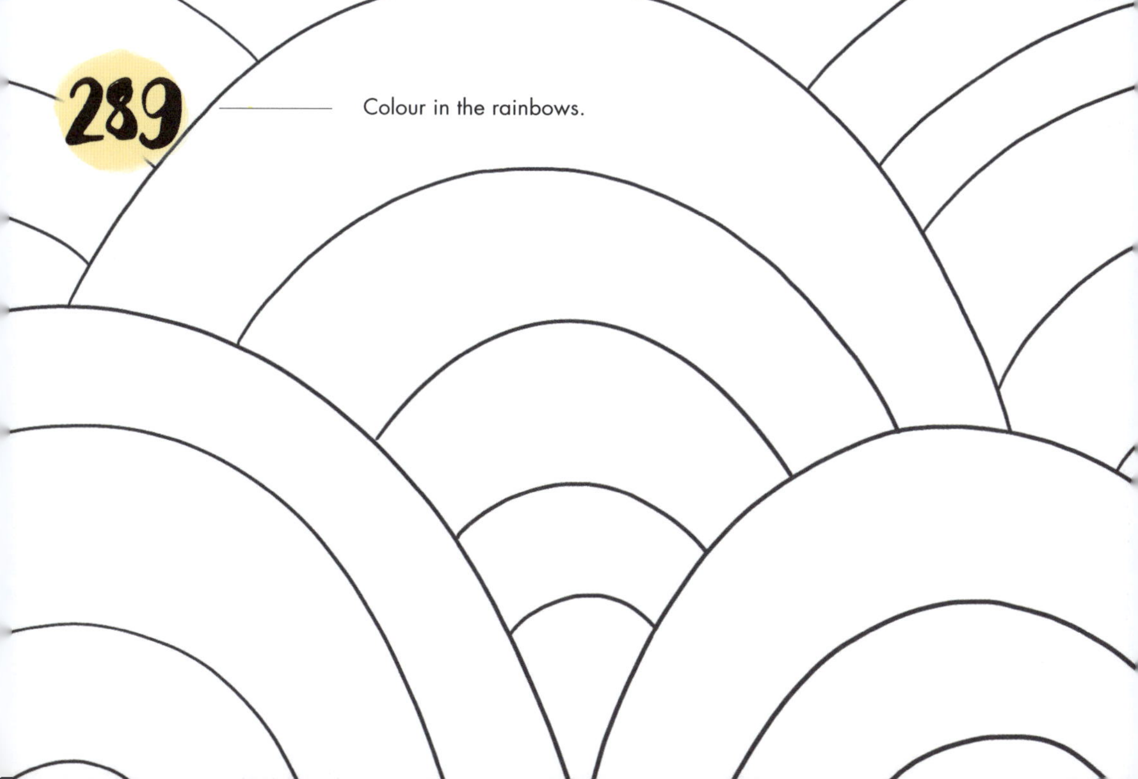

289 Colour in the rainbows.

290

Paint the colour of the sky at four different times. It could be different times of day, or during different weather conditions. Look for a variety of colours.

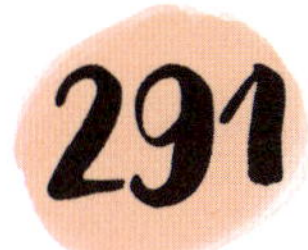

Use colour and art to calm yourself when you feel stressed. Take a few deep breaths and choose some relaxing colours. Create a tranquil piece of art.

Tip: Don't worry what it looks like, just go with the flow and enjoy taking a moment for yourself.

292

Fill the page using coloured pastels.

293

The mood of your drawing will be affected by the colour palettes you choose. Design colour palettes to describe each mood below. This is about how the colours make *you* feel – there's no wrong answer.

Hopeful	
Intimate	
Content	
Romantic	
Tense	
Excited	
Tranquil	

Tip: *Consider using these palettes to evoke an atmosphere in future artworks.*

294

Create an expressive drawing of a scene – either from life or from a photograph. Allow yourself to react emotionally to what you see or the weather you experience, and choose colours and marks in response to how the scene makes you feel.

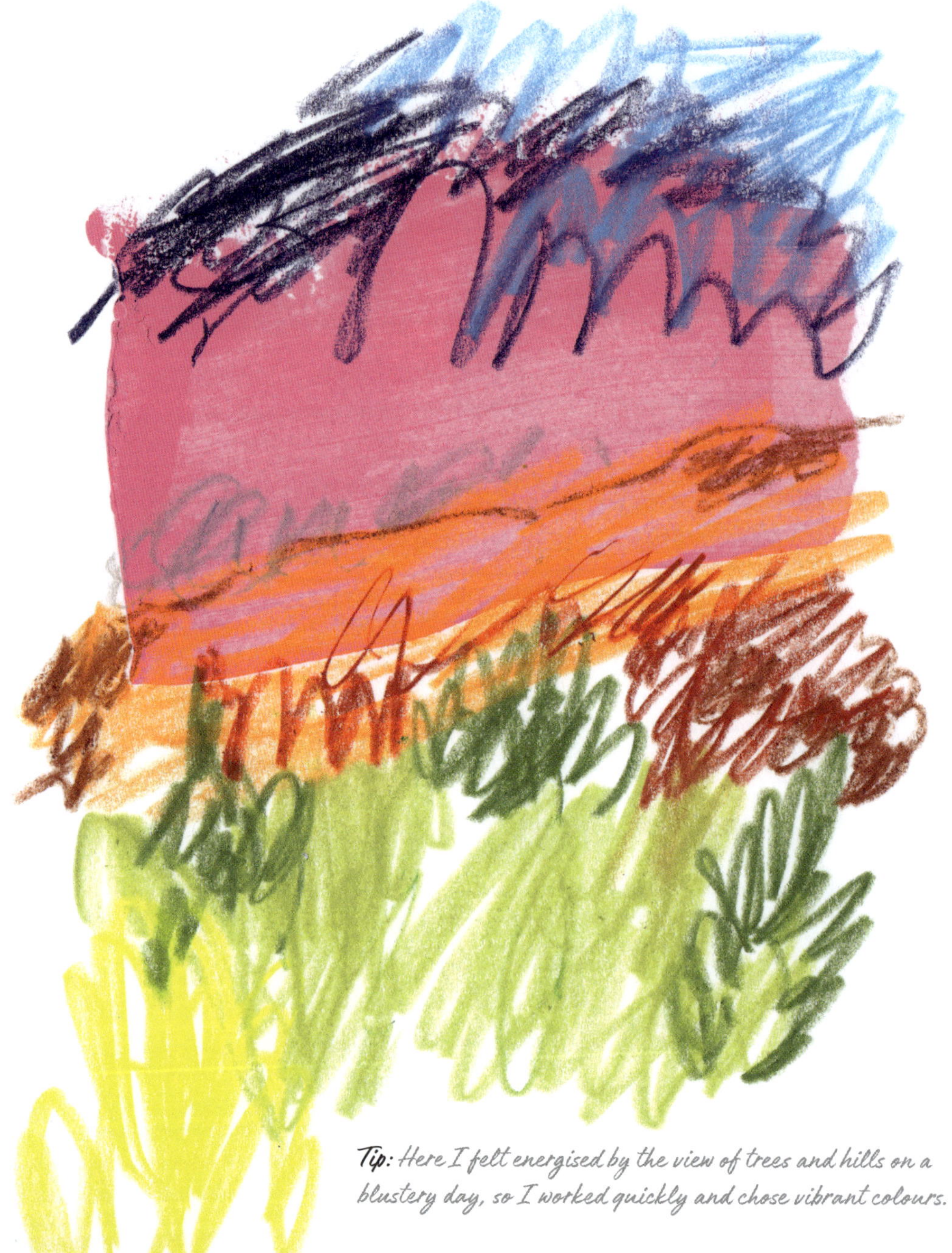

Tip: Here I felt energised by the view of trees and hills on a blustery day, so I worked quickly and chose vibrant colours.

295

Design some colourful outfits. Consider adding texture, pattern and print.

296

Create a portrait of yourself or anyone else from life or from a photo. Use sepia tones – oranges, browns, faded and washed-out colours. Concentrate on capturing the areas of tone within the face.

Tip: Squinting your eyes while looking at an image can help identify which areas are light and dark.

297

You don't have to use a harmonious palette when creating art. Sometimes you may want to make something that is lively and eye-catching, and a colour palette that features lots of contrast is perfect for that. Create collages that explore bold colours, jarring compositions and graphic shapes.

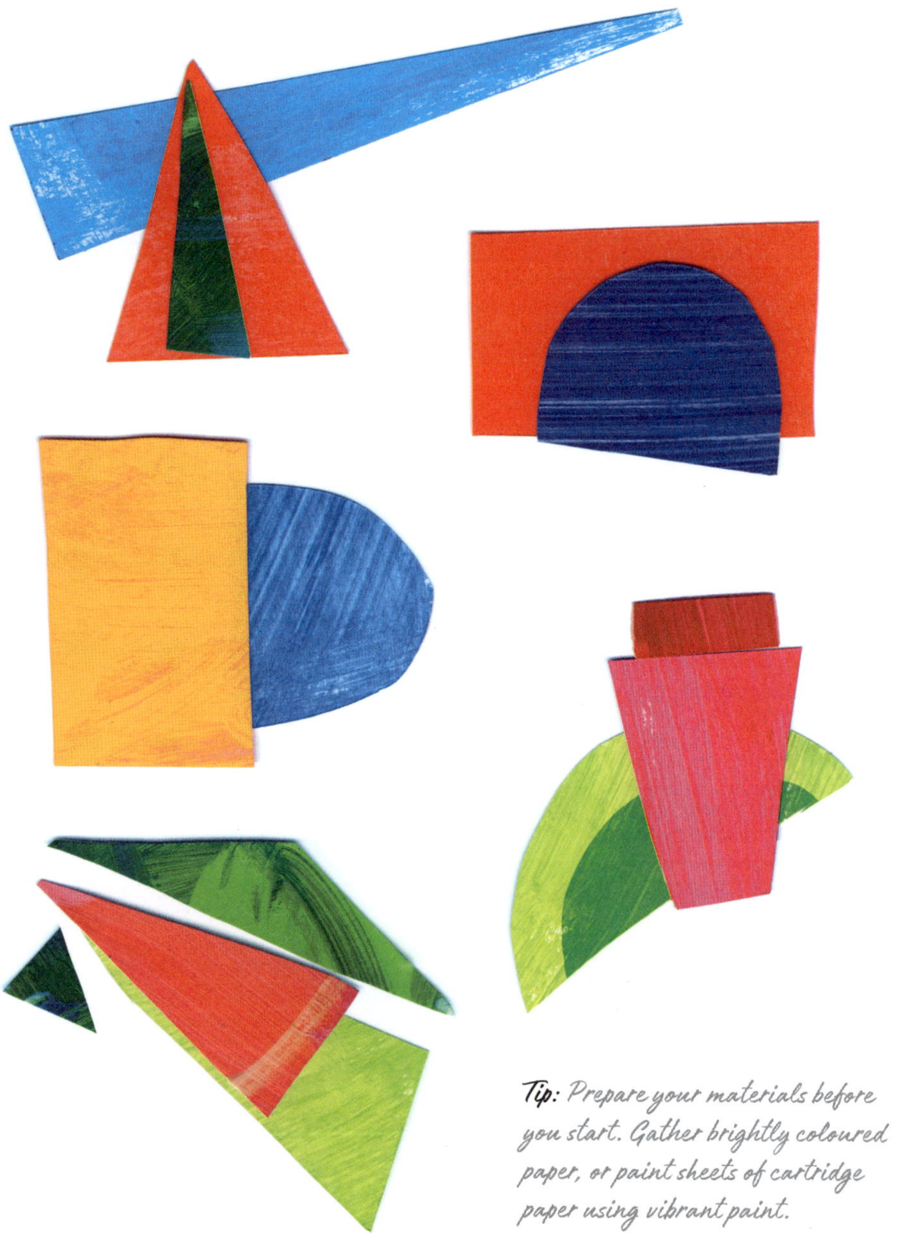

Tip: Prepare your materials before you start. Gather brightly coloured paper, or paint sheets of cartridge paper using vibrant paint.

298

Sketch some landscapes (from life or imagination) using colours to help describe the atmosphere of the location.

299 —— Draw three green things from observation.

300

It can be fun to paint with just a limited range of colours. This removes some of the decision making, giving you more opportunity to be playful. Create a piece of art using a small number of paint colours as a starting point. Begin by choosing three.

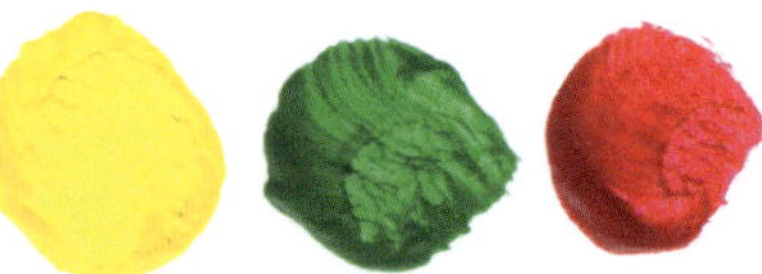

Then mix together those three colours in different quantities to form a range of colours.

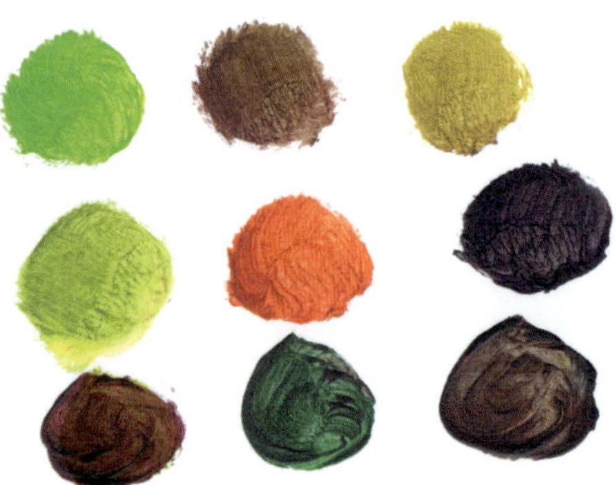

Tip: *You may find it easiest to mix the colours on a palette, rather than on the page. You can use an old ceramic plate for this, or a piece of card. I used acrylic paint.*

Paint an image using the colours in your palette. You don't need to make it look realistic, use any colour you feel inspired by. It can be helpful to identify the light, medium and dark tones within your palette and in the scene or object you are drawing.

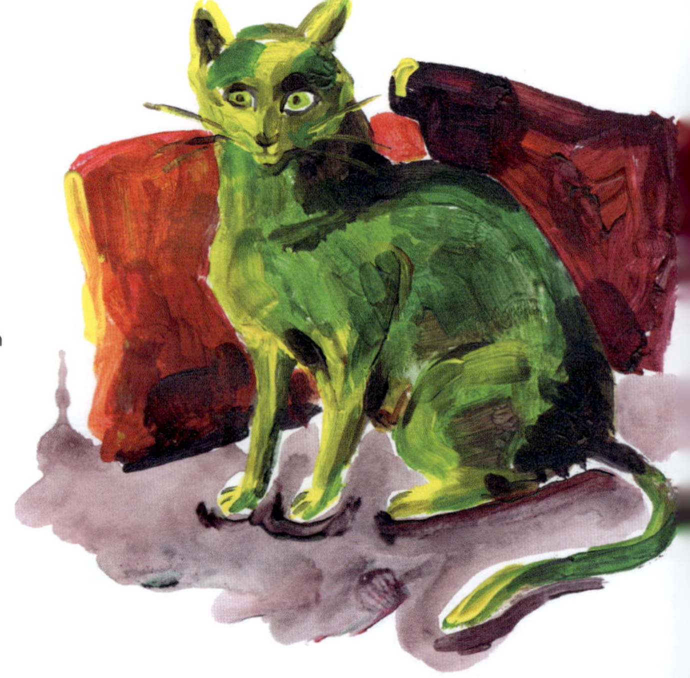

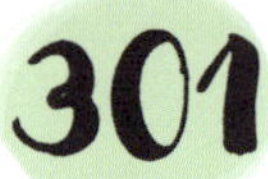

Observe the wing of this butterfly and create the other wing using any art material you like. Perhaps explore blending colours, or create a more abstract design using collaged paper.

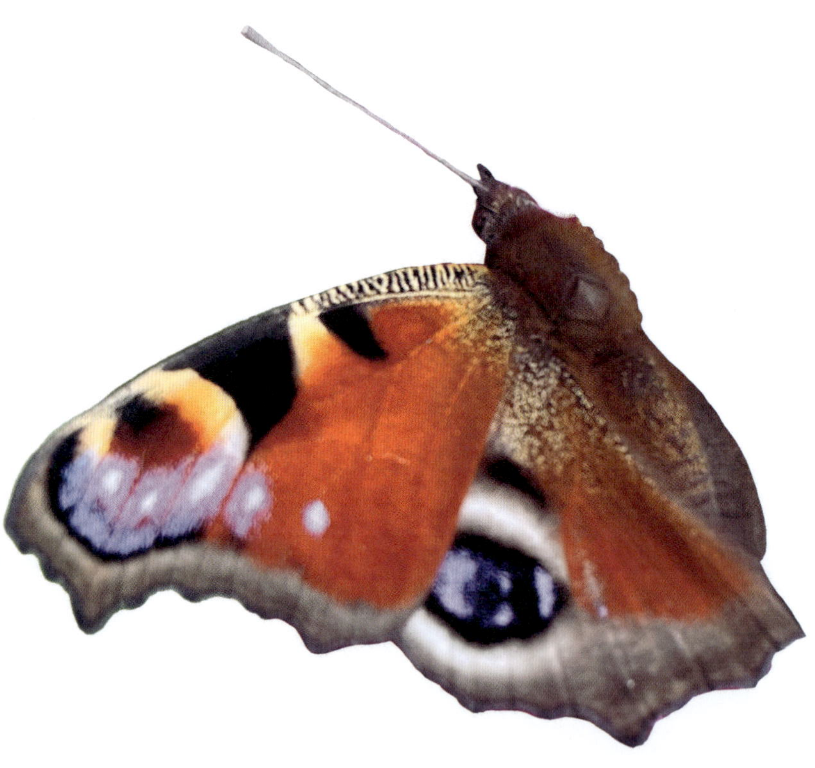

302

Create bold, simple shapes like these, then turn them into animals or people.

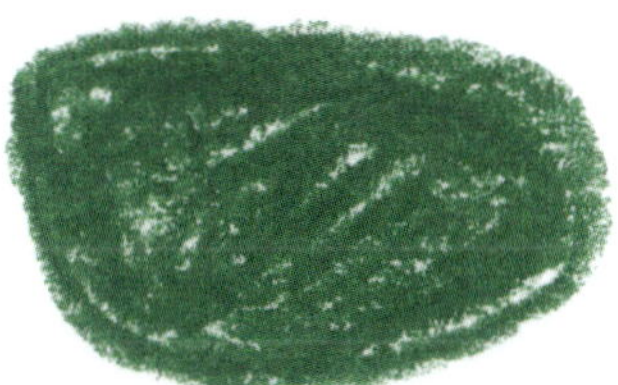

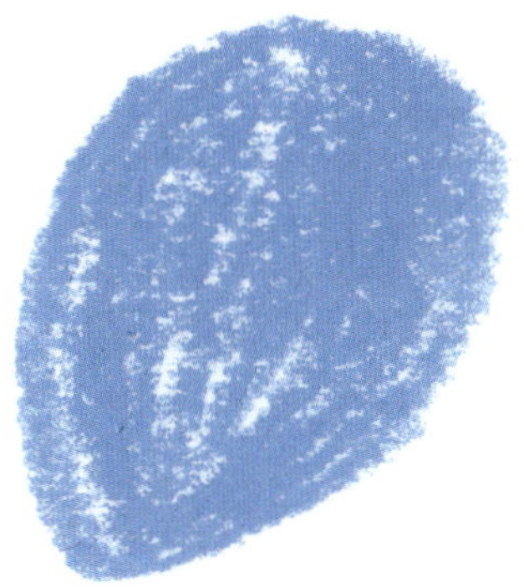

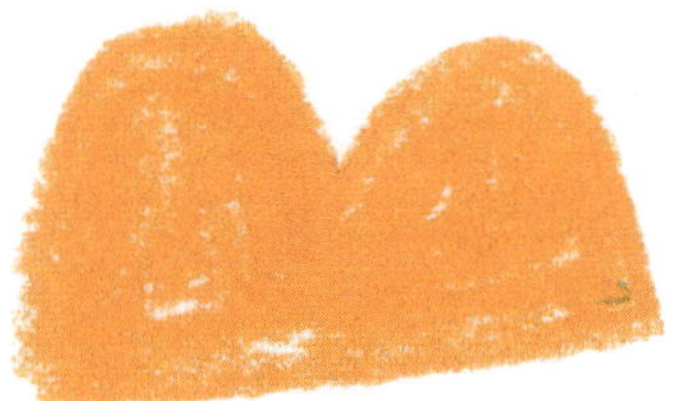

Colour each of these images differently. Explore a variety of colour combinations and enjoy using colours that aren't realistic.

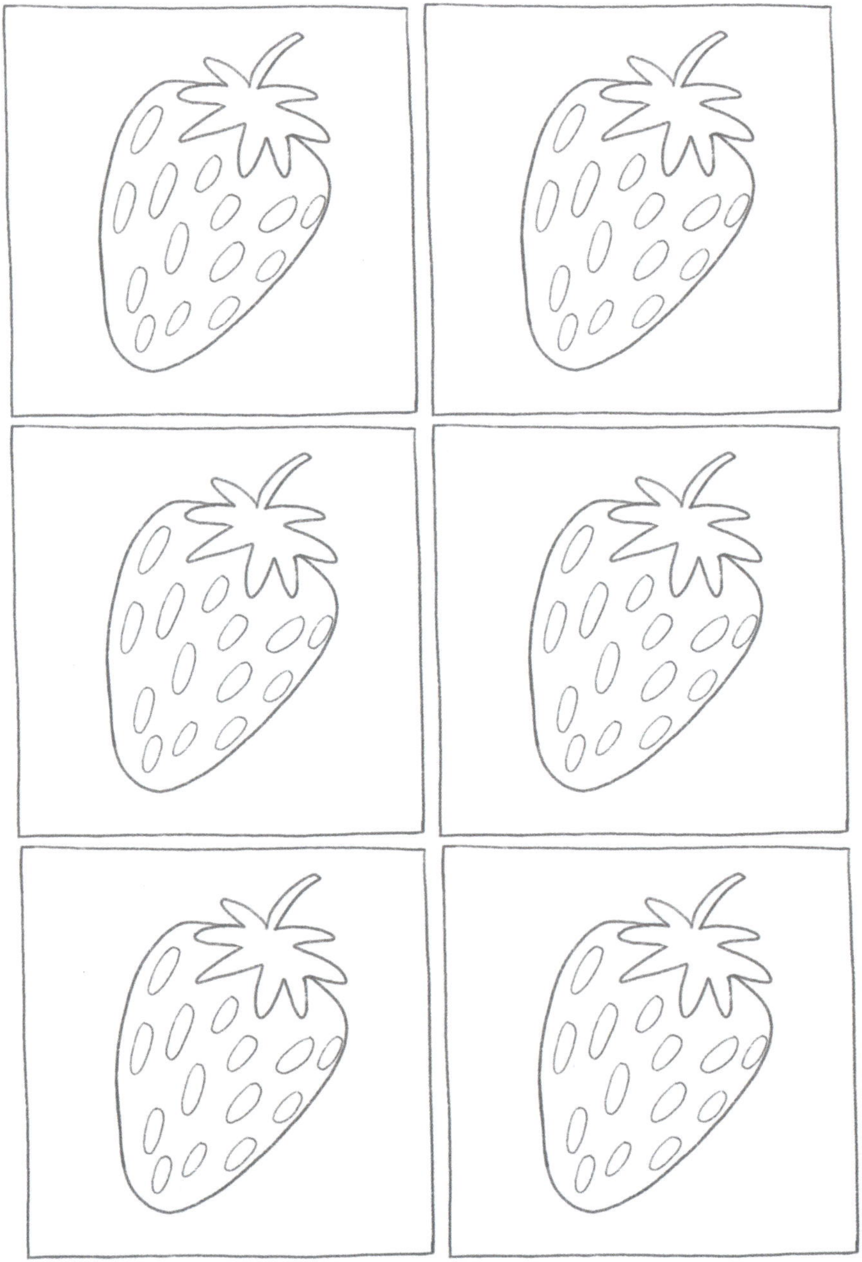

304

Draw an object using your favourite colours.

305

Add colour to the rest of this scene. You could use collage or bold strokes of paint.

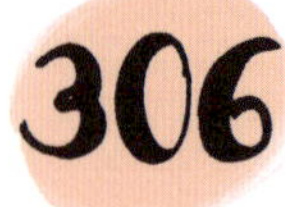

Use mark-making and considered use of colour to express how you feel today.

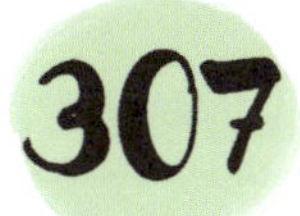

Colour can be used to make bold compositions even more eye-catching. Draw three more objects, giving your artwork vibrant, coloured backgrounds and consider unusual compositions.

Tip: Perhaps the object fills the space or is cropped in an interesting way.

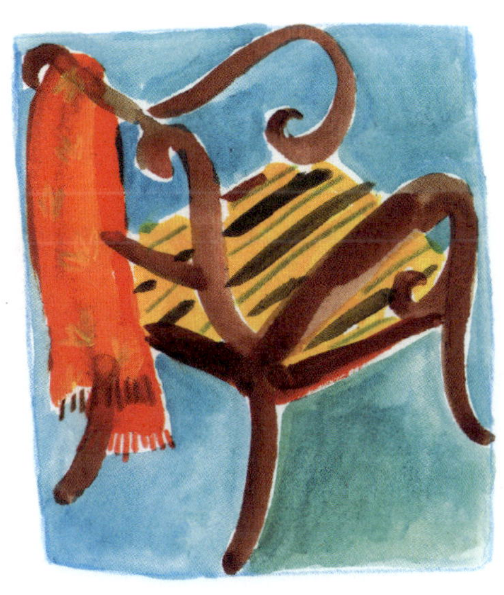

308

Fill the page with warm, earthy colours.
Perhaps it makes you feel calm and grounded.

309

Add the colourful surroundings to this scene – you'll be left with a white house that stands out against the background. Perhaps add colours to the doors too.

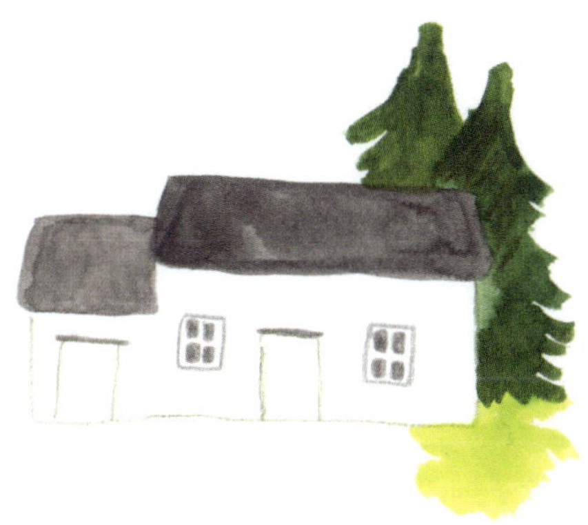

310

Add colours to this design.

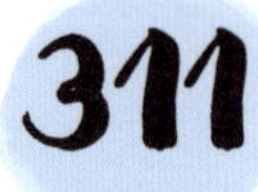

Find a painting by an artist that you love, and study the use of colour. Identify which colours are used in the piece and create your own version of it.

Tip: There's no need for this to be a detailed copy of the painting – it can be a simple representation.

312

Choose one (or a few) objects from nature and draw them, paying close attention to the variety of colours you can see if you really look carefully.

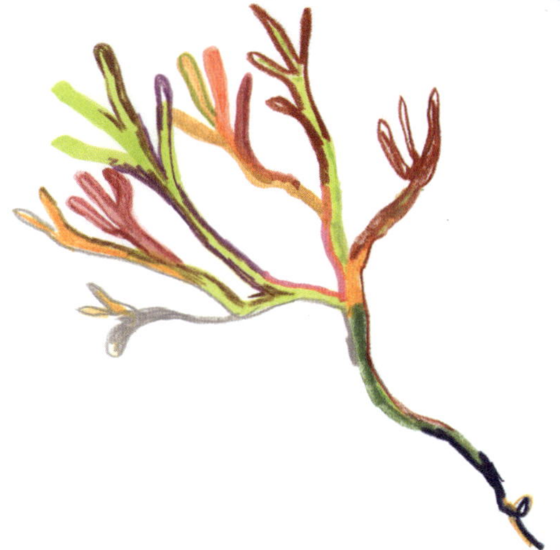

313

Create a woodland scene using collage.

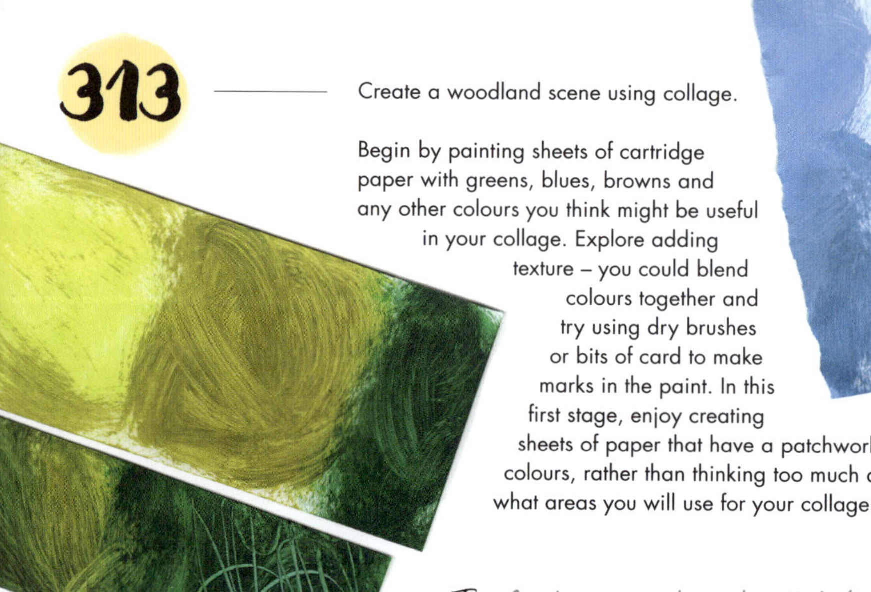

Begin by painting sheets of cartridge paper with greens, blues, browns and any other colours you think might be useful in your collage. Explore adding texture – you could blend colours together and try using dry brushes or bits of card to make marks in the paint. In this first stage, enjoy creating sheets of paper that have a patchwork of colours, rather than thinking too much about what areas you will use for your collage.

Tip: Acrylic or gouache work well, but you can use any paint you like. Be sure to let the paper dry fully before starting to cut it, otherwise the paper can rip.

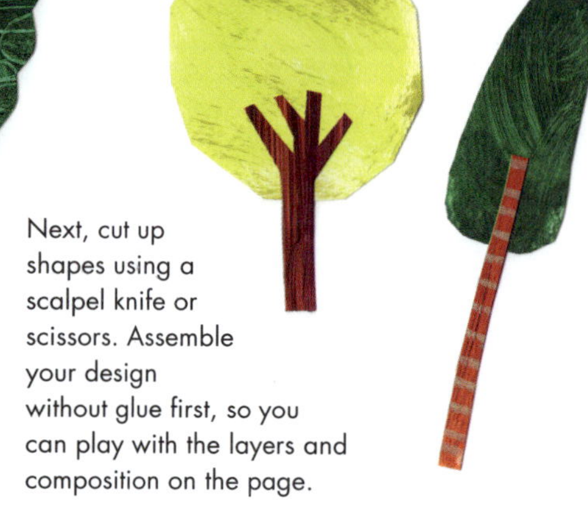

Next, cut up shapes using a scalpel knife or scissors. Assemble your design without glue first, so you can play with the layers and composition on the page.

Tip: Add more details using pastels.

Once you have a layout you like, stick the elements in place using a thin layer of PVA glue. You might need to flatten your drying image underneath some paper and a heavy book to make sure the bits of paper dry without curling.

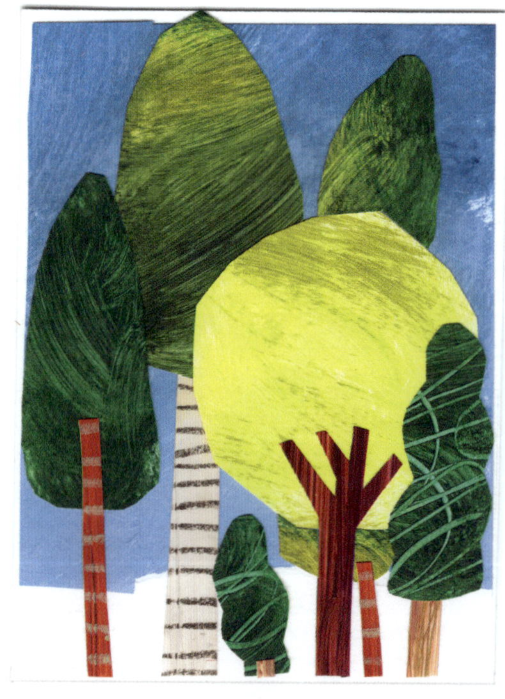

314

Look for colour in unexpected places – pour a glass of water and draw it, paying particular attention to the colours you can see in the glass and liquid.

315

Make sketches of people using pairs of complementary colours. These can create an unsettling, dynamic image.

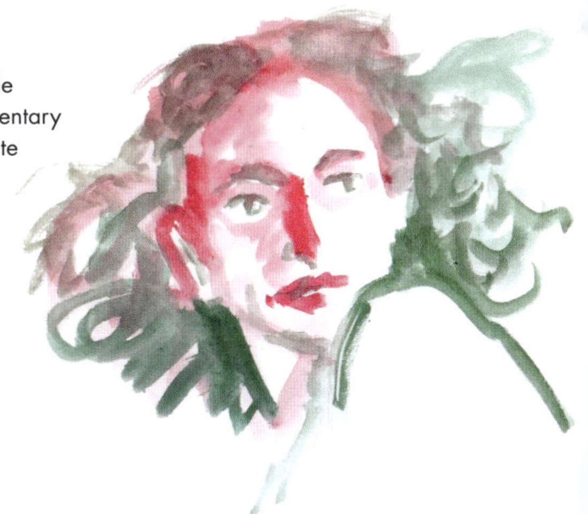

316

Lie down outside and spend some time looking up. Concentrate on the colours you can see. After 10 or so minutes, paint what you saw from memory. You may just remember big blocks of colour, and that's great!

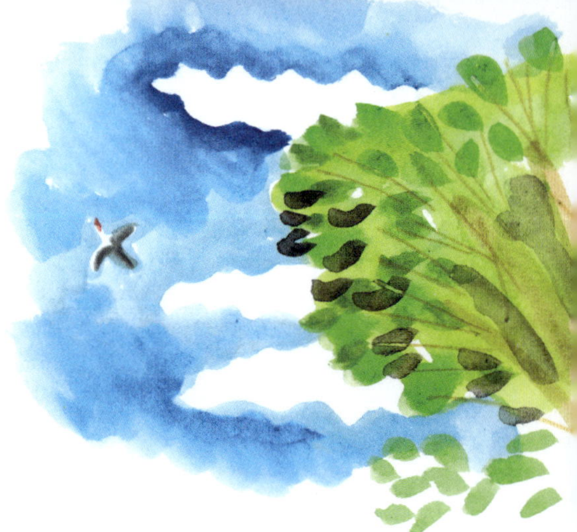

317

Add more greens then turn the image into a jungle.

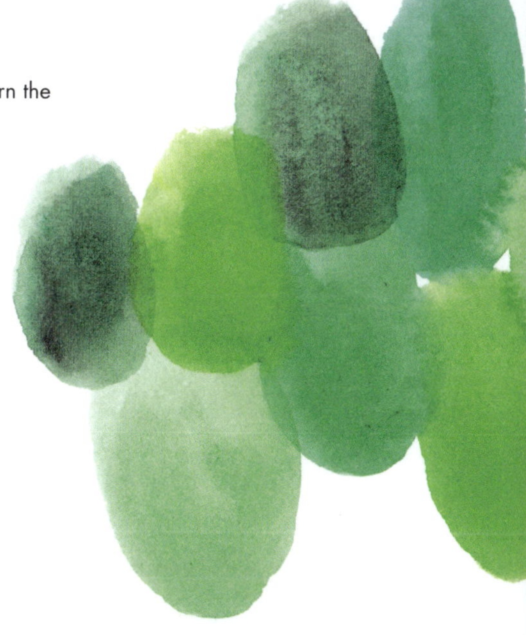

318

Purple can evoke luxury, moodiness, spirituality and magic. Consider how purple makes *you* feel, and create an image based on this shape.

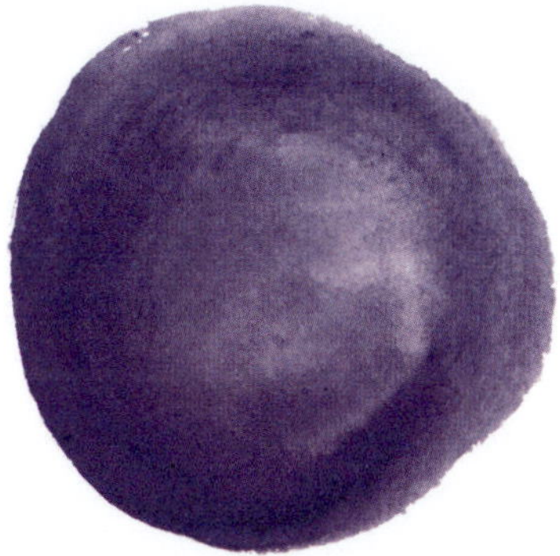

319

If you use shapes and subjects that you really enjoy, your art can be joyful, colourful and expressive. Choose an object that you love to look at and draw it lots of times on the opposite page. Delight in exploring its shape and using colour playfully.

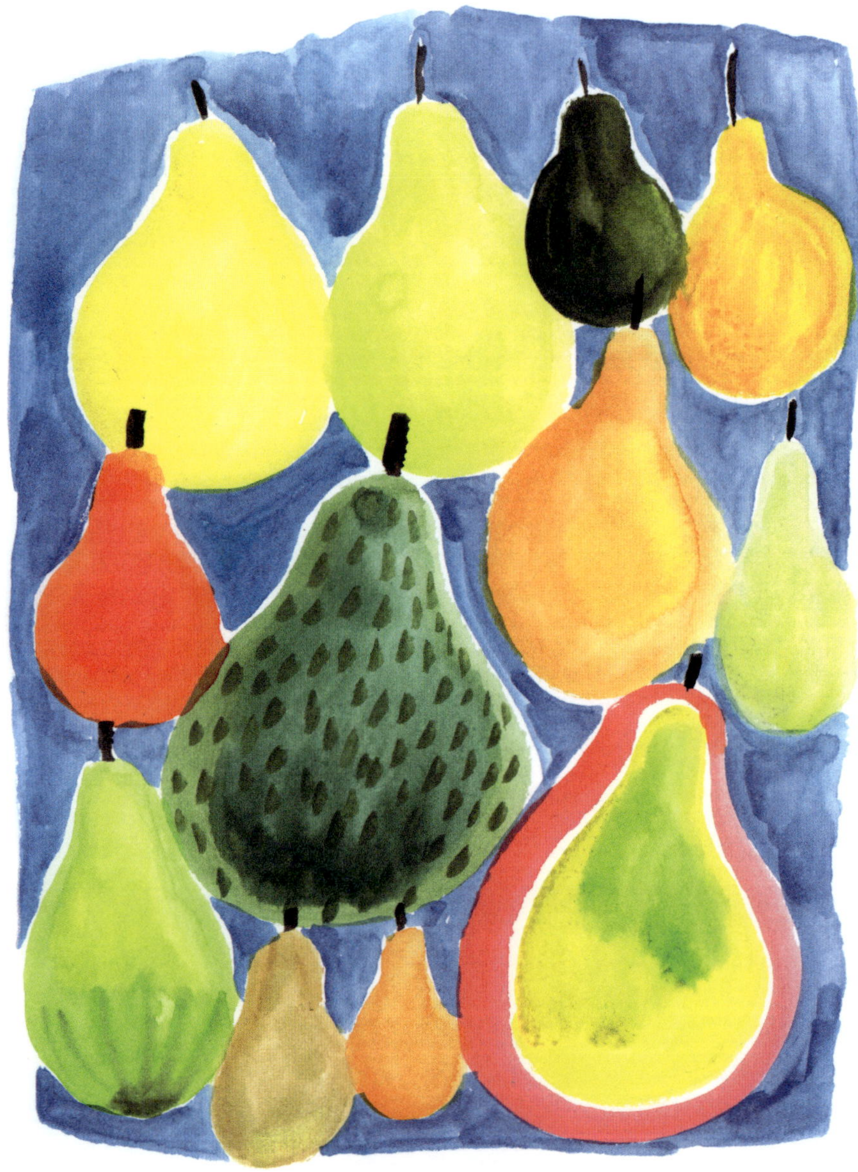

Tip: Learning to love using colour can be tricky – but choosing subjects you enjoy will give you a good start.

320

Set up a small still life using household objects. Draw what you see using lots of confident marks.

Tip: Consider what you've learnt about shadows being coloured rather than pure black.

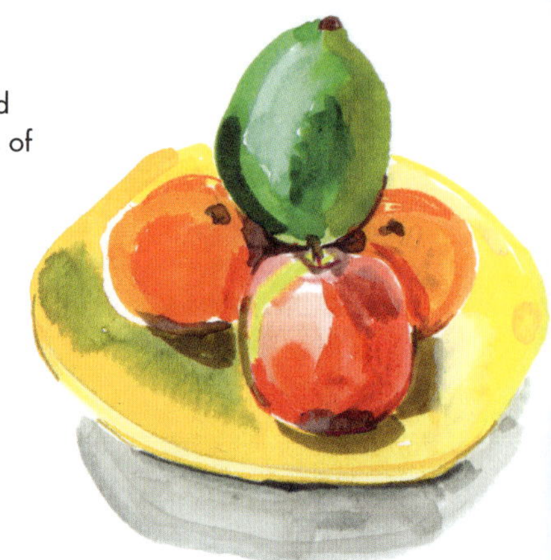

321 Create a colourful bird motif.

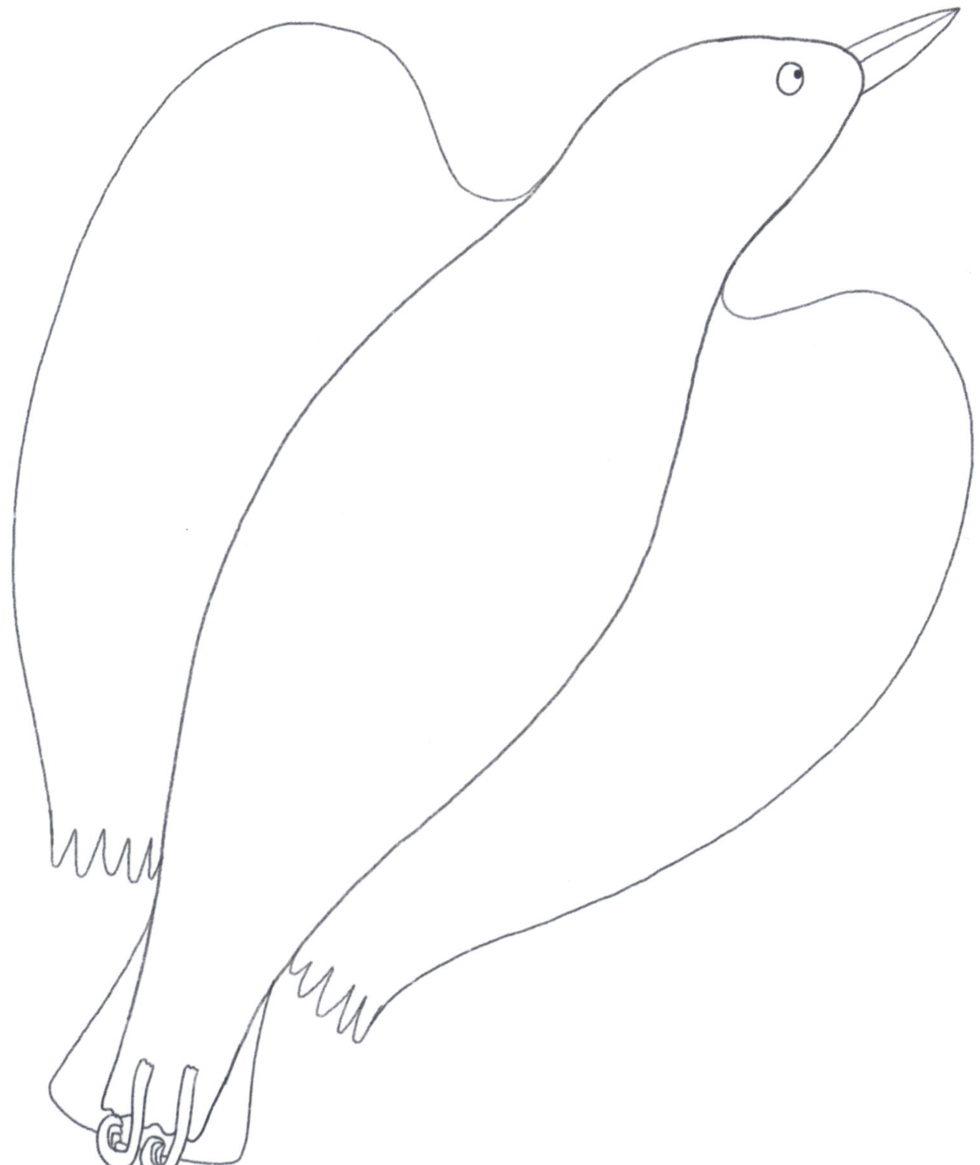

322

If we look into the distance, things that are further away – distant hills and buildings, for example – look less saturated. Add colour to these hills, making the colours less saturated the further back they are.

323

Add colours that have a vintage feel to the grid.

324

Fill the page with blue and violet zigzags.

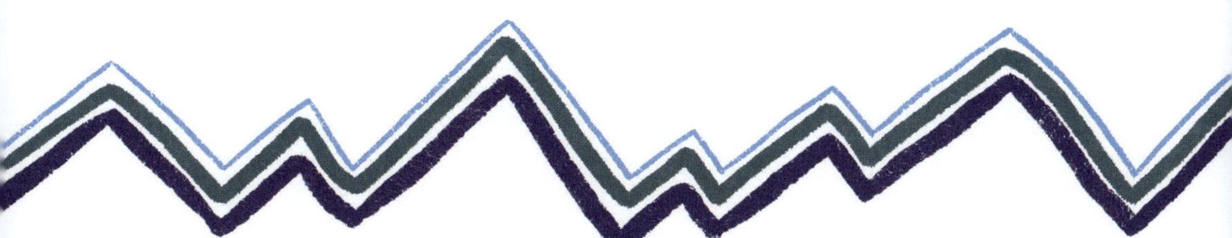

325

Visit a garden centre, garden or park and, as you walk around, notice the colour combinations that occur in nature. Look at flowers, stems and leaves and see how the combinations of colours can be so beautifully balanced. Make studies of what you see.

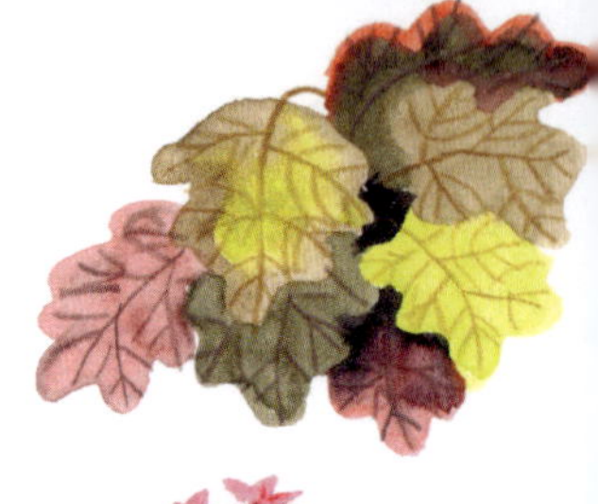

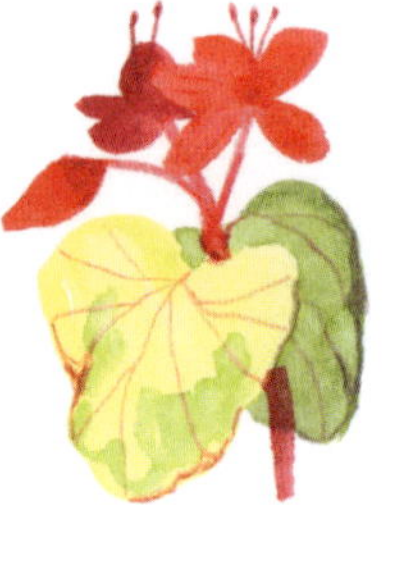

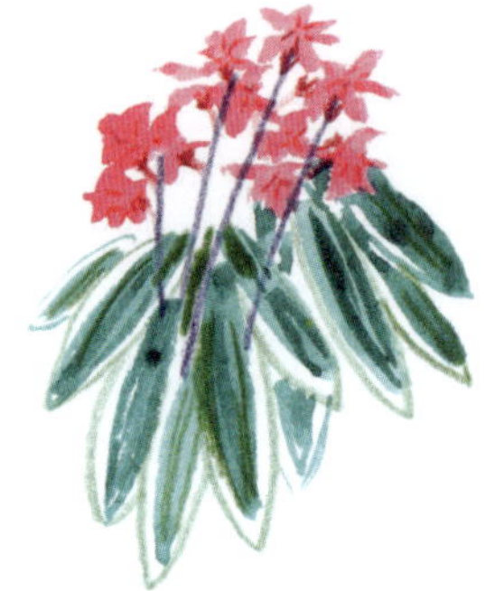

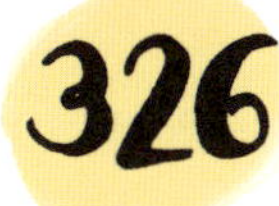

Using soft, muted colours – perhaps pastels and neutrals – add colour to these eggs. Explore adding textures and allowing colours to bleed into each other.

327

Colour this fruit using cheerful colours. Perhaps add a colourful, patterned tablecloth beneath them.

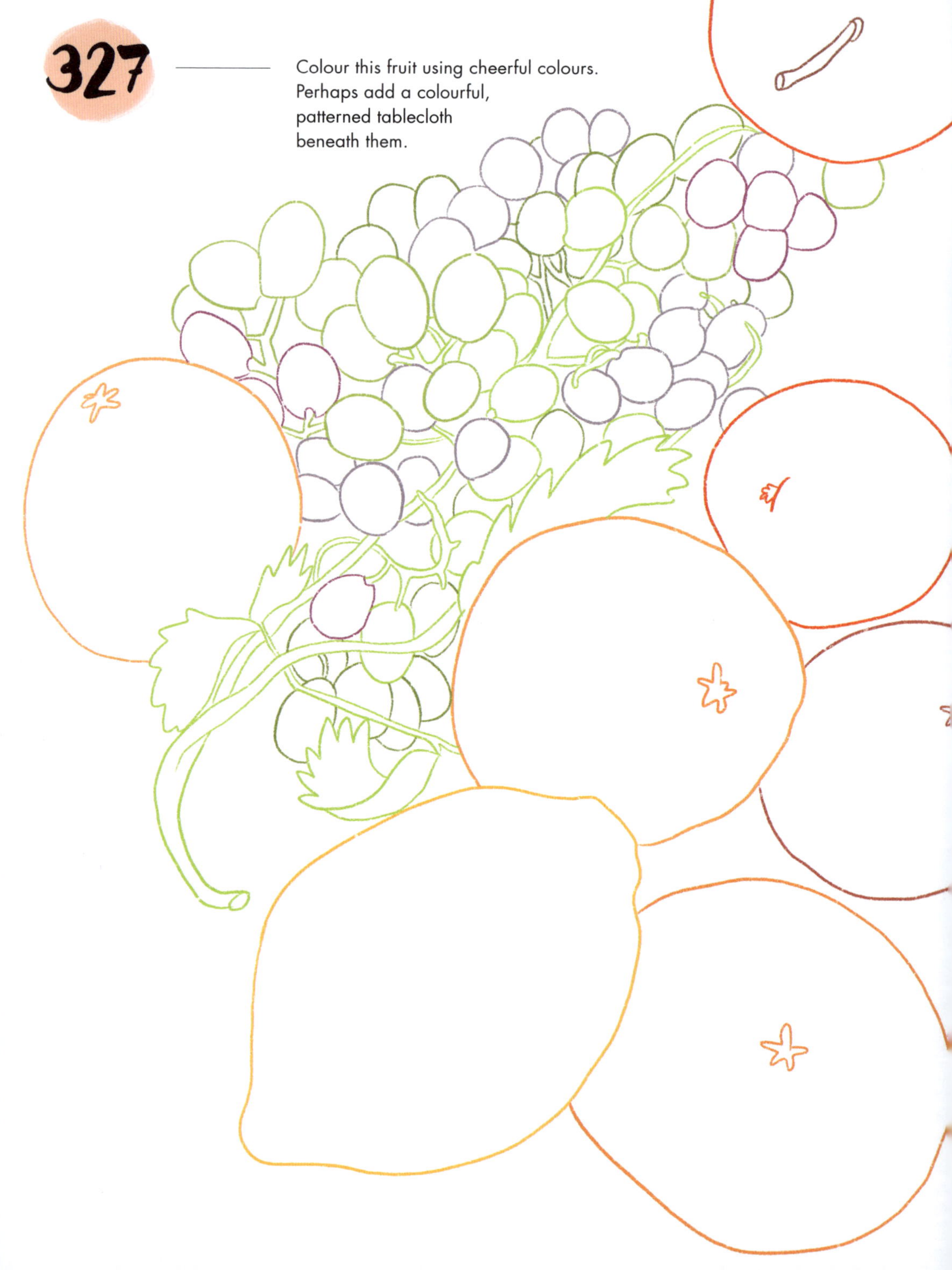

328

Draw five blue things from imagination.

329

Consider which colours evoke feelings of calm. Create an abstract drawing using serene shapes and colours.

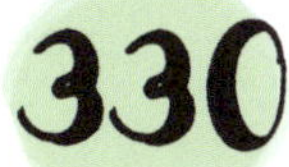

Visit a woodland, park or garden and draw what you see, using this background as a starting point.

Tip: *Look for clean and dirty colours that you could add to your image. Perhaps there are a lot of dirty colours and one small pop of bright, clean colour.*

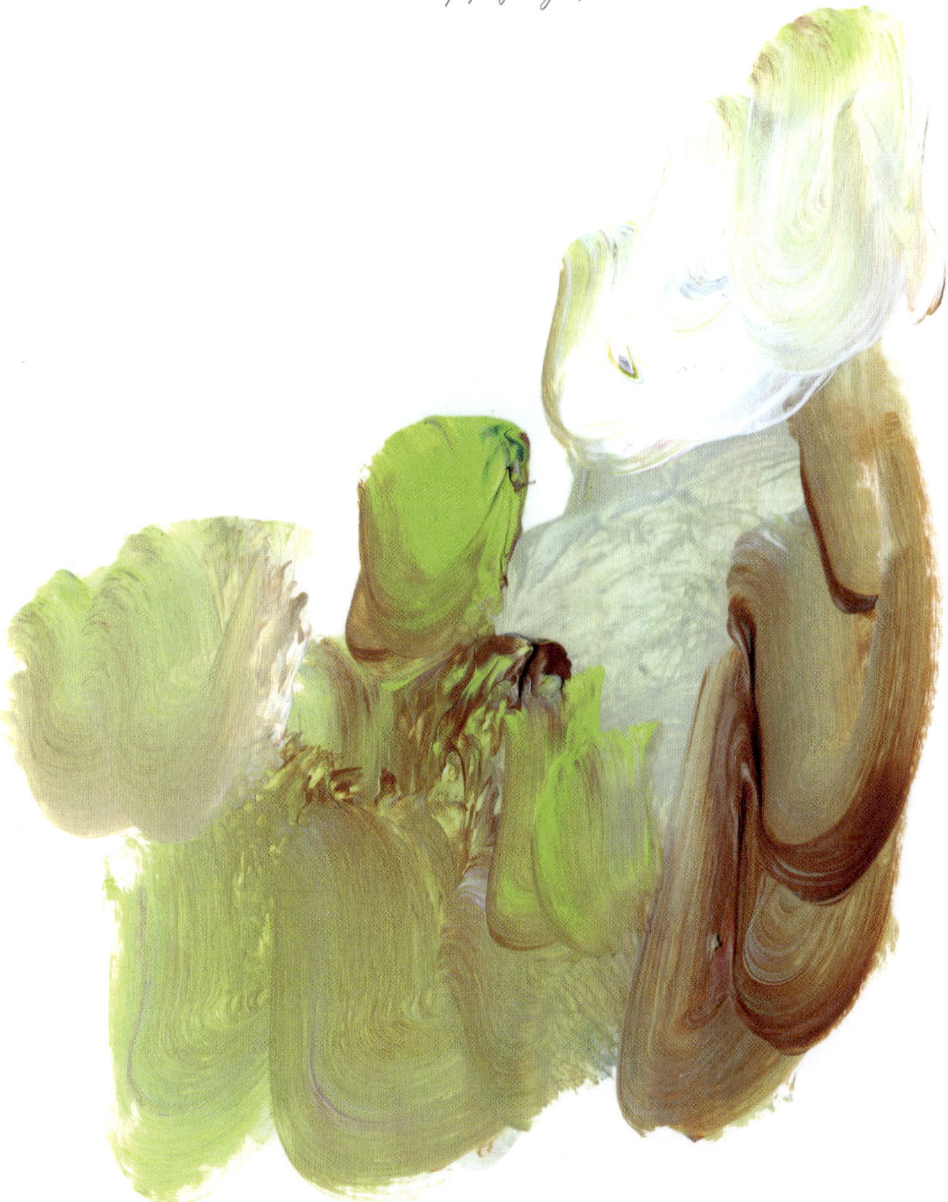

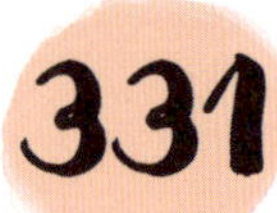

Orange can evoke friendliness, happiness and warmth. Be inspired by how orange makes *you* feel and create a piece of art based on this shape.

332

Add an image to this turquoise.

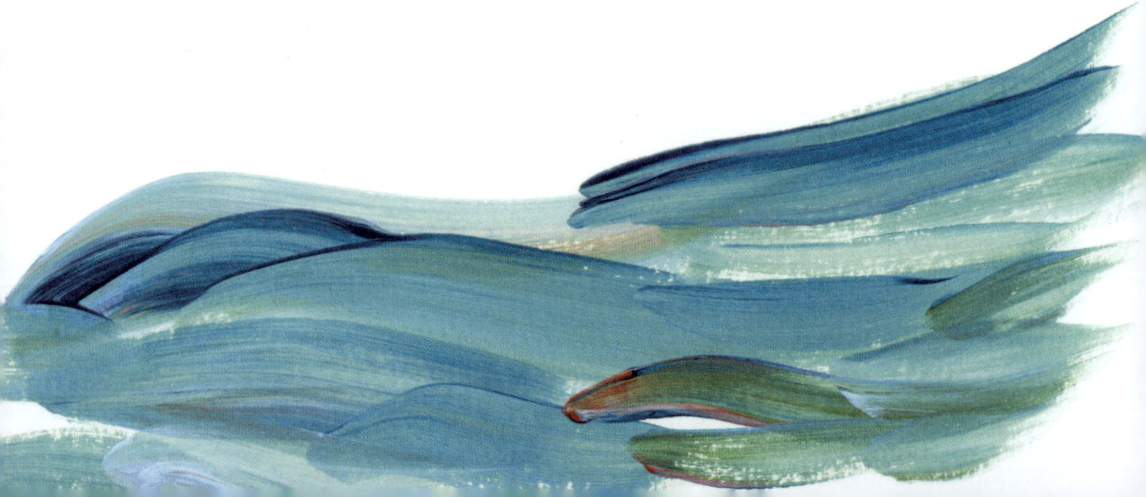

333 Add bright pastel waves.

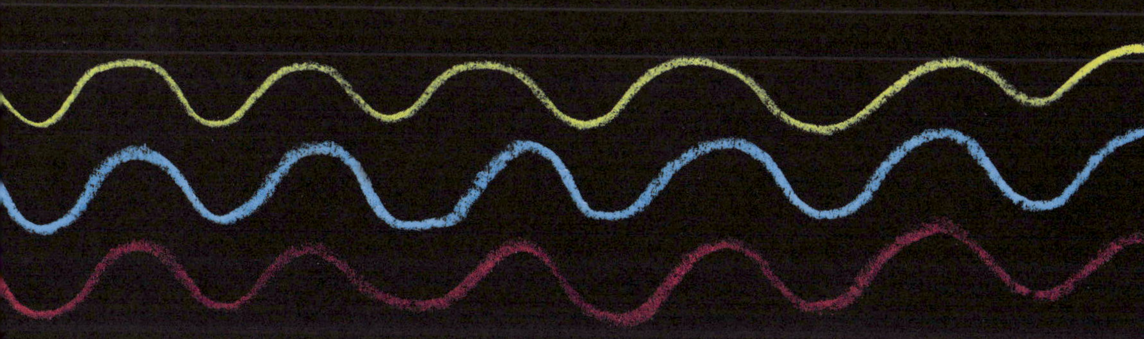

334 You can use colour and shape to depict movement in your art. Draw something kinetic – for example a firework – and use colour to illustrate how it travels through the air. It can be an abstract image, rather than needing to be realistic.

335

Draw an object or scene using a thick black or brown outline. Then add colour to your drawing, making bold, confident marks using vibrant colours.

Tip: Starting with a bold outline will immediately make your art eye-catching!

336

Start by painting a wash of bright colour across the page. Then add small amounts of other colours until you've filled the page. Enjoy choosing colours that work well together, and consider where you add marks so that your composition feels balanced.

Tip: Acrylic paint or gouache would be effective here. Or use watercolour for your background and pastels on top once the paint has dried.

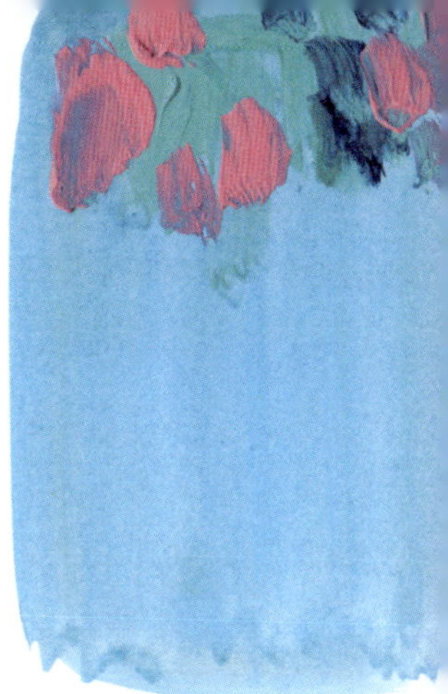

337

Design a colour scheme for a room in your house that evokes a specific feeling of your choice.

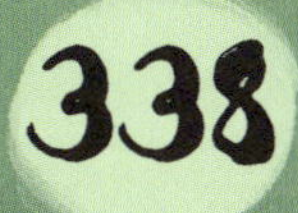

Make a piece of art from observation, using these two coloured backgrounds as starting points. Perhaps draw a potted plant that you can see, creating the pot in the bottom half and the plant in the top half.

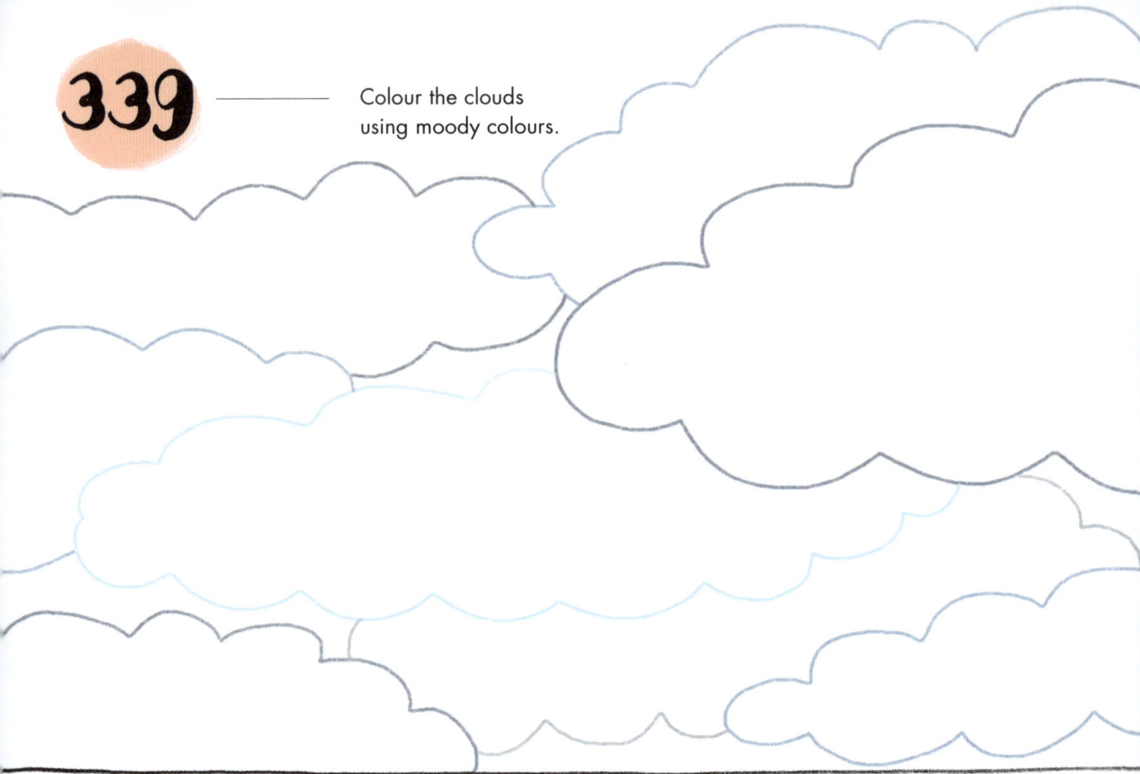

340

Design a pair of colourful shoes.

341

Choose two to five coloured pencils, pens or pastels and draw a person, concentrating on capturing their outline. There's no need to add tone or blocks of colour, just enjoy letting your materials glide across the page.

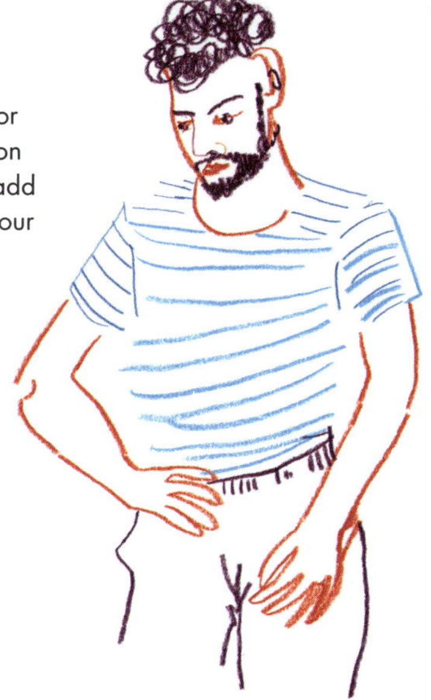

342

Draw a view from your home – inside or outside – using as many colours as possible. You could explore using a variety of materials too. Aim for your creation to be energetic and full of life.

343

Turn these green feathers into a bird.

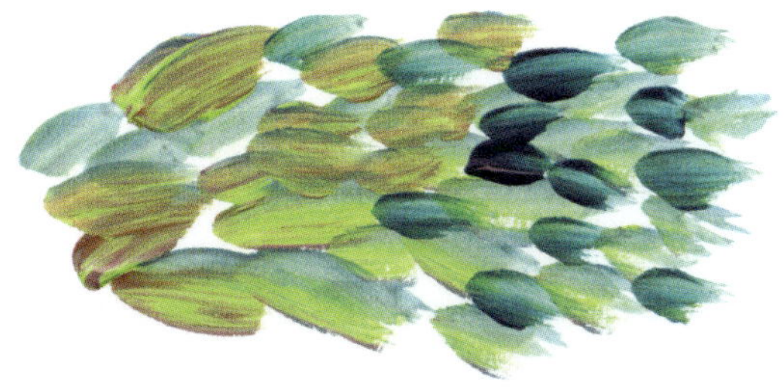

344

Create a palette of colours to describe your mood today.
Don't worry if you don't know exactly why you chose each colour – just go with your instincts.

345

It can be striking when a lot of one colour is used confidently. Look around your home for a scene or object which includes a few similar colours, and use this as inspiration for a piece of art. Be bold and unapologetic with your use of one colour – aim to create an arresting image.

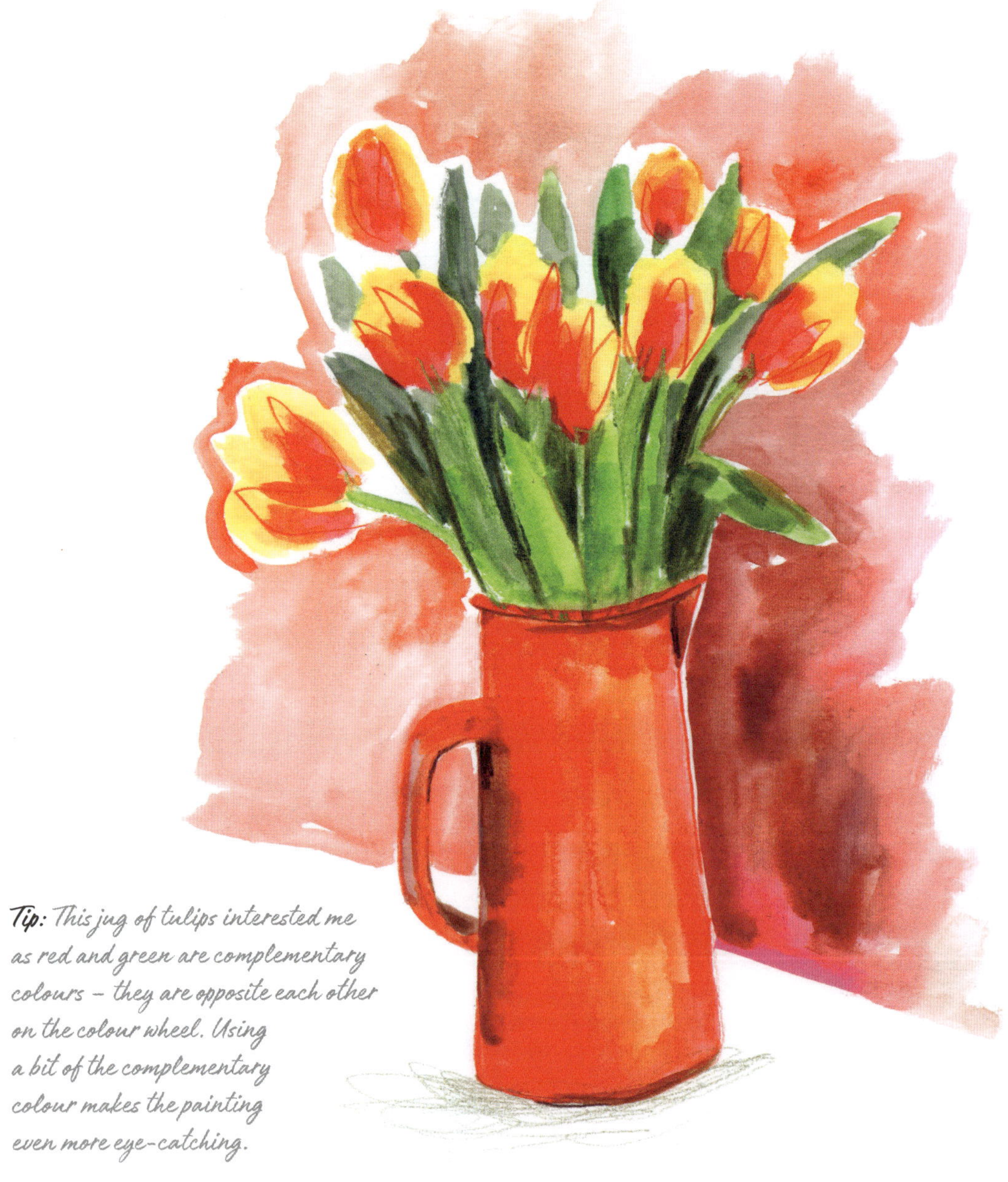

Tip: This jug of tulips interested me as red and green are complementary colours – they are opposite each other on the colour wheel. Using a bit of the complementary colour makes the painting even more eye-catching.

346 Continue adding triangles, then fill them in using any colour you like.

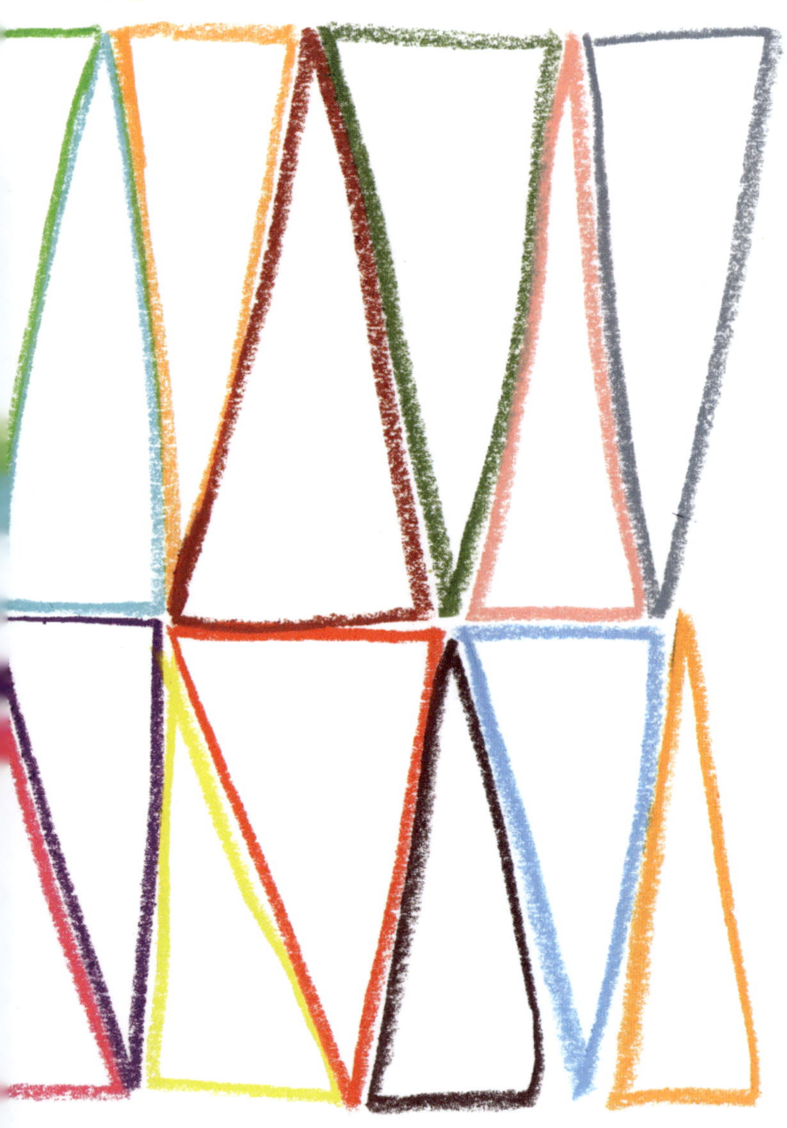

347

Inspiration for paintings can come from anywhere. There can be beautiful colour combinations in industrial machinery, buildings and everyday objects that catch your eye. Paint a view or scene that isn't traditionally depicted in art but interests you.

348

Explore bright, vibrant colour combinations here. Draw a circle of colour and then add a second colour around the outside.

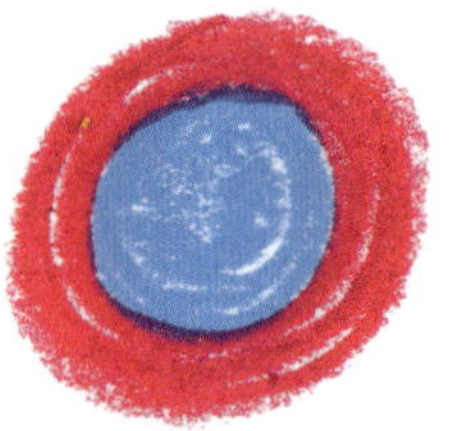

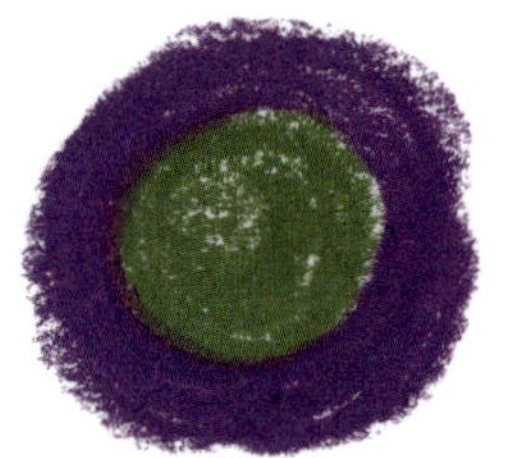

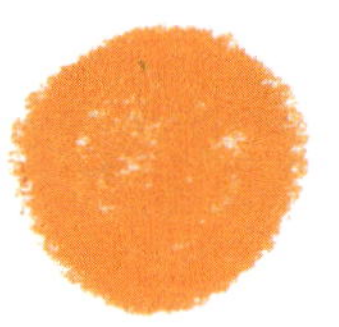

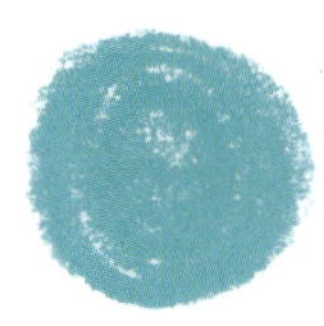

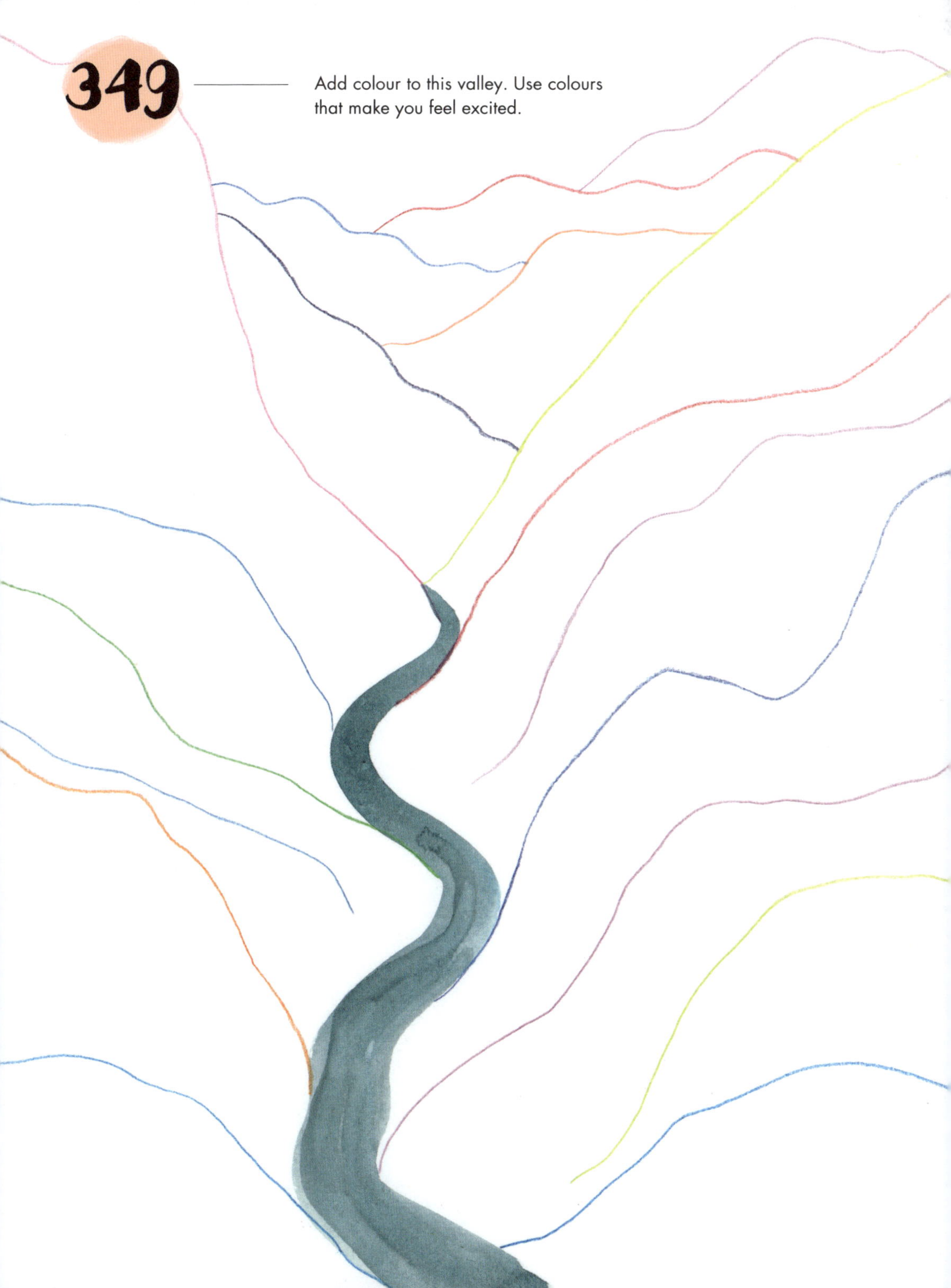
349
Add colour to this valley. Use colours that make you feel excited.

350

Draw the same scene at different times of day and observe how varying the colours can be. The same view can be inspiration for many pieces of art, as the light and weather changes.

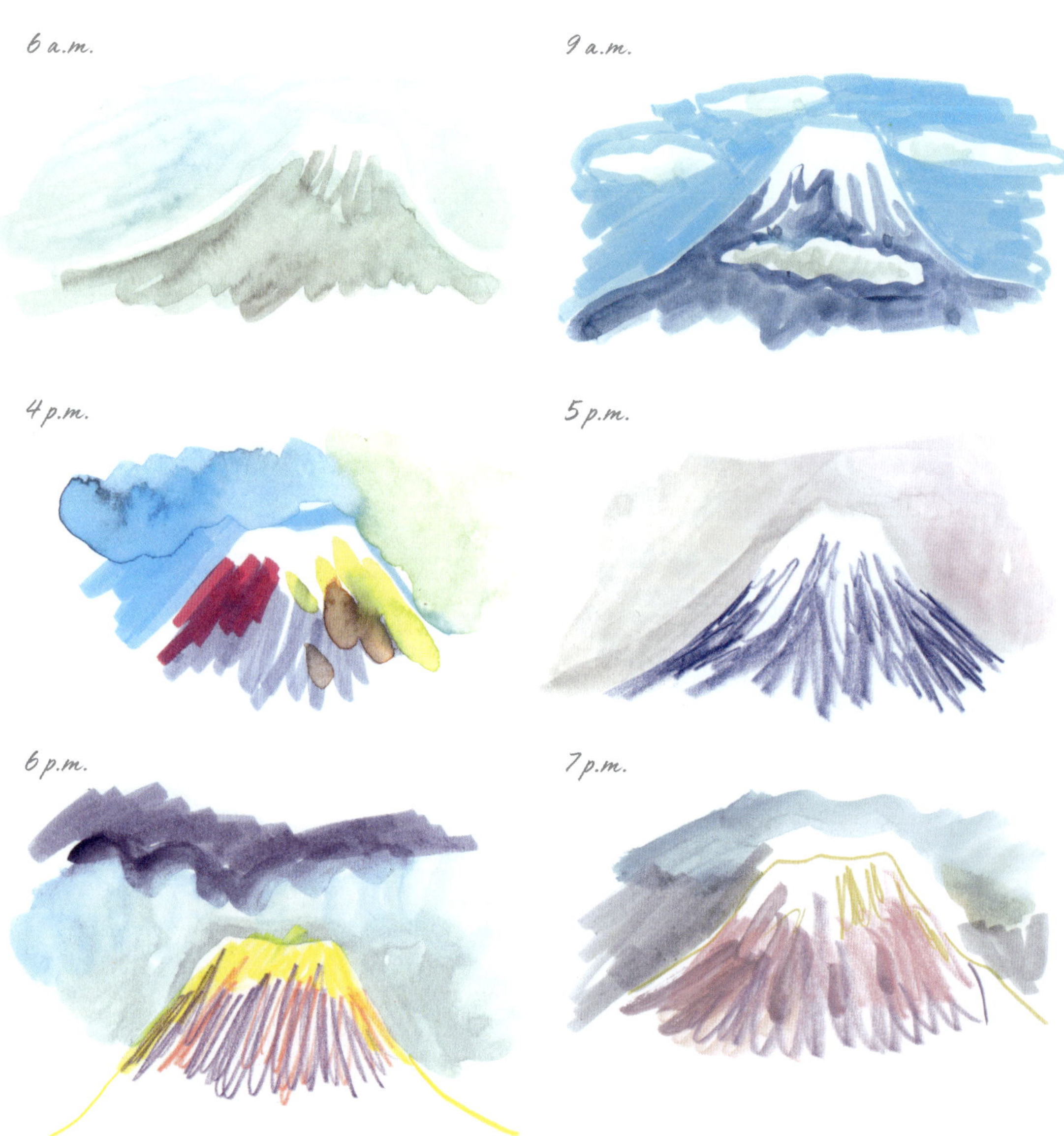

Tip: Light can change quickly, especially at sunrise and sunset! You may want to have some materials prepared in front of you, ready to quickly grab as soon as you need them.

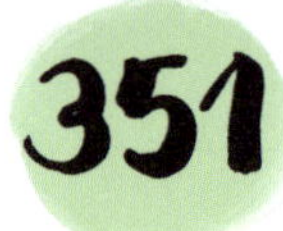

There is more than one colour in the sea and in a river or lake. Look at a body of water – in person or in a photo or video. Draw it, being sure to capture all the colours you observe. Consider how the weather has an affect on the tones you see in the water.

352

Fill the page with multicoloured diamonds.

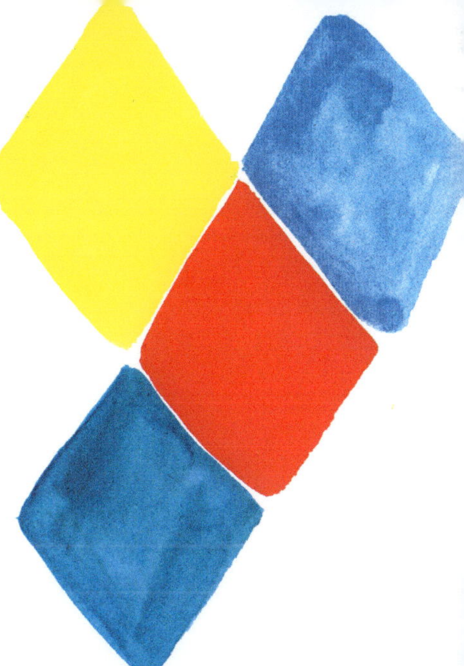

353

The colours we wear can affect how we feel.
Design an exuberant costume here.

354

Paint a scene that features a lot of tone (areas of light and dark). Use colour to depict tonal areas instead of greys and blacks.

Tip: Consider using tints and shades of colours, or perhaps complementary colours, to create striking shadows.

355 Add colour.

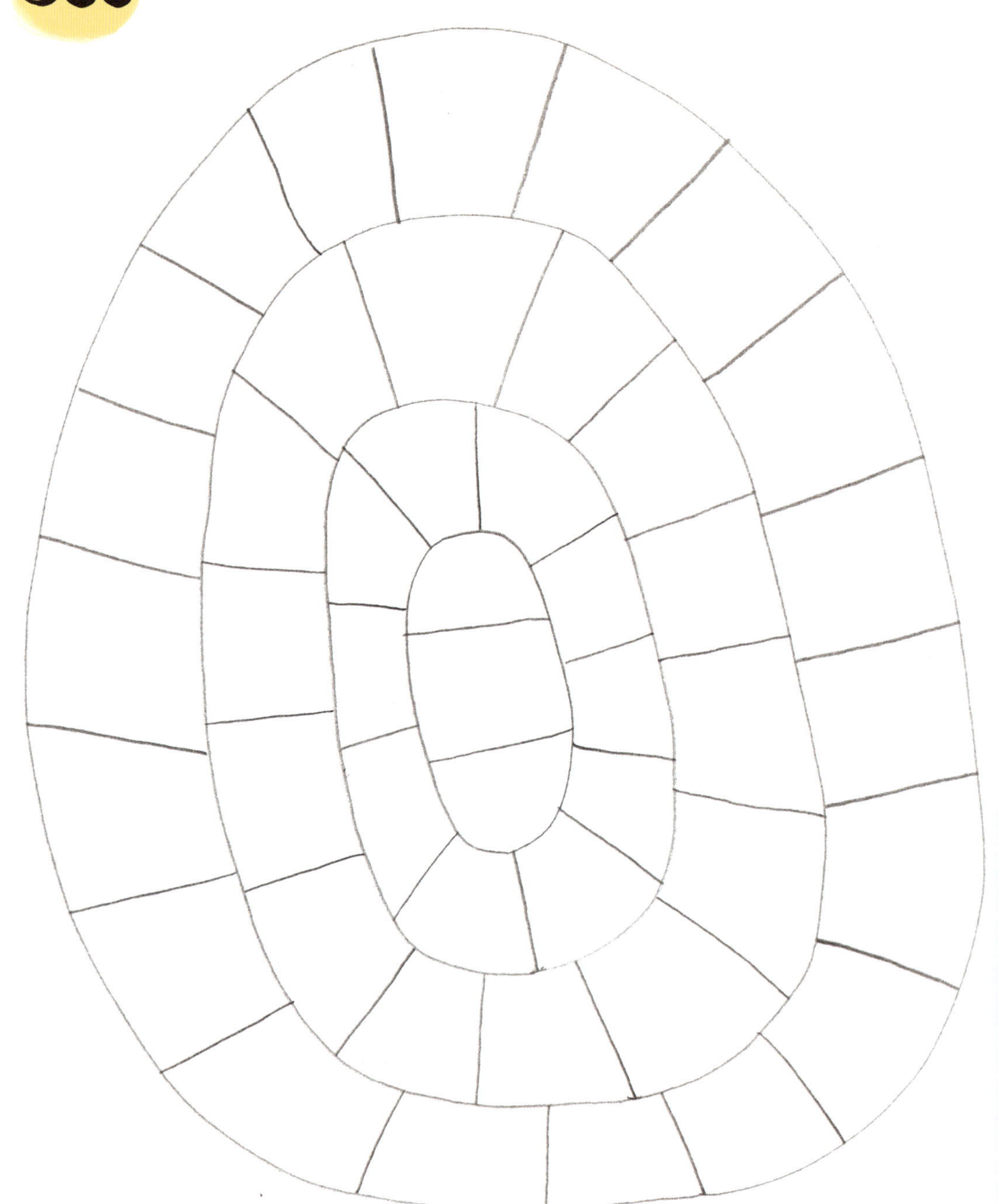

356

Paint a human figure using analogous colours to create a harmonious image. The colours you use don't need to be realistic, and can instead represent colours that are a similar tone.

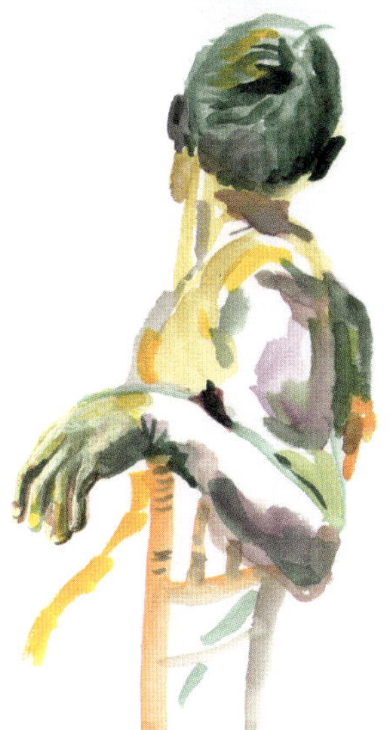

357

When painting, you don't need to mix paints before starting – and sometimes more spontaneous artwork can be created by using paints straight from the tube. Create a still life scene using objects or food from your home. It can be as simple as you like. Begin by looking carefully at the scene in front of you, and gather a palette of colours you'd like to use.

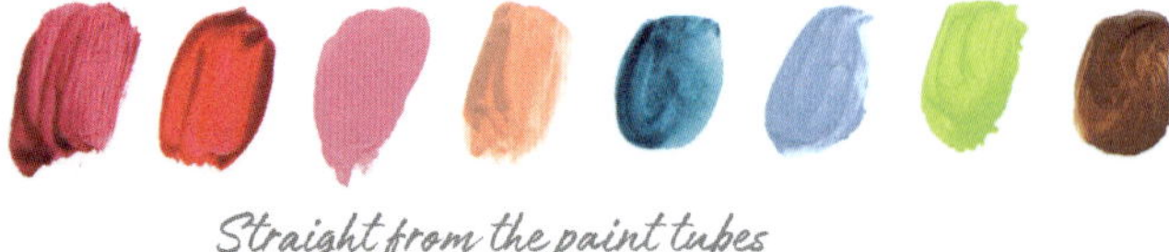

Straight from the paint tubes

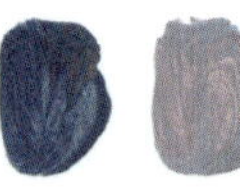

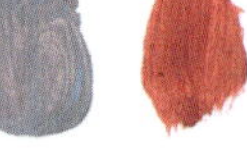

Mixed colours

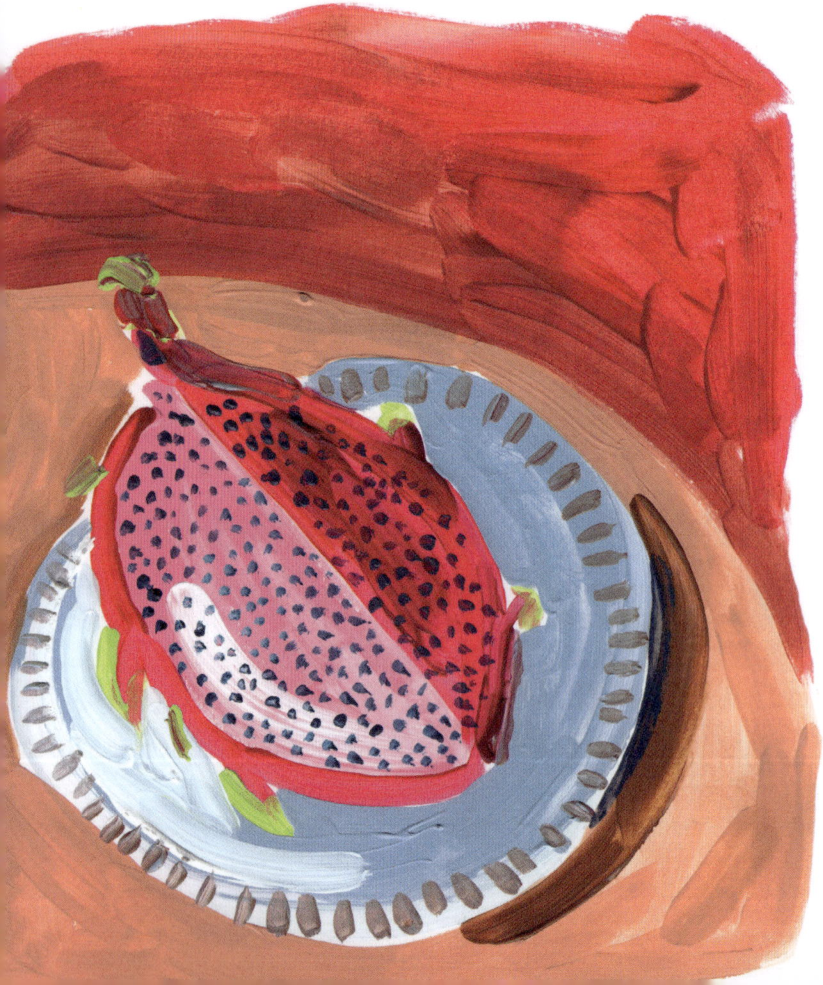

You may like to create some colour studies first – refer back to activity 231 before starting, or just go for it and paint the scene. Use big, bold shapes and work quickly, enjoying the colours and the ease of using them straight from a palette.

Tip: *Wash and dry your brush well between colours so that you keep them clean and prevent your colours from getting murky.*

358 — Paint a sunrise.

359

Paint a sunset. Consider how the colours differ from those you chose for your sunrise.

Use neutral, earthy colours to create a relaxing, peaceful image.

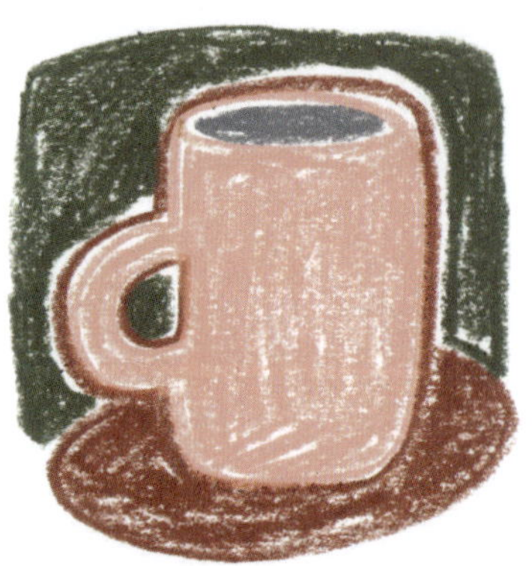

361

We may naturally assume that a drop of water always looks blue, but if we look more closely, a water droplet actually looks a similar colour to the object it's on or in front of. Make a study of water droplets on a flower, based on the image below, paying particular attention to the colours.

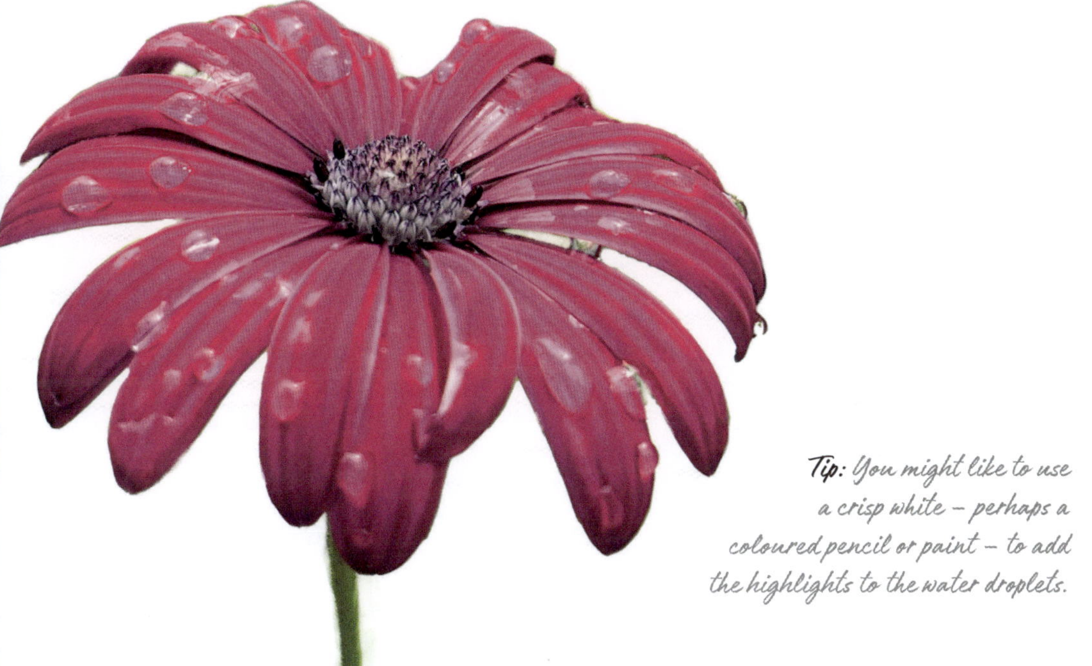

Tip: You might like to use a crisp white – perhaps a coloured pencil or paint – to add the highlights to the water droplets.

362

Use a pre-prepared, painted background to inspire a piece of observational art. Begin by painting colour onto the white page, allowing it to dry completely. Choose any colour you like, in any shape.

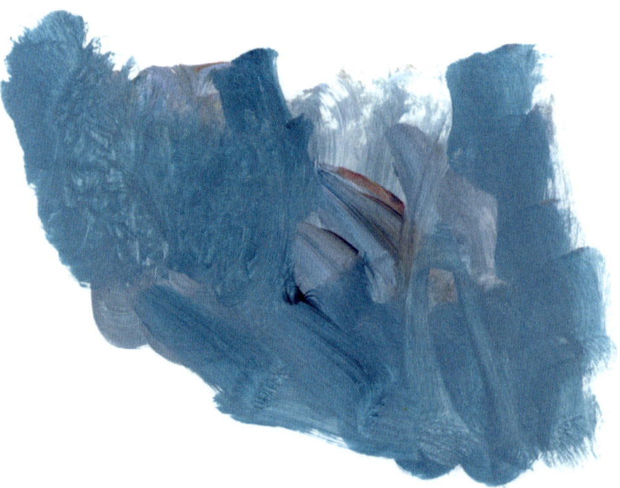

Then go for a walk with your coloured page and create a drawing or painting on top of this colour, using the colour as inspiration for a background, or as part of your image.

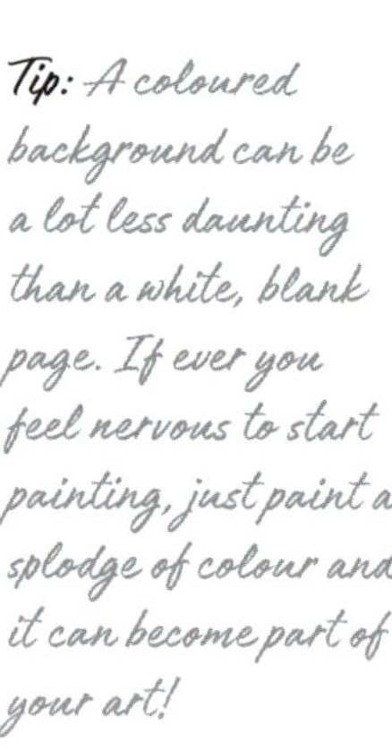

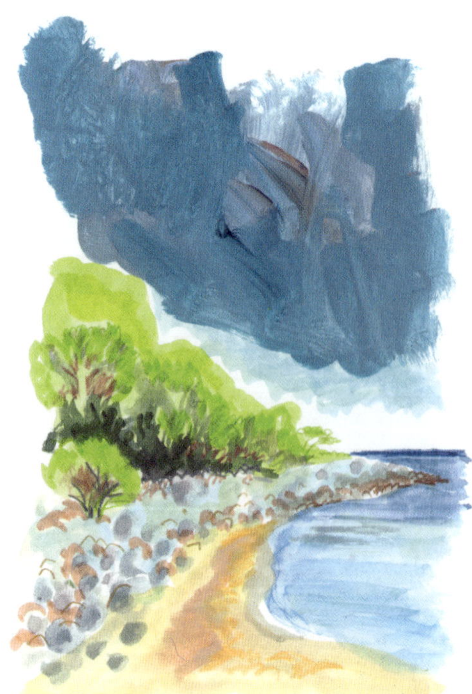

363

Create a nature-inspired pattern on a dark background.

364

Colour is used carefully in the design of logos to evoke certain feelings and create an identity. Design a logo for an imaginary product using colours deliberately. What do the colours mean to you?

365

Share your creations, and the joy of colour, by making some colourful greetings cards to send to your loved ones. Create an abstract piece of art using colours you love, and let it dry.

Tip: You may prefer to use a separate piece of card for your creations and use the opposite page to explore colour palette options.

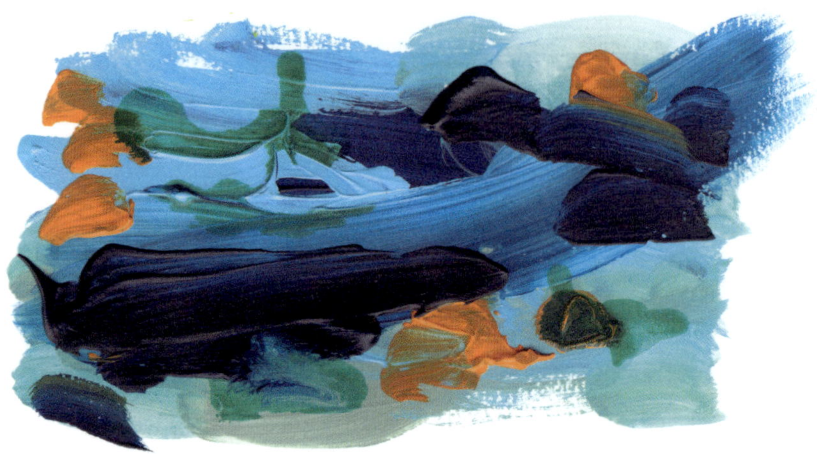

Then cut your colourful abstract into smaller, mini abstracts. Stick these onto a piece of folded card to create your greetings cards.

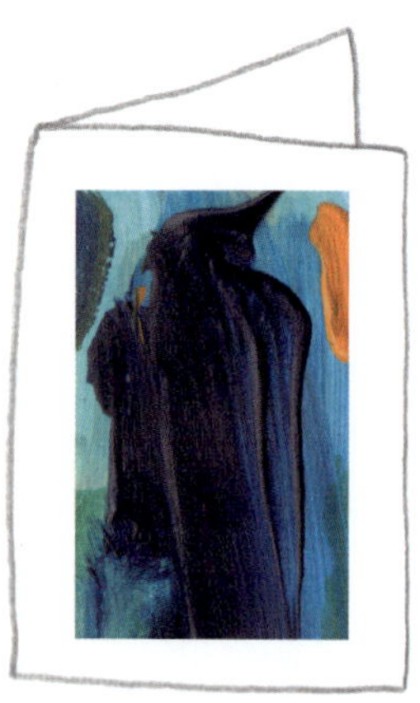

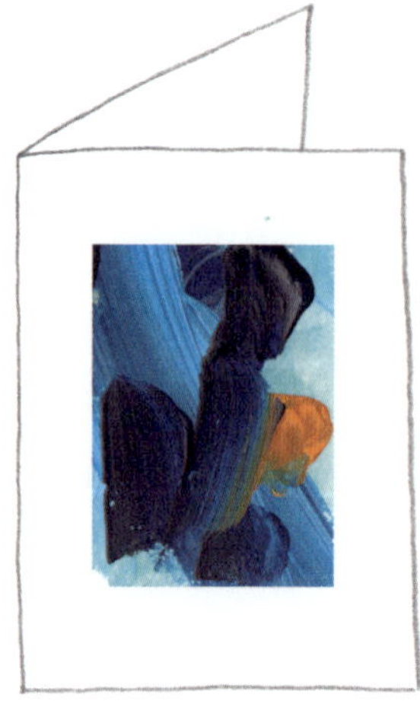

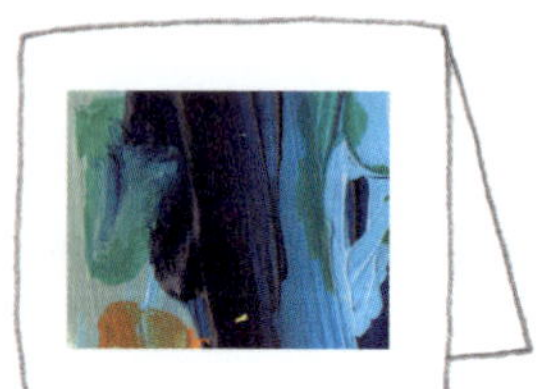

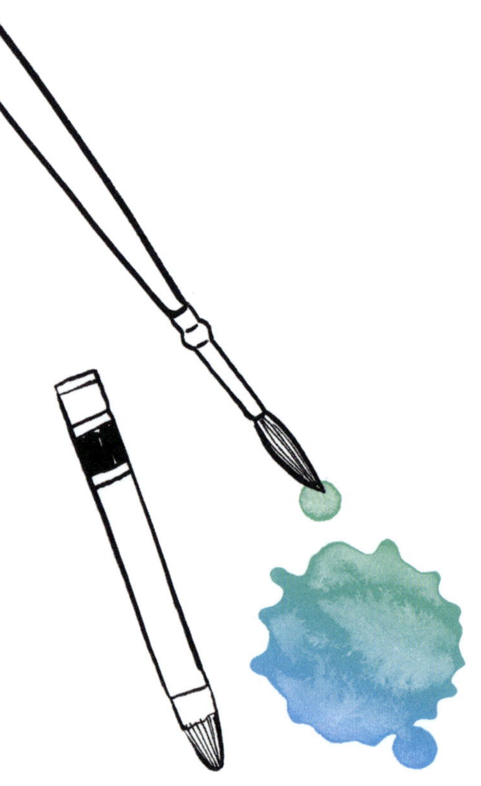

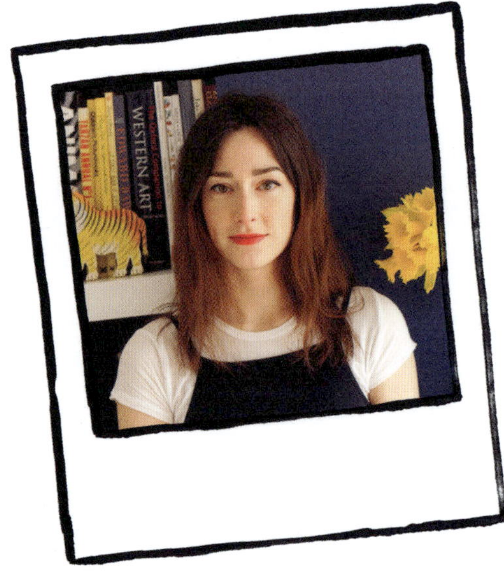

About the Author

Lorna Scobie grew up in the English countryside, climbing trees and taking her rabbit for walks in the fields. She is an author, illustrator and designer, now based in south-east London.

Lorna always has a sketchbook close to hand, just in case. She enjoys spontaneity in art, and the 'happy accidents' that can happen along the way. Her favourite place to draw is outside among nature, on trips around the world.

This is the sixth book in Lorna's *365 Days* series, following on from *365 Days of Art, 365 Days of Drawing, 365 Days of Creativity, 365 Days of Art in Nature* and *365 Days of Feel-good Art.*

If you'd like to keep up to date with Lorna's work, she can be found on Instagram: **@lornascobie**

www.lornascobie.com

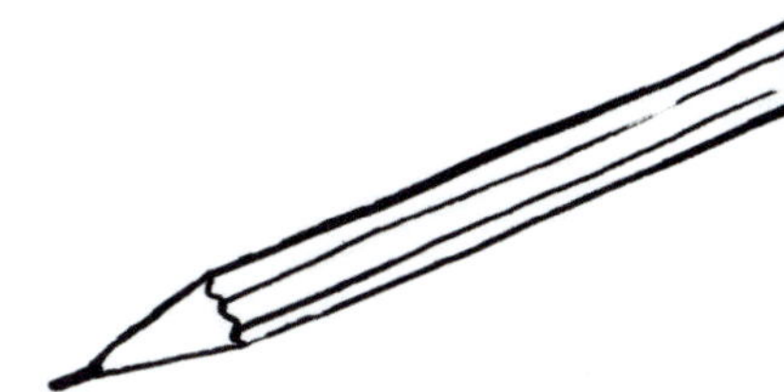

Thank you

To Tom, Coco, Isla and Charlie – for inspiring me to do what I love. And to Kajal and Chelsea and my super publishing team.

Dedicated to my mum, Emily, who has always surrounded me with joyful colour and art.

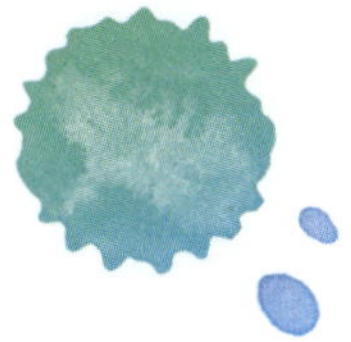

Quadrille, Penguin Random House UK,
One Embassy Gardens, 8 Viaduct Gardens,
London SW11 7BW

Quadrille Publishing Limited is part of the Penguin Random House group of companies whose addresses can be found at global.penguinrandomhouse.com

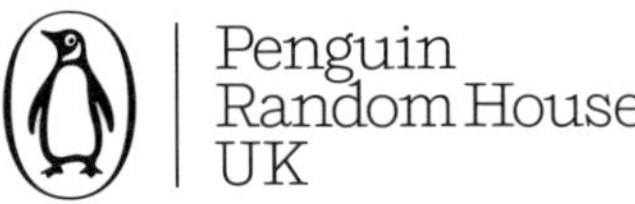

Published by Quadrille in 2025

www.penguin.co.uk

A CIP catalogue record for this book is available from the British Library

ISBN 9781837834716
10 9 8 7 6 5 4 3 2 1

Managing Director: Sarah Lavelle
Publishing Director: Kajal Mistry
Editorial Director: Harriet Butt
Managing Editor: Chelsea Edwards
Proofreader: Gaynor Sermon
Production Manager: Sabeena Atchia

Colour reproduction by F1

Printed in China by C&C Offset Printing Co., Ltd.

The authorised representative in the EEA is Penguin Random House Ireland, Morrison Chambers, 32 Nassau Street, Dublin D02 YH68.

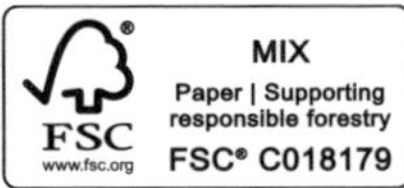

Penguin Random House is committed to a sustainable future for our business, our readers and our planet. This book is made from Forest Stewardship Council® certified paper.